DEDICATION

To the memory of my wonderful grandmother, Adeline Souza, who always gave me an abundance of unconditional love. I will always be grateful for the many investments she made in my life.

CONTENTS

PREFACE .... **ix**

PART 1: THE TOP STOCKS FOR 1998 .... **1**

STOCK PICKS—AN INTRODUCTION 3

CHRYSLER

Seth Glickenhaus 9

CISCO SYSTEMS

Kevin Landis 13

COHU

Scott Black 17

COMPUTER SCIENCES

Elizabeth Bramwell 21

CROMPTON & KNOWLES

John Wallace 25

DELL COMPUTER

James Collins 29

DEPARTMENT 56

Donald Yacktman 33

FANNIE MAE

David Dreman 37

HARDING LAWSON ASSOCIATES

William Nasgovitz 41

HERMAN MILLER

Louis Navellier 45

INTERNATIONAL PAPER

James O'Shaughnessy 49

ISIS PHARMACEUTICALS

Michael Murphy 53

MANPOWER

Jean-Marie Eveillard 57

McDONALD'S

Elaine Garzarelli 61

MEMTEC

Vivian Lewis 65

NORTHERN TRUST

John Rogers 69

PHILIP MORRIS

Robert Sanborn 73

PLAYTEX
Cappy McGarr 77
PRE-PAID LEGAL SERVICES
Michael DiCarlo 81
Q-ENTERTAINMENT
Andrew Addison 85
RATIONAL SOFTWARE
Garrett Van Wagoner 89
SCIENTIFIC-ATLANTA
Susan Byrne 93
TOKIO MARINE & FIRE INSURANCE
Martin Whitman 97
WELLS FARGO
Shelby Davis 101
ZOOM TELEPHONICS
Al Frank 105

PART 2: THE TOP MUTUAL FUNDS FOR 1998 109

A FEW WORDS ABOUT MUTUAL FUNDS 111

AGGRESSIVE GROWTH FUND
BARON ASSET
Robert Bingham 117
HARBOR CAPITAL APPRECIATION
Harold Evensky 121
TEMPLETON GLOBAL SMALLER COMPANIES
Eric Roseman 125

GROWTH FUND
CLIPPER FUND
Catherine Voss Sanders 129
DREYFUS AGGRESSIVE VALUE
Thurman Smith 133
YACKTMAN FOCUSED
Michael Stolper 137

GROWTH & INCOME FUND
MATTHEWS ASIAN CONVERTIBLE SECURITIES
Stephen Savage 141
T. ROWE PRICE DIVIDEND GROWTH
Walter Frank 145
T. ROWE PRICE EQUITY INCOME
Michael Hirsch 149

INTERNATIONAL FUND
ARTISAN INTERNATIONAL
Bob Markman 153
OAKMARK INTERNATIONAL
Louis Stanasolovich 157

PART 3: UP CLOSE WITH THE EXPERTS 161
GETTING TO KNOW WALL STREET'S FINEST 163
ANDREW ADDISON
The Addison Report..........165
ROBERT BINGHAM
Bingham, Osborn & Scarborough 167
SCOTT BLACK
Delphi Management 169
ELIZABETH BRAMWELL
Bramwell Capital Management 171
SUSAN BYRNE
Westwood Management 173
JAMES COLLINS
Insight Capital..........175
SHELBY DAVIS
Davis Selected Advisers 177
MICHAEL DiCARLO
DFS Advisors 179
DAVID DREMAN
Dreman Value Advisors 181
JEAN-MARIE EVEILLARD
SoGen Funds..........183
HAROLD EVENSKY
Evensky, Brown & Katz 185
AL FRANK
The Prudent Speculator 187
WALTER FRANK
Moneyletter..........189
ELAINE GARZARELLI
Garzarelli Investment Management 191
SETH GLICKENHAUS
Glickenhaus & Co. 193
MICHAEL HIRSCH
Freedom Capital Management 195
KEVIN LANDIS
Technology Value Fund 197
VIVIAN LEWIS
Global Investing 199
BOB MARKMAN
Markman Capital Management..........201
CAPPY McGARR
McGarr Capital Management 203
MICHAEL MURPHY
California Technology Stock Letter 205

WILLIAM NASGOVITZ
Heartland Advisors 207
LOUIS NAVELLIER
Navellier & Associates 209
JAMES O'SHAUGHNESSY
O'Shaughnessy Capital Management 211
JOHN ROGERS
Ariel Capital Management 213
ERIC ROSEMAN
Global Mutual Fund Investor 215
ROBERT SANBORN
The Oakmark Fund 217
STEPHEN SAVAGE
Value Line Mutual Fund Survey 219
THURMAN SMITH
Equity Fund Research 221
LOUIS STANASOLOVICH
Legend Financial Advisors 223
MICHAEL STOLPER
Stolper & Company 225
GARRETT VAN WAGONER
Van Wagoner Capital Management....................227
CATHERINE VOSS SANDERS
Morningstar Investor 229
JOHN WALLACE
Robertson Stephens Investment Management 231
MARTIN WHITMAN
Third Avenue Funds 233
DONALD YACKTMAN
Yacktman Asset Management....................235
UPDATE ON WALL STREET'S PICKS FOR 1997 237
GLOSSARY OF INVESTMENT TERMS....................241
INDEX 245

PREFACE

It's not easy gaining access to Wall Street's top minds. After all, most manage multibillion dollar portfolios and won't even consider taking you on as a private client unless you have $1 million or more to invest. It's even harder to convince these folks to let you pick their brains for a while, maybe over lunch or dinner, to learn their investment secrets and favorite stock or fund ideas for the coming months.

Fortunately, I have come to know many of the investment world's biggest stars personally. I'm privileged to enjoy the kind of access to these luminaries that few have. And now, for the third year in a row, I'm pleased to let you in on their investment insights and strategies for the year ahead in *Wall Street's Picks for 1998.*

This is by far the most timely and user-friendly investment guide on the market today. Instead of focusing on a bunch of abstract theories or listing hundreds of possible investment choices, like many other publications, *Wall Street's Picks for 1998* cuts through the financial jargon to bring you specific and current recommendations from the very best minds in the business.

In Part 1 of this new edition, you will learn the number one favorite stock ideas for the year ahead, according to such gurus as David Dreman, Elaine Garzarelli, Seth Glickenhaus, Al Frank, Jean-Marie Eveillard, Elizabeth Bramwell, Louis Navellier, Shelby Davis, Donald Yacktman, Michael DiCarlo, Martin Whitman, Michael Murphy, Garrett Van Wagoner, and many more. These are all successful investment managers who are at the top of their profession and consistently generate outstanding returns for their clients.

In essence, I asked each panelist to name the single stock they would own in 1998 if they could only choose one. The answers are revealed in the form of in-depth reports on each selection, including a background on the company, the reason for the recommendation, financial figures and charts, and a discussion of what kind of performance to expect as the year unfolds.

Because many readers are more interested in mutual funds, I have interviewed some of the country's leading fund analysts for Part 2. Following a general discussion about how funds work and why they are such great investment vehicles, you will find promising specific recommendations in various categories from such renowned fund authorities as Michael Hirsch, Walter Frank, Bob Markman, Stephen Savage, Michael Stolper, and Catherine Voss Sanders.

As I've said before, the idea behind this book is to bring together an investment dream team to help you develop a first-rate portfolio. It's the kind of inside information that used to be reserved exclusively for Wall Street's heavy hitters.

This kind of knowledge can't be found in any other book or magazine on the market today.

Of course, no pick is guaranteed to go up, and some may fall dramatically in price, despite my panel's optimistic expectations. That's all part of the risk you take when you become a part-owner of a company through purchasing stock. However, judging from the past performance of those featured on my panel, most of these choices should be very rewarding in 1998. They certainly have been over the past few years.

As usual, Part 3 features a complete biography of each adviser, describing his or her background, investment philosophy, market outlook, and other bits of advice you can use to make more money in the market. I want to thank nationally syndicated personal finance columnist, Humberto Cruz, for calling *Wall Street's Picks* one of only three investment books available today that survives the marketing hype. Humberto agreed with me that Part 3 is perhaps the most valuable part of the book, because the insights these living investment legends share can help make you richer for many years to come.

Additionally, even though this book is written in reader-friendly language, if you're ever confused by any financial verbiage that seems like a bunch of gobbledygook, simply turn to the back where you'll find a glossary full of definitions for some of the more commonly used investment terms and phrases you will encounter in the pages that follow.

If you're a regular reader of this series, you know that my list of panelists and picks changes dramatically from year to year. In fact, this time around the only stock making a repeat appearance is McDonald's. This is the third year in a row McDonald's has been selected by one of my experts, which means if you originally bought it based on Art Bonnel's suggestion in the 1996 edition, you made a great choice. (By the way, if you want to know how last year's contributors feel about the prospects for their picks going into 1998, their latest buy, sell and hold ratings can be found immediately following Part 3.)

For now, sit back, relax and enjoy what I hope will be a very prosperous journey into the world of Wall Street's best advice on how to invest your money over the next 12 months.

—Kirk Kazanjian

part 1

THE TOP STOCKS FOR 1998

STOCK PICKS — AN INTRODUCTION

Before we discuss this year's stock selections, it makes sense to review some of the important principles that should guide all of your investment decisions. To begin with, as all smart investors know, basing portfolio decisions solely on the economy, specific items in the news, or the direction of the Dow is a recipe for disaster. In fact, the richest and most successful investors view the New York, American, Nasdaq and other exchanges not as stock markets but, rather, markets of stocks, where the key to great profits is finding individual companies with stories and valuations so compelling, their share prices are bound to go up regardless of what happens with the overall economy or underlying indexes.

Those who try to time the market usually end up making the least amount of money. That's because no one has created a foolproof system for predicting where stocks are headed. Though some look back and boast about how accurate they were at calling certain tops, bottoms, and crashes, they rarely mention the number of times their advice was wrong.

Investors versus Traders

It has often been said that *investors*, those who buy quality companies and stay in the market regardless of outside influences, drive Cadillacs, while *traders*, people who jump in and out on a regular basis, ride around in Chevys. History suggests this is true. Statistics show the majority of all market gains come on only a handful of trading sessions each year. Therefore, if you are out on those days, you can expect nothing more than mediocre returns, or even losses.

For the decade of the 1980s, the Standard & Poor's 500 index produced an average annual return of 17.6 percent. However, if you were in cash on the top ten trading days during that period, the figure dropped to 12.6 percent. Had you been on the sidelines for the 20 best days, you would have earned a mere 9.3 percent. And, if you missed the 30 biggest advancing sessions, your return would have plummeted to just 6.5 percent, less than what you would have earned in a money market fund. Clearly, not being fully invested is costly, since stocks tend to move in lumps. They rise or fall, and then remain stagnant for awhile, before rallying up or down again.

This is further proof that market timing rarely makes sense. Sure, it would be great to avoid every correction and bear market. But that's impossible to do. Those who make the right calls often owe their success more to luck than anything else. It's a point driven home by the great investor Sir John Templeton. When I asked for his market outlook a few years ago, he replied, "In the 52 years I was in the investment industry, I have never been able to answer that question. I just searched for those stocks whose prices were lowest in relation to earnings." In other words, he had a strategy and stuck with it, regardless of what was happening with the "market."

Take it from Sir John: The secret to investment riches is finding the right stocks to be in at any given time. After all, though the major indexes may fall or go nowhere, some individual issues always manage to skyrocket. For example, back in 1994, the S&P 500 and Nasdaq each squeezed out a mere 1 percent gain, including dividends. Yet Microtouch Systems soared 555 percent, Cooper Companies leaped 227 percent, LSI Logic rose 154 percent, and Rock Bottom Restaurants jumped a full 128 percent for the year, proving that even though the overall market may be stagnant, it's possible to make a lot of money through superior stock selection.

Building Wealth with Equities

By now you've figured out that creating wealth with stocks requires you to construct a stable of spectacular companies with bright future prospects. But how can you, as an individual investor far removed from the inner workings of Wall Street, find these jewels for yourself? That's what Part 1 is all about.

Over the past several months, I personally spoke with dozens of the world's top investment experts and asked, "If you could only choose one stock to hold in 1998, what would it be and why?" The panelists represent leading mutual fund managers, newsletter editors, investment advisers, and market strategists, all of whom have a slightly different style or area of expertise, giving you a truly diversified list of potential holdings.

Next, I followed up on these responses by doing further analysis on the selections, such as culling through annual reports, financial statements, and historical price charts. This provided some perspective as to where the stocks have been and where they might be going. Additional insight came from talking with corporate officers about any developments that might make the picks either more or less compelling.

All of this revealing information was then put together in the form of an easy-to-read research report. There are a total of 25 different companies, which are listed in alphabetical order. Be aware that this isn't a beauty contest to see who can pick the best performer, nor are these stocks you should buy in January and sell in December. Instead, they are quality companies that each expert considers to have great prospects for 1998 and beyond.

Dissecting the Information

Each discussion starts off with a table showing the company's ticker symbol, trading exchange, and business industry, along with such data as current price, PE ratio, book value, and earnings per share. Next is a profile of the company that includes specific reasons why it was selected. You'll also find graphs showing the stock's daily price patterns for the past 12 months, total return versus the S&P 500, and performance compared to its peer index. There's even a box containing important balance sheet numbers (like current assets, liabilities and shareholder's equity) going back two years. You should also pay attention to each stock's estimated beta factor, which is included in the statistical box at the top of every profile. This measures its price volatility compared to the S&P 500, which has a beta of 1. Simply put, a stock with a beta of 0.6 is less volatile than the market overall, while one with a rating of 1.6 is much riskier. At the end of each profile, you'll find the address and phone number you can use to request more information from the company. In addition, this year I have also included each company's Internet address, if it has one.

Please understand that these reports present predominately positive comments about the various companies. This stands to reason, since the advisers are very upbeat about these stocks and their future prospects. However, there are always negatives to every story, and I have taken care to bring some of them to your attention. Make sure you evaluate the potential downfalls of each idea before investing. Remember, not every optimistic expectation by my panel of experts will come to fruition.

When choosing equities, it usually makes sense to stick with companies reporting steady annual earnings growth, a characteristic shared by most of the stocks in this book. In addition, generally speaking, the lower the current percentage of institutional ownership in a stock, the better. That's because institutions account for more than 70 percent of all daily trading activity. If they only own a small amount of the stock, it shows the potential for them to buy more, and unless institutions are gobbling up shares in large quantities, it will be difficult for the price to substantially rise. High ownership by inside management is another bullish sign. It indicates that those in the know have enough faith in the firm to put their own money on the line. You'll learn more about stock-picking strategies by reading the biographies in Part 3. In many respects, this is one of the most important sections of the book, since the insights and advice these market masters provide are invaluable.

Stock Selection

It should be noted that each stock has been selected for a different reason, from low valuation to high future earnings potential, based on the adviser's particular style. In fact, every panelist has a unique process for selecting stocks. This information is spelled out for you in every discussion and should be an important consideration as you decide which ideas make the most sense for you, given your risk tolerance and overall objectives.

You'll notice the recommendations once again cover the gamut in terms of market capitalizations, industry groups, and geographic locations. There are some very big blue chips, namely Fannie Mae and Chrysler; smaller high-tech outfits with more risk, like Isis Pharmaceuticals and Rational Software; and international concerns, among them Tokio Marine & Fire Insurance and Memtec.

Asset Allocation

As you stroll through these pages, keep several things in mind, including asset allocation. You need to consider whether you even belong in stocks and, if so, to what extent.

Let me first make it clear that only investment capital should be put into the market. In essence, this is money above and beyond what you need to live on. Think of it as funds you could afford to lose without dramatically altering your lifestyle. Granted, no one invests to lose. But, because the stock market is inherently risky, this is a good attitude to have. That way you won't be scared out just when you should be jumping in.

After you've identified your investment capital, you must outline your goals. If you're saving for retirement, or a similar long-term objective that's at least five to ten years away, stocks should comprise a significant amount of your portfolio. They are the only investment class to consistently stay ahead of inflation, while providing the highest rates of return throughout history. (We'll delve deeper into the subject of asset allocation in Part 2.)

Once you determine what percentage to devote to stocks, you should understand that smaller and international issues generally carry more risk than those that are larger and better known. Keep this in mind as you evaluate which companies to purchase. If you consider yourself to be conservative, you might want to stick with only blue chips. If you're more moderate, perhaps several large companies sprinkled with a few small-caps and an international issue make sense. The brave, those shooting for huge gains and willing to take a potential rollercoaster ride in this pursuit, could concentrate almost entirely on smaller names with big prospects.

How many stocks do you need in your portfolio? Ask ten different people and you'll get ten different answers. One rule of thumb is you should never put more than 5 percent of your total assets into any single investment and/or industry. Therefore, to really reduce your downside exposure, you need at least 20 different issues. On the other hand, Warren Buffett, who is among the greatest investors ever, only holds a handful of stocks and has racked up enormous gains by concentrating on a select group of companies he knows well.

Just make sure you don't buy too many stocks in the same sector. If you own 30 high-technology stocks, your diversification is virtually nil. Spread your choices over many different areas, so when one is out of favor, you can profit from another. Fortunately, the selections in this book are highly diversified in terms of size, industry, and even geographic location.

A good technique for developing a nice mix involves constructing your portfolio around a core. In other words, you choose a handful of great, mostly blue chip, companies that you plan to hold for the long haul, and build some more speculative names around them.

Remember, you will have to pay a commission for each stock you buy or sell. These charges can add up quickly and eat into your profits. You can save money by using a quality discount broker. Some brokers on the Internet will execute trades for as little as $12, so be certain to shop around. I'm sure you'll agree there's no use paying those high full-service brokerage fees when you're acting on your own investment advice (with the help of a few well-connected friends).

Limit or Market Orders?

Another decision you will face is whether to place market orders or limit orders for your stock selections. When you place a market order, you agree to pay whatever the prevailing price is at the time your order is executed, which may be more or less than the amount quoted by your broker.

On the other hand, limit orders allow you to set the terms. Here's why: All stocks trade at a spread, which is the difference between the bid and offer price. If a stock is trading at a bid of 15 and offered at 15 1/2, the spread is 50 cents. With a limit order, you can specify that you will only buy the stock at 15. Otherwise, it would likely clear at market, or 15 1/2. Be advised, however, that while limit orders can save you money, they may take longer to execute, especially for thinly traded issues.

Limit orders are also used to set much lower price targets. For example, if you like a stock today that trades at 20, but only want to get in if it drops to 16, you can place a good-till-canceled (GTC) limit order for 16, which means the trade won't clear unless the issue hits your price point of 16. This may not ever happen, so be realistic if you place such an order.

Conversely, you can set stop-loss limit orders once you've purchased a stock on the New York or American Stock Exchanges to cushion your potential loss. Let's say you buy a stock for 20 and want to sell if it falls more than 10 percent. You can place a stop-loss order for 18, which means the stock will automatically be sold if it reaches that level. (This technique should be used with caution, given that the market is quite volatile today and stocks tend to bounce around by several points during each trading session. If you're not careful, you could be sold out of a position, even though the stock closes the day at a much higher price.)

When You Should Buy or Sell

Unfortunately, when writing about the stock market, be it for a book such as this or for a daily Internet site, information and valuations can change dramatically in a matter of seconds. That's why I have tried to include each analyst's 1998 price target in every profile. If a stock has already reached this target by the time you read about it, you may want to determine whether this enthusiasm is sustainable, or simply move on to another pick that appears to be a better bargain. If the company has just introduced a new product or acquisition that will make a significant contribution to earnings, it may merit the higher valuation. (As mentioned earlier, it's wise to favor companies with rapidly growing earnings.) However, if nothing has changed, perhaps the price has moved ahead of itself or reached full value. On the other hand, if a stock is trading well-below its target price, it theoretically is an even more compelling buy, assuming nothing catastrophic or scandalous has happened to change the fundamentals in the interim.

The question of when to sell is more difficult. Some feel you should never get rid of a good company. Others suggest you let go when the price appreciates or depreciates to some arbitrary level, such as 20 or 30 percent above or below cost. You'll find plenty of advice on this subject in Part 3.

Needless to say, if something happens to cloud both the company's future prospects and your reasons for buying in the first place, this too may be a compelling reason to get out.

Before You Begin

A few final notes: Please don't invest in any stock just because a person you admire likes it. Simply use this validation as a starting point. Then call or write the company (the location, phone numbers, and addresses are provided for each stock), request an annual report and form 10-K, check out available research reports at your library or broker's office, talk with an investor relations representative, and ultimately make a decision as to whether the recommendation makes sense for *you*. Just because it's right for Garrett Van Wagoner or Elaine Garzarelli doesn't necessarily mean it belongs in your portfolio. Use these suggestions as a launching pad, but do a little legwork to confirm everything in your own mind and, for heaven's sake, make sure you understand what you're buying. If a company is engaged in some exotic technology, and you have no clue as to what it does, stay away. Keep an eye on how your ultimate stock selections perform, and remain informed about any new positive and negative developments surrounding them.

Be sure to read the quarterly and annual reports, and keep good records. This will make your life easier when it comes time to pay Uncle Sam for capital gains and dividend interest. It's also smart to periodically examine and calculate your total return figures to see how you're doing, especially compared to the S&P 500, which is the industry's standard benchmark. In essence, you should run your investment portfolio like a business. Once you make a purchase, you become a part-owner in the company and have a duty to run your affairs accordingly.

Finally, always remember there are no guarantees. While the following stocks truly represent the best ideas from some wonderful investors, the market never goes straight up. All equities carry a significant amount of risk. Also be aware that the various experts may own positions in the equities they recommend, either in personal and/or managed accounts. This is not necessarily a bad thing, it's just something you should know. With that in mind, let's begin naming names on which companies could make you rich in 1998.

CHRYSLER

Seth Glickenhaus
Glickenhaus & Co.

Company Profile

Chrysler has come a long way over the past few years. The automaker has reinvented its product lineup, improved its balance sheet, and produced some impressive financial results. Still, money manager Seth Glickenhaus says it remains unloved by Wall Street. "It has all of the criteria I look for in a stock," he says. "It has good management, free cash flow, is a low-cost producer, and has a huge amount of cash, something like $7.5 billion, which translates into $11 per share. It has also taken steps to significantly reduce debt."

The company sold more vehicles than ever before in 1996, breaking records in 13 different categories. Among its most popular vehicles are the Dodge Neon, Eagle Vision, Jeep Grand Cherokee, and Dodge Ram trucks. Chrysler's greatest success in the United States lately has come from sales of minivans, trucks, and sport-utility vehicles, which offer the highest profit margins. The company's share of the full-size truck segment has grown from 6.9 percent in 1992 to more than 20 percent today. In all, it shipped almost 3 million vehicles around the world last year.

Chrysler manufactures cars under the Chrysler, Dodge, Plymouth, Jeep, and Eagle brand names. In addition, it operates the Dollar Rent-A-Car system and a vehicle financing subsidiary. "The company has raised its dividends substantially over the past few years," Glickenhaus points out. In fact, dividends have been increased seven times, or 433 percent, since 1993. "Additionally, it bought back, are you ready for this, $1 billion worth of stock in 1995, $2 billion in 1996, and another $2 billion in 1997. This means it is shrinking its total market capitalization, which raises earnings per share. I would say the company will earn about $5.65 per share during 1998."

Chrysler's latest goal is to expand operations, overseas. "Almost going broke in the late seventies, being forced to sell off our international operations, and having to start over was actually a lucky break for us," Chrysler chairman Bob Eaton insists. "We don't have an expensive infrastructure overseas. We don't need one. We can grow in international markets mainly through exports. That maximizes our return on net assets and lets us leverage the development costs of our core products. We invest overseas when necessary to gain access to markets and only when it makes sense."

Which brings up another reason Glickenhaus likes the stock. "Chrysler outsources about 70 percent of its products, which costs it much less than paying United Auto Workers Union wages," he says. "Ford and General Motors do much more in-house, which means their overhead and expenses are higher."

Furthermore, Chrysler claims to have improved product quality by 39 percent since 1991 and is working to reduce the number of parts used to manufacture each vehicle.

Reason for Recommendation

Chrysler's earnings chart over the past five years looks like a seesaw—up one year and down the next. That's how the automobile industry is. It's cyclical and follows the economy. This is one reason portfolio managers have been selling the stock of late. They're looking for companies with more stable earnings. "Wall Street is at the mercy of money pouring into companies like Microsoft and Coca-Cola that don't even pay a good dividend and are selling at 40 to 50 times earnings," Glickenhaus says. Those companies are currently growing much faster than Chrysler, but Glickenhaus isn't sure how long that will last.

What if the pundits are right? After all, we could enter a recession, even a mild one this year, which would presumably have a negative impact on car sales. Glickenhaus isn't concerned. "Sales may be off a bit, but Chrysler's share of the market is growing," he reasons.

In 1997, the company began production of its first computer-generated engines, a family of aluminum block V-6 power plants, which will be used on the Chrysler Concorde and Dodge Intrepid models. These new sedans were developed in just 31 months, 7 months faster than the original versions introduced in 1993. Not only will the computer technology enable Chrysler to do more testing in less time, it will aid in the design process as well.

The company's goal for the future is to continue to grow profitability. Of course, a downturn in the economy during 1998 could put those plans on hold. What's more, the automobile business is highly competitive, and there's no guarantee Chrysler's models will remain popular among consumers. Glickenhaus, however, remains optimistic. "This is a really simple story," Glickenhaus adds. "Chrysler has great products with good profits. It is buying back stock and raising dividends. Eventually Wall Street is going to recognize this. This stock is so preposterously cheap right now, it's bound to go up. My target price for Chrysler in 1998 is $60."

Contact Information: Robert J. Eaton
Chairman of the Board, President and CEO
Chrysler Corporation
1000 Chrysler Drive
Auburn Hills, MI 48326
(810) 576-5741
http://www.chryslercorp.com

Chrysler Corporation

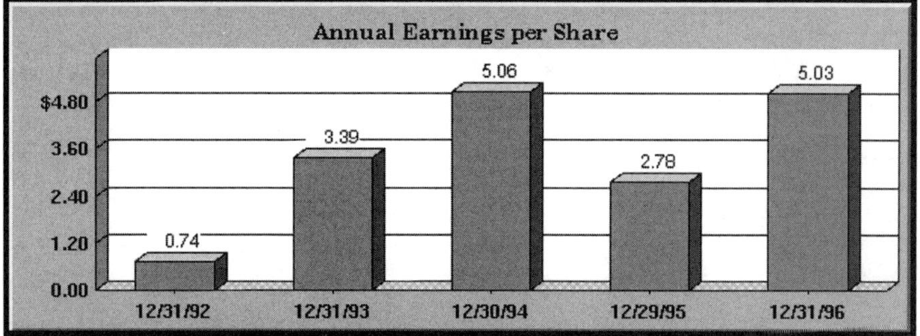

Chrysler Corporation

Symbol: C Exchange: NYSE

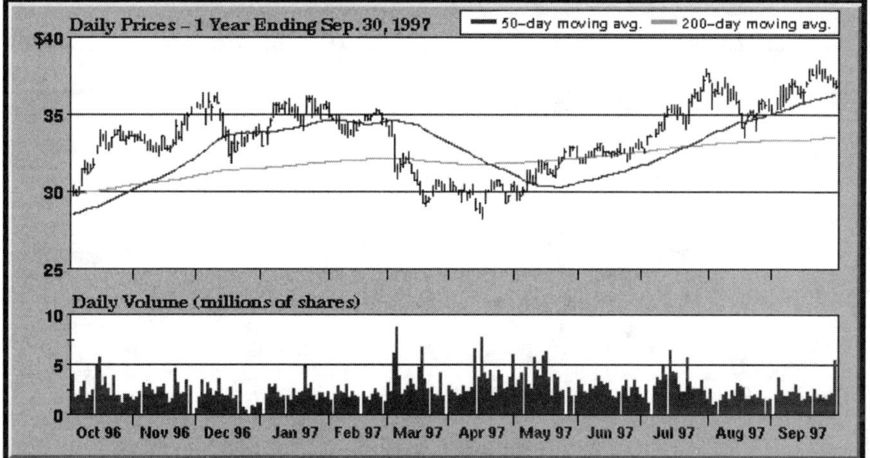

Latest Pricing Data (as of Sep. 30, 1997)		
Close (net change):	$36 13/16	(-3/16)
Day High & Low:	$37 1/4	$36 5/8
Volume & Avg. Volume:	5,461,000	3,041,811
52-Week High:	$38 9/16	Sep. 22, 1997
52-Week Low:	$28 1/8	Apr. 15, 1997
Latest Dividend:	$0.40	Sep. 11, 1997
Ind. Ann. Div. & Yield:	$1.60	4.35%
12 Month EPS:	$4.48	June 30, 1997
P/E Ratio & Beta Factor:	8.22	0.701
Shares Outstanding:	687.927 million	
Market Value:	$25.324 billion	
Institutional Holdings:	54.36%	
Number of Institutions:	976	
Primary Market:	NYSE	
Component of:	S&P 500	

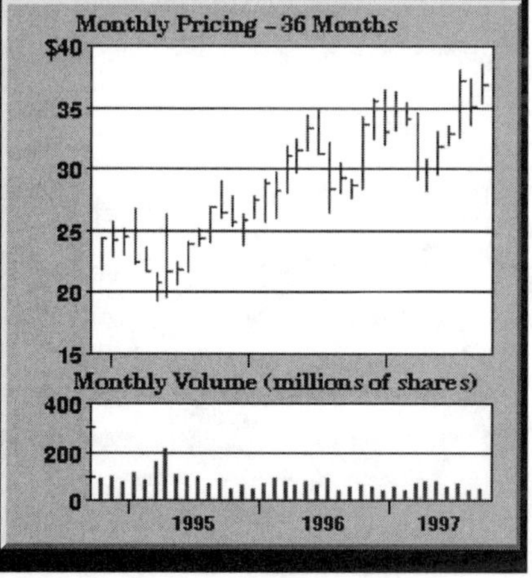

Currency: U.S. Dollars.

Source: IDD Information Services

Chrysler Corporation
Symbol: C

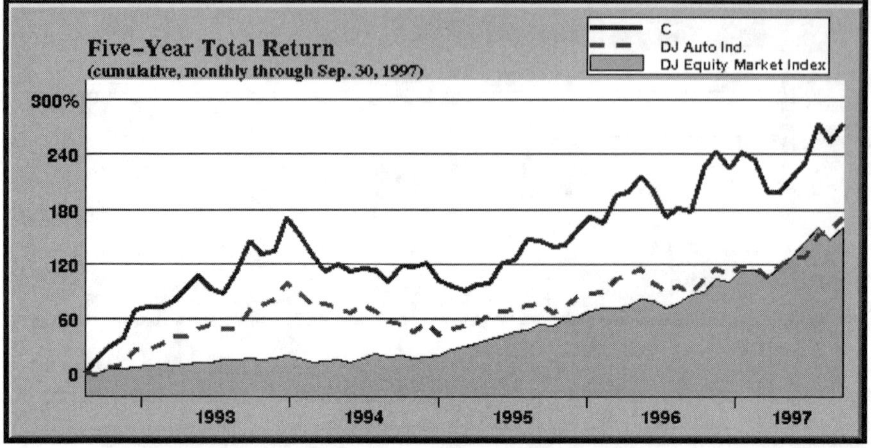

SELECTED INCOME STATEMENT AND BALANCE SHEET ITEMS

INCOME STATEMENT	12/31/92	12/31/93	12/30/94	12/29/95	12/31/96	LTM
Sales/Revenues	35,501	42,260	50,736	51,190	59,333	61,060
Cost of Goods Sold	28,740	32,382	38,032	41,304	45,842	46,157
Pre-tax Margin (%)	2.60	9.10	11.50	6.70	10.30	8.43
Operating Income	902.00	3,337.0	5,279.0	2,439.0	5,035.0	6,132.0
Net Income before Extras	505.00	2,415.0	3,713.0	2,121.0	3,720.0	3,190.0
Reported Net Income	505.00	2,415.0	3,713.0	2,121.0	3,720.0	3,190.0
Depreciation & Amortization	1,610.0	1,640.0	1,944.0	2,220.0	2,312.0	2,494.0
EPS from Net Income (Primary)	0.740	3.390	5.060	2.780	5.030	4.480
EPS from Net Income (Fully Diluted)	0.750	3.390	4.550	2.680	5.000	4.460
Dividend per Common Share	0.300	0.325	0.550	1.000	1.400	1.550
Dividend Yield (%)	1.88	1.22	2.24	3.63	4.24	4.71
Payout Ratio	0.41	0.10	0.11	0.36	0.28	0.35

BALANCE SHEET						
ASSETS						
Cash & Cash Equivalents	2,357.0	4,040.0	5,145.0	5,543.0	5,158.0	
Inventories	3,090.0	3,629.0	3,356.0	4,448.0	5,195.0	
Total Current Assets	19,540	21,564	27,315	29,184	29,341	
Total Assets	40,653	43,830	49,539	53,756	56,184	
LIABILITIES & EQUITY						
Short Term Debt	2,117.0	4,580.0	5,456.0	4,335.0	6,212.0	
Long Term Debt	13,434	6,871.0	7,650.0	9,858.0	7,184.0	
Total Liabilities	33,115	36,994	38,845	42,797	44,613	
Shares Outstanding	591.784	704.120	710.200	756.600	702.500	
Common Stockholder Equity	7,536.0	6,834.0	10,692	10,959	11,571	
Total Stockholder Equity	7,538.0	6,836.0	10,694	10,959	11,571	

Note: Figures in Millions of $ except: per share items, margins, yields, and ratios.

Source: IDD Information Services

CISCO SYSTEMS

Kevin Landis
Technology Value Fund

Company Profile

If you've ever cruised through the information superhighway, you've undoubtedly used equipment manufactured by Cisco Systems. "When you send e-mail, it goes through your modem across the Internet to my modem," explains Kevin Landis, portfolio manager of the Technology Value Fund. "Cisco provides most of the products your e-mail has to travel through."

Cisco is the leading provider of what it calls "internetworking" solutions around the world. Its hardware and software products are used to link computers together, giving people instant access to information, regardless of where they are or what type of system they are using. "Cisco is clearly the dominant player in this business," Landis maintains. "In certain segments, it has a market share of greater than 80 percent."

The company was founded in 1984 by some computer scientists from Stanford University who wanted an easier way to connect computer systems together. Cisco's first product was shipped in 1986. Since then, it has grown into a multinational corporation with more that $5 billion in annual revenues, compared to just $28 million seven years ago. The company has some 10,200 employees, and a $1 investment in Cisco's IPO is now worth more than $100. The company is headquartered in San Jose, California and has manufacturing facilities in both North Carolina and Massachusetts.

Although it is still a young firm, Cisco's management team is seasoned. "John Chambers is the company's third CEO, so it clearly has gone through its entrepreneurial phase," Landis points out. "It is now a large company built for continued rapid growth. In other words, many companies can grow rapidly, but it's highly stressful. Cisco management seems to have put together a company that structurally can handle a high rate of change and growth without falling apart. That's not as easy as it sounds."

To demonstrate just how successful the company has been at growing its business, you need look no further back than 1996. During a period when the overall networking industry averaged growth between 30 and 50 percent, Cisco generated growth of 83 percent, easily outstripping its revenue increase of 67 percent in 1994 and 1995.

Cisco is the acknowledged king of the global internetworking marketplace. It defines the internetwork as "the tie that binds, the chain that links many disparate protocols, platforms, and computing environments together." In technological lingo, the internetwork encompasses all networks, including LANs and WANs, private and public nets, plus the Internet and corporate intranets.

Reason for Recommendation

The potential in the networking industry is enormous. But so is the competition. Some of Cisco's biggest rivals include Ascend Communications (one of *Wall Street's Picks for 1996* and *1997*), Bay Networks, and 3Com. The company's future growth is dependent on both the market and its ability to come up with new products in a timely manner. However, Landis maintains that Cisco has proven it knows what it takes to stay on top. "Evidence of that is when it sees a smaller company with a better product, it often buys that company and rapidly integrates its product in with its own," he says. In 1996, the company either acquired or made significant investments in at least a dozen other firms, highlighted by the purchase of StrataCom, Inc., the world leader in WAN switching technology and products. Cisco maintains that acquisitions will continue to be an integral part of its future.

To extend its market reach further, Cisco has developed a number of solutions targeted at its prime customers, including Internet service providers. These organizations use Cisco products to build their network infrastructures, deliver reliable Internet access to customers, and create and manage the services they provide.

Networking stocks, like most others in the technology sector, are highly volatile. As this book is being written, they are under enormous selling pressure and out of favor on Wall Street. That's one reason Landis is so attracted to Cisco. "This is the strongest networking company, and the entire group is selling at historically low levels," Landis says. "Cisco currently trades at 25 times earnings. That's a modest valuation for a company that ought to be able to grow from 25 to 35 percent each year for the next ten years."

Landis believes the stock will trade for around $100 by the end of 1998.

Contact Information: John T. Chambers
President and CEO
Cisco Systems, Inc.
170 West Tasman Drive
San Jose, CA 95134
(408) 526-4000
http://www.cisco.com

Cisco System Incorporated

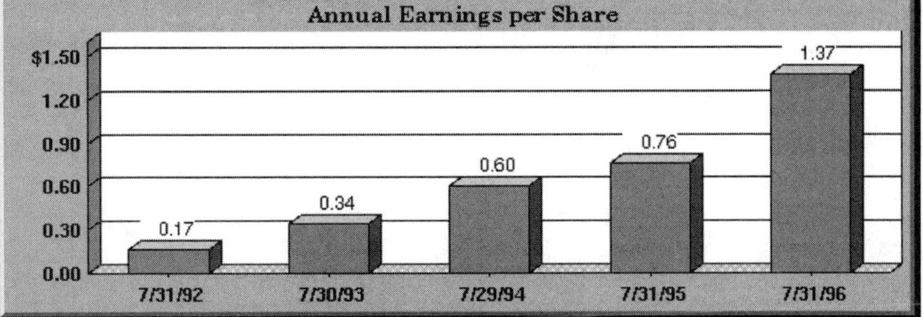

Cisco System Incorporated

Symbol: CSCO   Exchange: Nasdaq NMS

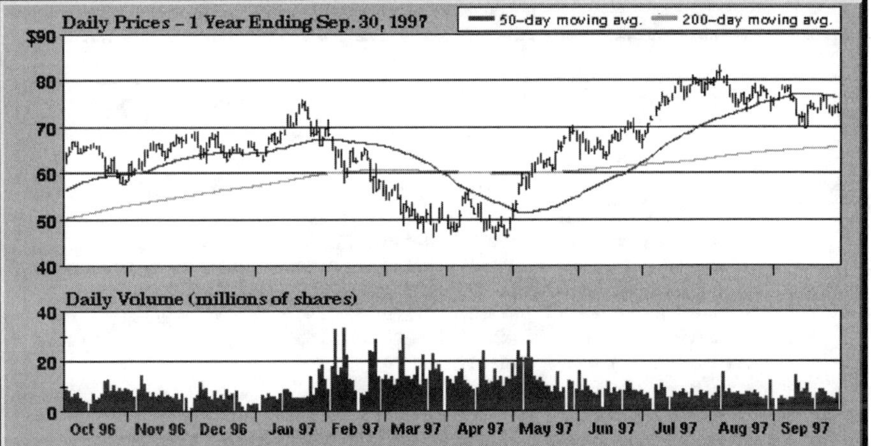

Latest Pricing Data (as of Sep. 30, 1997)		
Close (net change):	$73 1/16	(–1 1/16)
Day High & Low:	$74 3/4	$73
Volume & Avg. Volume:	7,005,000	7,969,420
52-Week High:	$83 1/4	Aug. 5, 1997
52-Week Low:	$45 1/4	Apr. 22, 1997
Latest Dividend:	$0.00	
Ind. Ann. Div. & Yield:	$0.00	N.A.
12 Month EPS:	$1.52	July 31, 1997
P/E Ratio & Beta Factor:	48.07	1.690
Shares Outstanding:	663.647 million	
Market Value:	$48.488 billion	
Institutional Holdings:	65.05%	
Number of Institutions:	1804	
Primary Market:	Nasdaq NMS	
Component of:	S&P 500	

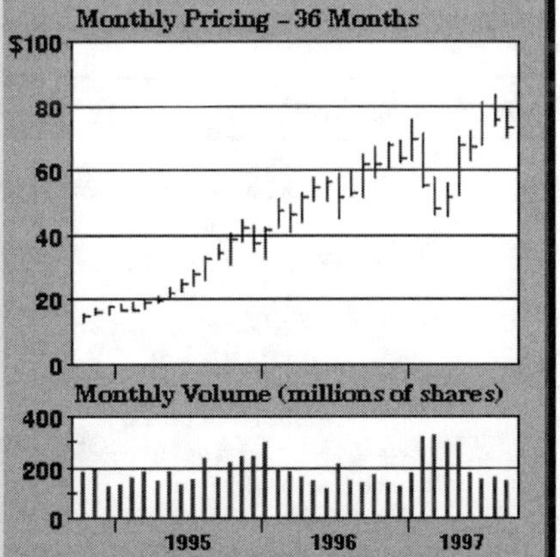

Currency: U.S. Dollars.

Source: IDD Information Services

Cisco System Incorporated
Symbol: CSCO

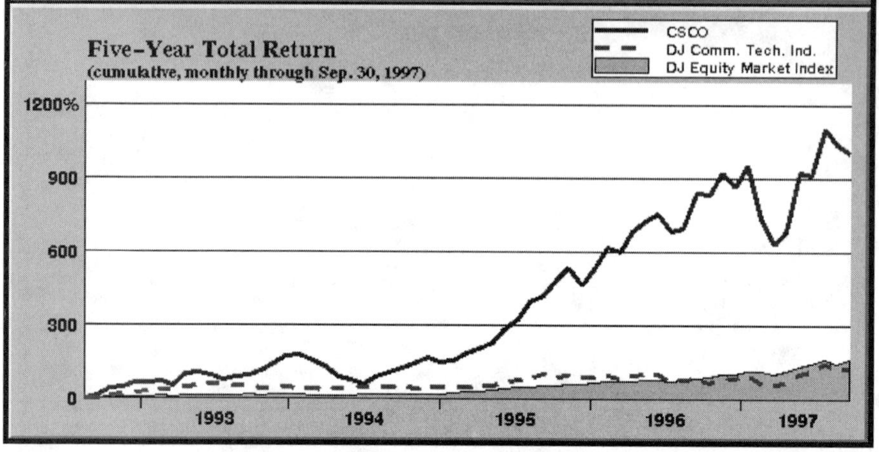

SELECTED INCOME STATEMENT AND BALANCE SHEET ITEMS

INCOME STATEMENT	7/31/92	7/30/93	7/29/94	7/31/95	7/31/96	LTM
Sales/Revenues	339.60	649.00	1,243.0	1,978.9	4,096.0	6,440.2
Cost of Goods Sold	104.50	196.90	382.00	585.70	1,277.3	N.A.
Pre-tax Margin (%)	40.10	42.40	41.00	34.30	35.80	N.A.
Operating Income	129.40	263.60	488.20	642.90	1,400.8	N.A.
Net Income before Extras	84.400	172.00	314.90	421.00	913.30	1,048.7
Reported Net Income	84.400	172.00	314.90	421.00	913.30	1,048.7
Depreciation & Amortization	6.700	13.600	30.800	58.500	132.60	N.A.
EPS from Net Income (Primary)	0.170	0.340	0.600	0.760	1.370	1.520
EPS from Net Income (Fully Diluted)	0.170	0.340	0.600	0.760	1.370	1.520
Dividend per Common Share	0.000	0.000	0.000	0.000	0.000	0.000
Dividend Yield (%)	N.A.	N.A.	N.A.	N.A.	N.A.	N.A.
Payout Ratio	N.A.	N.A.	N.A.	N.A.	N.A.	N.A.

BALANCE SHEET					
ASSETS					
Cash & Cash Equivalents	40.000	27.200	53.600	204.80	279.70
Inventories	9.100	23.500	27.900	71.200	301.20
Total Current Assets	247.10	268.30	507.70	996.00	2,159.6
Total Assets	323.90	595.20	1,053.7	1,757.3	3,630.2
LIABILITIES & EQUITY					
Short Term Debt	0.000	0.000	0.000	0.000	0.000
Long Term Debt	0.000	0.000	0.000	0.000	0.000
Total Liabilities	78.400	120.00	205.50	378.60	810.70
Shares Outstanding	480.888	494.832	515.394	544.492	649.284
Common Stockholder Equity	245.60	475.20	848.20	1,378.7	2,819.6
Total Stockholder Equity	245.60	475.20	848.20	1,378.7	2,819.6

Note: Figures in Millions of $ except: per share items, margins, yields, and ratios.

Source: IDD Information Services

COHU

Scott Black
Delphi Management

Company Profile

Cohu is one of the largest suppliers of semiconductor test-handling equipment in the world. This electromechanical equipment is designed to automatically handle and sort integrated circuits while they are being tested for such things as proper functioning and voltage prior to being shipped to end-users.

"In other words, when the logic comes off the assembly lines, like DRAMs, you have to test the electronic circuits," explains Scott Black of Delphi Management. "You must have a device that actually picks the logic up and puts it in a place to be tested. Cohu is the dominant player in this business, with about a 40 percent share of the U.S. market."

The company designs, manufactures, markets, and services this test-handling equipment from both its Delta Design subsidiary in San Diego, California and Daymarc operation in Littleton, Massachusetts. It has sales, service, and technical personnel throughout the United States, Asia, and Europe. "Cohu's three biggest customers are Intel, Texas Instruments, and Motorola," Black shares. "It also sells a lot to Siemens in Europe."

There are two primary types of handling technologies: gravity-feed and pick-and-place. "Pick-and-place is the high end of the business, and Cohu dominates in this area," Black says. "But its Massachusetts subsidiary uses the gravity-feed technology." The company claims the two product lines are complementary, with virtually no overlap.

Handlers are complex electromechanical systems used continuously in high-production environments. Many are in service around the clock. Therefore, it is essential that the equipment be functional at all times. For this reason, Cohu has engineers stationed around the world, including Southeast Asia, where more than half of all integrated-circuit testing takes place.

"The company's balance sheet is bulletproof," Black exclaims. "It has $53 million in cash and no debt. Here's a company that made $24 million after taxes in 1996 and generated free cash flow of $25 million. That's awesome."

But 1996 was by no means a banner year for Cohu. After five years of unprecedented growth, semiconductor manufacturers suddenly found themselves with too much capacity and sharply reduced capital spending. Semiconductor equipment suppliers are feeling the effects of this slowdown in the form of lower order rates, reduced backlog, and uncertainty about future purchasing plans from customers. As a result, the company was forced to lay off part of its workforce, while implementing several cost reduction programs.

Reason for Recommendation

"I really think we're coming off the bottom of the cycle," Black offers. "Intel's got two major plants coming online, one in Ireland and the other in Israel. It's also going to ramp up the Pentium Pro. In addition, I think you're going to see manufacturers push up the technology on 64K DRAMs. As you move to this next level, you need more semiconductor equipment, both on the back and front end. You've got to be able to test these circuits. This creates a derived demand for Cohu's product."

Aside from the test-handling business, Cohu manufactures closed-circuit television cameras, although this segment accounted for less than 11 percent of consolidated net sales in 1996. "It made all of the high-resolution cameras for the Washington Metro and those that are on the air fields in Saudi Arabia," Black adds.

Despite the recent slowdown, Cohu's top-line growth from 1992 to 1996 compounded at an annual rate of 43 percent. "I don't expect that kind of growth going forward," Black admits. "I think the overall semiconductor industry is probably going to grow closer to 15 percent a year. But it's coming off the bottom, and there's great operating leverage in this business right now."

That's why Black is such a big believer in Cohu. "One risk with this stock is they could lose market share to another competitor, but that is highly doubtful," Black contends. "We could also have a recession and not get any growth in the semiconductor and computer business. That would cause this stock to fizzle. After all, 60 percent of the demand for semiconductors comes from the personal computer industry. If there are order postponements because of weak worldwide economies, Cohu would feel the long-term effects."

Still, Black maintains he can sleep well at night owning this stock because Cohu has no debt and plenty of cash, which takes away much of the financial risk. "It has a solid management team, and I've known the founder for 17 years," he says. It should be noted that when Black first selected this stock for the book, it traded for around $20 a share. It then went on to double in a matter of weeks. Therefore, Black only recommends purchase of Coho at $40 or less, believing it still has a shot at reaching $80 by the end of 1999.

Contact Information: Charles A. Schwan
President and CEO
Cohu, Inc.
5755 Kearny Villa Road
San Diego, CA 92123-1170
(619) 277-6700
http://www.cohu.com

Cohu Incorporated

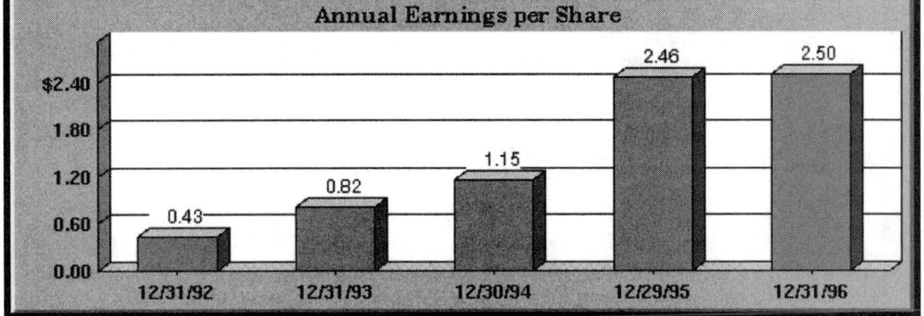

Cohu Incorporated

Symbol: COHU Exchange: Nasdaq NMS

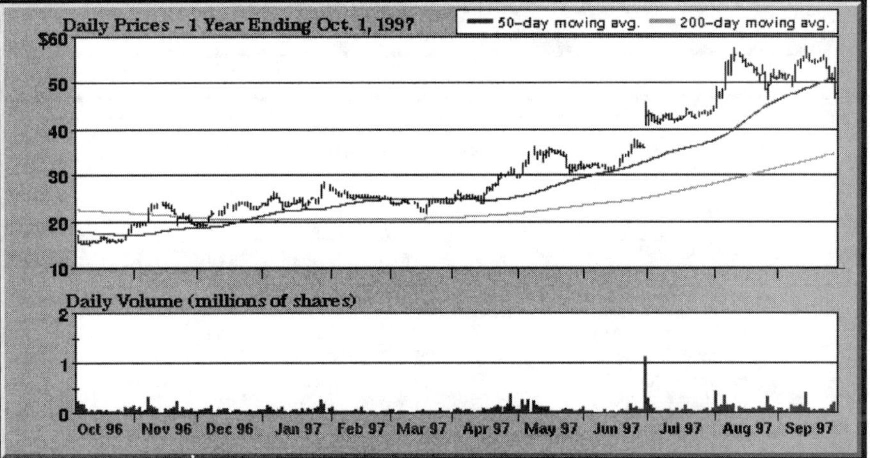

Latest Pricing Data (as of Oct. 1, 1997)		
Close (net change):	$47 5/8	(–3)
Day High & Low:	$53 1/4	$46 1/2
Volume & Avg. Volume:	213,100	80,082
52–Week High:	$11 5/8	Sep. 30, 1997
52–Week Low:	$6 3/4	Nov. 25, 1996
Latest Dividend:	$0.06	Sep. 3, 1997
Ind. Ann. Div. & Yield:	$0.24	0.50%
12 Month EPS:	$2.09	Jun. 30, 1997
P/E Ratio & Beta Factor:	22.79	1.000
Shares Outstanding:	9.272 million	
Market Value:	$442 million	
Institutional Holdings:	37.05%	
Number of Institutions:	65	
Primary Market:	Nasdaq NMS	

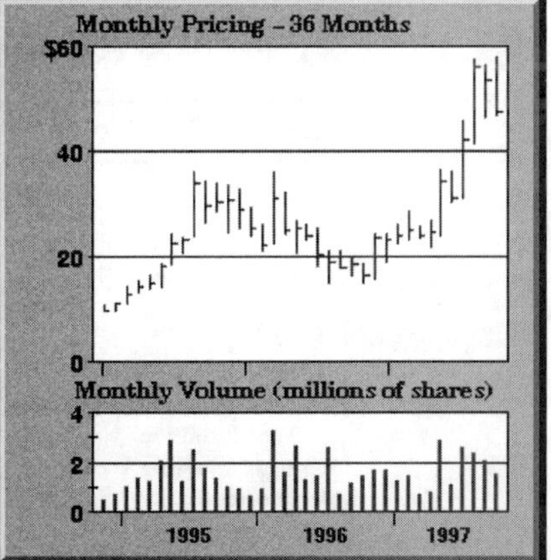

Currency: U.S. Dollars.

Source: IDD Information Services

Cohu Incorporated
Symbol: COHU

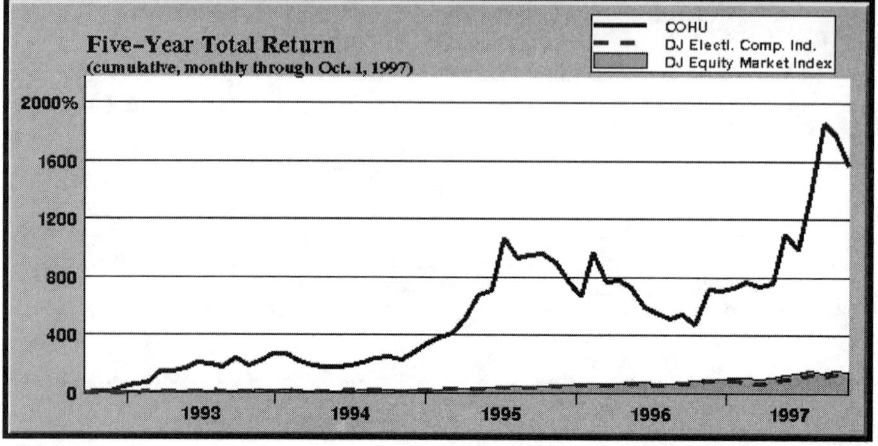

SELECTED INCOME STATEMENT AND BALANCE SHEET ITEMS

INCOME STATEMENT	7/31/92	7/30/93	7/29/94	7/31/95	7/31/96	LTM
Sales/Revenues	339.60	649.00	1,243.0	1,978.9	4,096.0	6,440.2
Cost of Goods Sold	104.50	196.90	382.00	585.70	1,277.3	N.A.
Pre-tax Margin (%)	40.10	42.40	41.00	34.30	35.80	N.A.
Operating Income	129.40	263.60	488.20	642.90	1,400.8	N.A.
Net Income before Extras	84.400	172.00	314.90	421.00	913.30	1,048.7
Reported Net Income	84.400	172.00	314.90	421.00	913.30	1,048.7
Depreciation & Amortization	6.700	13.600	30.800	58.500	132.60	N.A.
EPS from Net Income (Primary)	0.170	0.340	0.600	0.760	1.370	1.520
EPS from Net Income (Fully Diluted)	0.170	0.340	0.600	0.760	1.370	1.520
Dividend per Common Share	0.000	0.000	0.000	0.000	0.000	0.000
Dividend Yield (%)	N.A.	N.A.	N.A.	N.A.	N.A.	N.A.
Payout Ratio	N.A.	N.A.	N.A.	N.A.	N.A.	N.A.

BALANCE SHEET					
ASSETS					
Cash & Cash Equivalents	40.000	27.200	53.600	204.80	279.70
Inventories	9.100	23.500	27.900	71.200	301.20
Total Current Assets	247.10	268.30	507.70	996.00	2,159.6
Total Assets	323.90	595.20	1,053.7	1,757.3	3,630.2
LIABILITIES & EQUITY					
Short Term Debt	0.000	0.000	0.000	0.000	0.000
Long Term Debt	0.000	0.000	0.000	0.000	0.000
Total Liabilities	78.400	120.00	205.50	378.60	810.70
Shares Outstanding	480.888	494.832	515.394	544.492	649.284
Common Stockholder Equity	245.60	475.20	848.20	1,378.7	2,819.6
Total Stockholder Equity	245.60	475.20	848.20	1,378.7	2,819.6

Note: Figures in Millions of $ except: per share items, margins, yields, and ratios.

Source: IDD Information Services

COMPUTER SCIENCES

Elizabeth Bramwell
Bramwell Capital Management

Company Profile

Computer Sciences Corporation uses information technology to solve various business problems for its clients. "It's a financial information technology outsourcing company," says Elizabeth Bramwell of Bramwell Capital Management. "It plays into the theme that companies want to focus on their core businesses and outsource everything else." Computer Sciences Corporation, or CSC, offers a full range of services, from consulting to actual system design and integration. It has more than 44,000 employees who work in some 600 offices worldwide.

The company began as the brainchild of Roy Nutt and Fletcher Jones, who were 20-something aerospace computer analysts back in 1959. The two formed CSC with $100 and a contract from Honeywell to develop a business-language compiler called FACT. They saw an opportunity to provide computer manufacturers with software that could increase the productivity of programmers, while making it easier to use their machines. Back then, there were fewer than 3,000 computers in the entire world, compared to 200 million today. CSC later became the first software company to be listed on the New York Stock Exchange in 1968. The company initially focused on getting business from the federal government, before putting more emphasis on the commercial market in the mid-1980s. "Right now, it does about 71 percent of its business with the commercial sector and 29 percent with the federal government," Bramwell notes. "This company is growing at about 15 percent a year. It has picked up some really large outsourcing contracts recently with such companies as JP Morgan, DuPont, and CNA." CSC has also been on a buying spree, acquiring companies like Continuum, Planmetrics, American Practice Management, DAN Computer Management, and The Pinnacle Group in the past year. "Continuum basically has software for facilitating the processing of insurance claims, which really helps to bring down the cost of processing medical claims," Bramwell observes. "CSC integrated these various organizations into its existing structure and it seems to work very well."

CSC has managed some of the world's toughest projects over the past three decades, from advancing the nation's air traffic control system, to developing Europe's largest online tax system. It even created a private data network for the U.S. Treasury Department. Its clients come form a wide array of industries, including aerospace, automotive, banking, manufacturing, pharmaceuticals, retail, transportation, and utilities. "I think the company is well-positioned for doing systems integration on different computer systems for consulting and general outsourcing," Bramwell contends. "I also feel it's positioned for dealing with the year-2000 updates, which is going to be a really big issue going forward."

Reason for Recommendation

This brings us to the major reason Bramwell likes CSC as we enter 1998. The year-2000 issue gets more serious as each day goes by. As you may have heard, many computers are not designed to handle the year 2000 in their internal calendars. They read the "00" as 1900. If something isn't done soon, many major systems will come crashing down at the start of the new millennium.

CSC is involved in coming up with solutions for dealing with this problem, which Bramwell insists both the private sector and government will have to address right away. "The solution has to be in place by the beginning of 1999, because the biggest problem of all will be testing it to make sure all of these systems integrate properly," she cautions. "It's global in nature. The chain will be as strong as its weakest link." The weakest link right now may be the U.S. government, which Bramwell says apparently doesn't have a clue about how its going to solve this dilemma. "The government is farther behind than anyone, yet it has all of this massive data to protect for things like Social Security and the military," she observes. "I recently heard one U.S. Senator talk at a luncheon and I asked what the government planned to do to update its databases for the year 2000. He didn't have a clue as to what I was talking about. The other analysts and I looked at each other in absolute horror, because companies are spending hundreds of billions of dollars on this problem."

But Bramwell is quick to point out she didn't choose CSC merely as a year-2000 play. "There is an enormous trend among companies to get costs down by farming out data processing and using third parties like CSC to update all their systems," she says, adding that while the company has a number of smaller competitors, none are as capable or growing as fast as CSC. "I expect 16 to 17 percent annual growth going forward and think the stock should trade for at least 20 times earnings." Based on her 1998 earnings estimate of $3.90 per share, that would put the stock at around $80 by the end of the year.

Contact Information: Van B. Honeycutt
Chairman, President and CEO
Computer Sciences Corporation
2100 East Grand Avenue
El Segundo, CA 90245
(310) 615-0311
http://www.csc.com

Computer Sciences Corporation

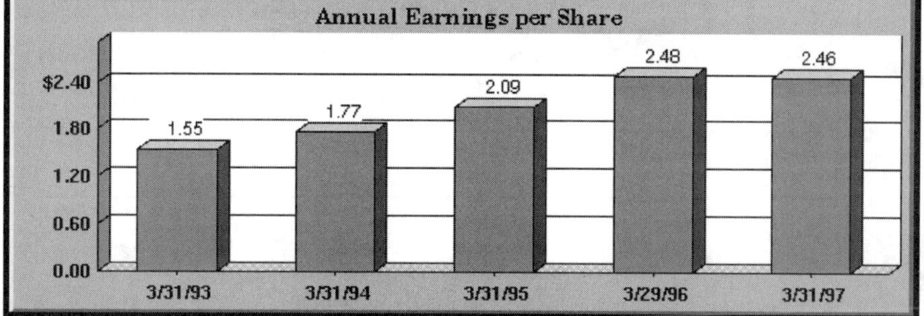

Computer Sciences Corporation

Symbol: CSC Exchange: NYSE

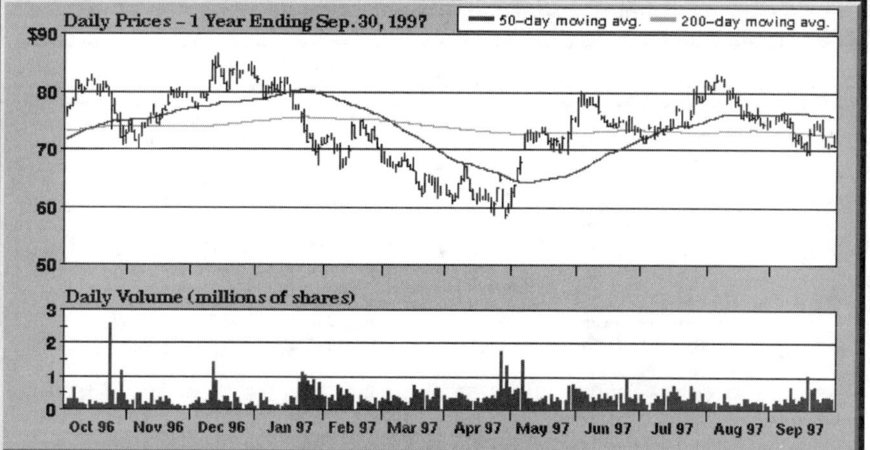

Latest Pricing Data (as of Sep. 30, 1997)		
Close (net change):	$70 3/4	(−1/4)
Day High & Low:	$72 5/8	$70 3/4
Volume & Avg. Volume:	325,500	278,300
52-Week High:	$86 1/2	Dec. 12, 1996
52-Week Low:	$57 7/8	Apr. 28, 1997
Latest Dividend:	$0.00	
Ind. Ann. Div. & Yield:	$0.00	N.A.
12 Month EPS:	$2.55	June 30, 1997
P/E Ratio & Beta Factor:	27.75	1.040
Shares Outstanding:	76.777 million	
Market Value:	$5.432 billion	
Institutional Holdings:	69.85%	
Number of Institutions:	614	
Primary Market:	NYSE	
Component of:	S&P 500	

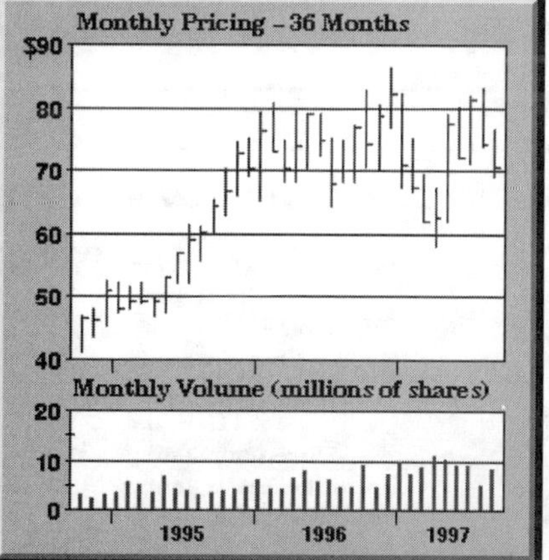

Currency: U.S. Dollars.

Source: IDD Information Services

Computer Sciences Corporation
Symbol: CSC

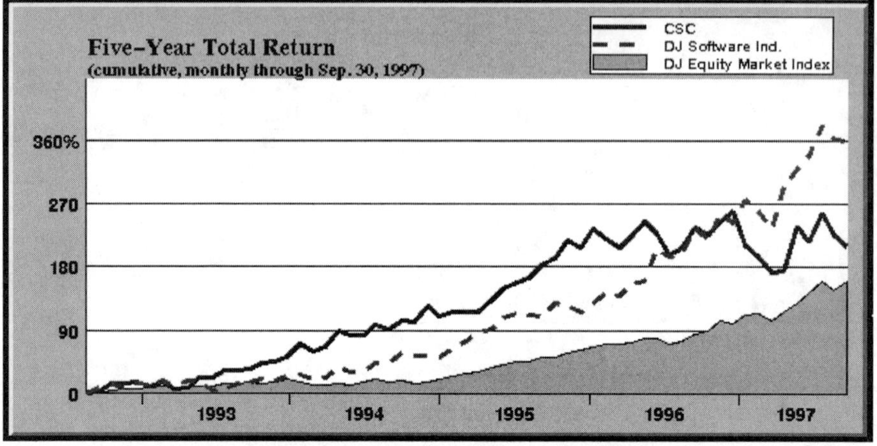

SELECTED INCOME STATEMENT AND BALANCE SHEET ITEMS

INCOME STATEMENT	3/31/93	3/31/94	3/31/95	3/29/96	3/31/97	LTM
Sales/Revenues	2,479.8	2,582.7	3,372.5	4,242.4	5,616.0	5,800.9
Cost of Goods Sold	1,977.7	2,065.0	2,685.6	3,349.7	4,413.2	4,547.3
Pre-tax Margin (%)	5.20	5.80	5.20	5.50	5.40	1.80
Operating Income	144.40	160.00	203.10	261.70	384.50	396.00
Net Income before Extras	78.100	90.900	110.70	141.70	192.40	199.70
Reported Net Income	78.100	90.900	110.70	141.70	192.40	199.70
Depreciation & Amortization	118.70	130.70	172.60	252.10	333.20	350.40
EPS from Net Income (Primary)	1.550	1.770	2.090	2.480	2.460	2.550
EPS from Net Income (Fully Diluted)	1.550	1.770	2.090	2.480	2.460	2.550
Dividend per Common Share	0.000	0.000	0.000	0.000	0.000	0.000
Dividend Yield (%)	N.A.	N.A.	N.A.	N.A.	N.A.	N.A.
Payout Ratio	N.A.	N.A.	N.A.	N.A.	N.A.	N.A.
BALANCE SHEET						
ASSETS						
Cash & Cash Equivalents	111.50	126.80	155.30	104.90	110.70	
Inventories	0.000	0.000	0.000	0.000	0.000	
Total Current Assets	747.80	857.10	1,081.5	1,144.3	1,612.4	
Total Assets	1,453.6	1,806.4	2,333.7	2,595.8	3,580.9	
LIABILITIES & EQUITY						
Short Term Debt	16.700	50.500	137.40	70.300	29.900	
Long Term Debt	295.30	273.30	310.30	405.50	630.80	
Total Liabilities	758.20	1,000.7	1,185.1	1,290.2	1,911.2	
Shares Outstanding	49.913	51.910	55.171	56.030	76.593	
Common Stockholder Equity	695.40	805.70	1,148.6	1,305.7	1,669.6	
Total Stockholder Equity	695.40	805.70	1,148.6	1,305.7	1,669.6	

Note: Figures in Millions of $ except: per share items, margins, yields, and ratios.

Source: IDD Information Services

CROMPTON & KNOWLES

John Wallace
Robertson Stephens Investment Management

Company Profile

"This is the typical stock I love to own," says John Wallace, portfolio manager of the Robertson Stephens Growth & Income fund. "It's underowned, underfollowed, but has a couple of visible catalysts that I don't think are appreciated yet."

First, some background. Crompton & Knowles is a specialty chemical manufacturing company with several different businesses. The largest, which accounts for 27 percent of sales, is involved in manufacturing rubber chemicals and polymers. "It makes a lot of mundane stuff, like the black sealants you see around your car's doors and windows," Wallace observes. "It also makes the roofing membranes that you lay on top of a roof before you put your shingles down."

C&K's other primary businesses include one that produces chemicals for crop protection and another that develops ingredients for sweeteners and colors. Now back to that catalyst Wallace was talking about. "It is really twofold," he says. "Management and a restructuring story. The restructuring is just now beginning and will start to accelerate during 1998."

Here's the story: In 1996, C&K merged with Uniroyal Chemical. The current president, chairman and chief executive officer of C&K, Vincent Calarco, who joined the company in 1985, used to be head of the chemicals division at Uniroyal. "This means he knows where all of the bodies are buried," Wallace maintains.

The Uniroyal merger tripled the size of the company and markedly expanded its global reach. Calarco calls it the most significant strategic move in the company's 156-year history. "By completing the merger with Uniroyal, we set Crompton & Knowles on course for extending its success with new businesses and new products in markets around the world," Calarco says. "The merger supports our declared corporate objectives to expand our asset base in specialty chemicals, significantly increase worldwide market positions, add new platforms for growth, and enhance our company's earnings power. The new Crompton & Knowles is a $1.8 billion, broadly based, specialty chemicals company dedicated to meeting customer needs through technology, service, and performance."

Reason for Recommendation

Wallace points out that a lot of the company's divisions are slow growers. "It has a die business, which has been under a lot of competitive pressure over the last year," he says. "I will admit, though, that Calarco has cut costs while increasing profitability, and Crompton & Knowles has done quite well." However, the company's stock peaked at $25 back in 1993. What could make it move higher? Wallace's other catalyst: a meaningful restructuring that he believes will start to accelerate this year.

"By restructuring, I mean Calarco can do a lot of things to help drive the earnings and cash flow of this company a lot higher than what Wall Street is looking at," he contends. "What we've got here is the potential divestiture of some of its slower growth businesses. We could have a turnaround in the Uniroyal Chemical business, which is more cyclically oriented. And we could have a divestiture of the nonstrategic businesses."

The problem is, Calarco has been held back from doing any of this until 1998. "When they merged the two companies, they did a pooling of interest," Wallace points out. "Calarco is precluded from selling anything until August of 1998. A lot of people on Wall Street know this can happen, though they're not going to buy the stock if they have to wait for him to take action. But if he executes this restructuring game plan, the stock has the potential to go a lot higher." Wallace adds that Calarco owns 1.75 million shares of the company's stock, meaning he has a strong incentive to make this strategy work. Wallace looks for the company to earn $1.45 a share in 1998, climbing to near $2 in 1999.

There are several things that could cripple this catalyst. For one, the company has a lousy balance sheet. "Uniroyal was undercapitalized, so the company has a negative net worth of about $96 million and debt of approximately $1 billion," Wallace admits. "That's going to be scary to a lot of people. But the company generates free cash, and I think it will be able to pay off this debt to the tune of $100 million a year for the next few years."

There's also a chance the marriage of these two companies won't go as smoothly as planned, the economy could worsen and hurt the chemicals business, or the divestiture might not happen as expected. All of these would damage the stock. But if Wallace's scenario pans out, and the catalyst becomes a reality, he expects the stock to trade above $30 within the next two years.

Contact Information: Vincent A. Calarco
Chairman, President and CEO
Crompton & Knowles Corporation
One Station Place, Metro Center
Stanford, CT 06902
(203) 353-5400

Crompton and Knowles Corporation

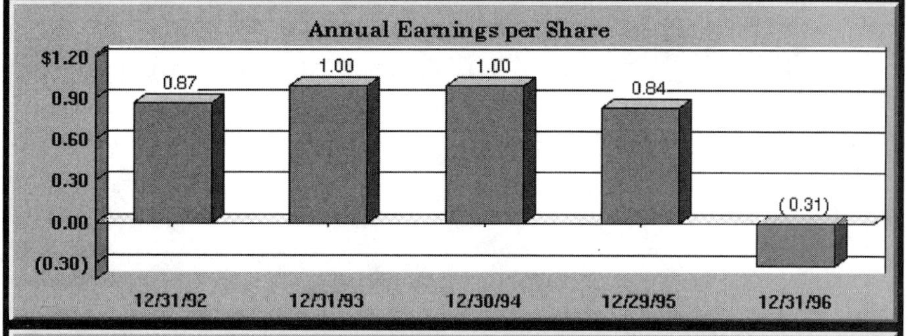

Crompton and Knowles Corporation

Symbol: CNK Exchange: NYSE

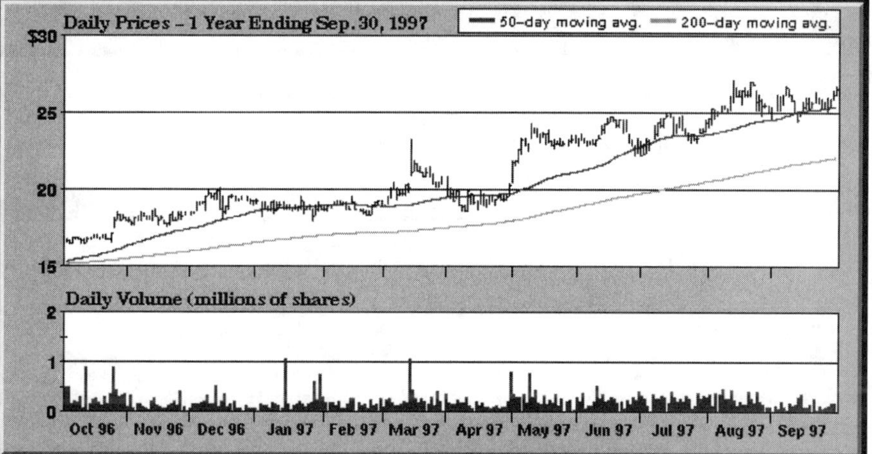

Latest Pricing Data (as of Sep. 30, 1997)		
Close (net change):	$26 9/16	(+5/16)
Day High & Low:	$26 3/4	$26 1/8
Volume & Avg. Volume:	162,900	254,852
52-Week High:	$27 1/8	Aug. 12, 1997
52-Week Low:	$16 3/8	Oct. 9, 1996
Latest Dividend:	$0.05	May 7, 1997
Ind. Ann. Div. & Yield:	$0.05	0.19%
12 Month EPS:	($0.17)	June 30, 1997
P/E Ratio & Beta Factor:	N.A.	0.471
Shares Outstanding:	73.200 million	
Market Value:	$1.944 billion	
Institutional Holdings:	76.94%	
Number of Institutions:	258	
Primary Market:	NYSE	

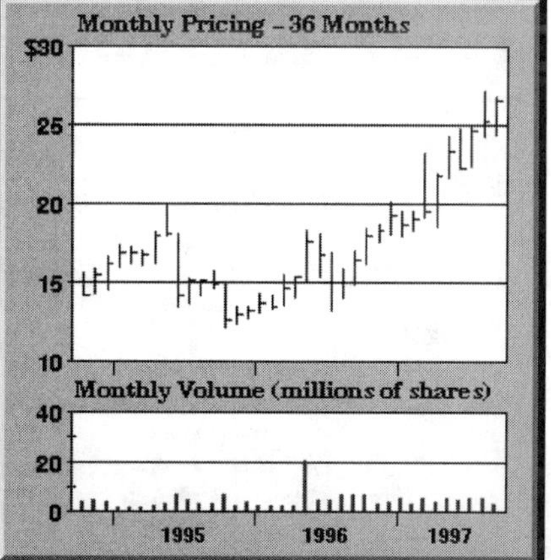

Currency: U.S. Dollars.

Source: IDD Information Services

Crompton and Knowles Corporation
Symbol: CNK

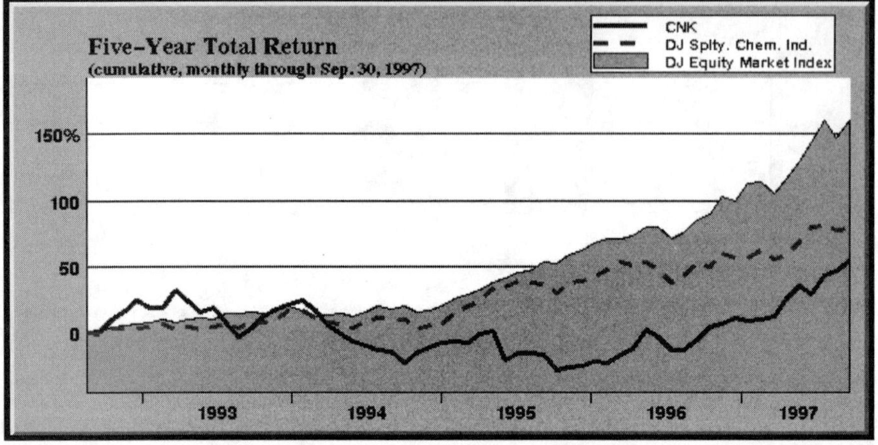

SELECTED INCOME STATEMENT AND BALANCE SHEET ITEMS

INCOME STATEMENT	12/31/92	12/31/93	12/30/94	12/29/95	12/31/96	LTM
Sales/Revenues	517.70	558.30	589.80	665.50	1,804.0	1,841.9
Cost of Goods Sold	357.10	380.90	403.80	473.70	1,170.6	1,197.4
Pre-tax Margin (%)	13.20	14.80	13.60	9.60	(0.50)	0.45
Operating Income	72.700	82.300	81.100	72.300	218.60	235.20
Net Income before Extras	43.300	52.000	50.900	40.500	(22.100)	(9.200)
Reported Net Income	43.300	52.000	50.900	40.500	(22.100)	(9.200)
Depreciation & Amortization	11.600	12.100	13.300	15.000	82.600	80.400
EPS from Net Income (Primary)	0.870	1.000	1.000	0.840	(0.310)	(0.170)
EPS from Net Income (Fully Diluted)	0.870	1.000	1.000	0.840	(0.310)	(0.170)
Dividend per Common Share	0.265	0.380	0.460	0.525	0.270	0.050
Dividend Yield (%)	1.19	1.73	2.83	3.96	1.40	0.22
Payout Ratio	0.30	0.38	0.46	0.63	N.A.	N.A.

BALANCE SHEET					
ASSETS					
Cash & Cash Equivalents	2.400	9.300	1.800	0.900	21.100
Inventories	115.70	113.90	157.40	154.90	362.30
Total Current Assets	207.40	220.40	260.70	291.50	742.20
Total Assets	350.70	363.20	432.30	484.10	1,657.2
LIABILITIES & EQUITY					
Short Term Debt	5.400	5.100	39.700	60.400	9.300
Long Term Debt	24.000	14.000	54.000	64.000	1,055.0
Total Liabilities	139.30	123.20	208.50	244.10	1,753.6
Shares Outstanding	51.082	52.176	50.406	53.015	72.940
Common Stockholder Equity	211.50	240.00	223.90	240.00	(96.400)
Total Stockholder Equity	211.50	240.00	223.90	240.00	(96.400)

Note: Figures in Millions of $ except: per share items, margins, yields, and ratios.

Source: IDD Information Services

DELL COMPUTER

James Collins
Insight Capital

Company Profile

What began in founder Michael Dell's college dorm in 1984 has turned into a $9 billion dollar business that has revolutionized the way people buy computers. Dell Computer markets its products directly to customers, which include corporations, the government, educational institutions, small businesses, and individuals. Roughly 90 percent of the company's revenues come from its corporate and government clients. Dell's products include desktops and notebooks, all of which are custom-designed based on the specific needs of each customer. Products can be purchased over the phone or through the Internet. Dell also sells some systems through mass merchants to supplement its direct-marketing strategy, and offers an extensive selection of peripherals and software.

The company was started on the belief that delivering custom-built computers is the best way to provide solutions that are most relevant to the end-user. This flexible manufacturing process allows Dell to keep minimal inventory levels, while providing customers with the latest equipment and processors. By contrast, their competitors are often forced to dramatically reduce the prices of their older, prebuilt models that quickly become obsolete as new technologies and faster processors are introduced. "The Dell salesman writes an order and puts down the features you want," explains James Collins of Insight Capital. "He then sends it off to the back room, and out the door it goes."

This method is not only more efficient, but also cuts down on the cost of doing business. "Dell has built its business through direct marketing, which cuts out a lot of the middle people and enhances profits. This is one of the best managed companies in the computer business," Collins insists. "Even when it gets into problems it gets out of them quickly. I like the company's marketing concept and aggressiveness. Plus, they're expanding rapidly in Europe and Asia." Dell launched its first international operation in the United Kingdom during 1987 and has since opened offices in 28 countries outside the United States. Its products are available in more than 140 countries and territories, and the company employs more than 10,000 people worldwide. "I didn't think it would have as much luck as it did in Europe, but it's done a very good job there," Collins admits. "Dell is even selling machines in Japan, which is saying a lot." At present, the company sends 67 percent of its computers to customers in America, with 26 percent in Europe and 7 percent in Asia.

"Dell has had dramatic growth in gross margins, due primarily to cutting costs on components," Collins observes. "It has been able to continue to grow its bottom-line profits, despite price cuts. It also has a very good product breadth and is on the cutting edge of what's new in PCs. These guys are right there all the time."

During the past year, revenues grew by 52 percent, operating income increased by 51 percent, and the company now has one of the strongest balance sheets in the business, with more than $640 million in cash and investments. This solid financial position allowed it to finance its growth through internal funds without taking on any additional debt or equity. And the company keeps exceeding even the most optimistic expectations on the Street. Of course, this hasn't gone unnoticed by investors. Dell stock rose more than 207 percent in 1996 and was continuing to skyrocket as this book went to print. This means that when the company comes out with a disappointing earnings report down the line, the stock will be highly vulnerable.

Reason for Recommendation

Nevertheless, Collins believes Dell stock has more steam left in the coming months. Part of his enthusiasm rests with his belief that corporate America will continue to buy newer computers directly through manufacturers like Dell, instead of going to the store for a prepackaged model. "Companies are upgrading because of Windows NT, and you see a lot of the stuff being bought directly from Dell," Collins maintains. "In my own office, I replace all of my computers every 18 months."

There's also the question of whether the PC industry in general will continue to grow. "I think it will, though it may be slower than in the past," Collins predicts. "After all, Intel keeps bringing out these new chips which give you all kinds of new things you didn't have before. Americans are high-tech oriented and can't wait to get the next gizmos on their machines, so I can't see any reason why the business will slow down." In Collins's mind, the biggest risk of all is that economic growth in the United States will slow, causing both companies and individuals to cut back on investments in equipment like computers. "If economic growth weakens both here and in Europe, you get a double whammy," he warns. For this stock to continue to climb higher, Collins's optimistic expectations must come to fruition. Otherwise, this stock, which seems to defy gravity, could come crashing back down to earth.

Contact Information: Michael Dell
Chairman and CEO
Dell Computer Corporation
2214 West Braker Lane, Suite D
Austin, TX 78758-4053
(512) 338-4400
http://www.dell.com

Dell Computer Corporation

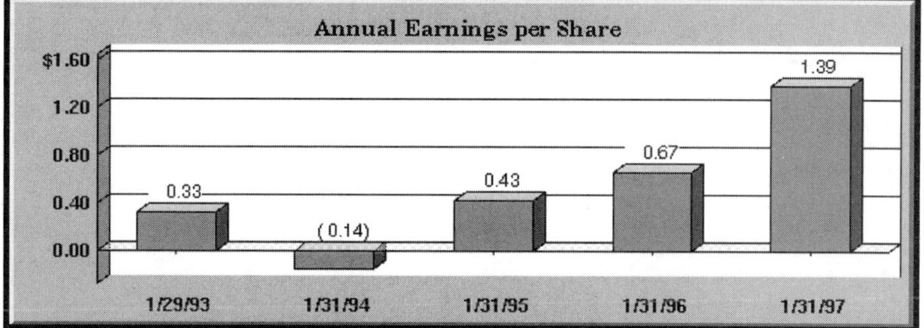

Dell Computer Corporation

Symbol: DELL Exchange: Nasdaq NMS

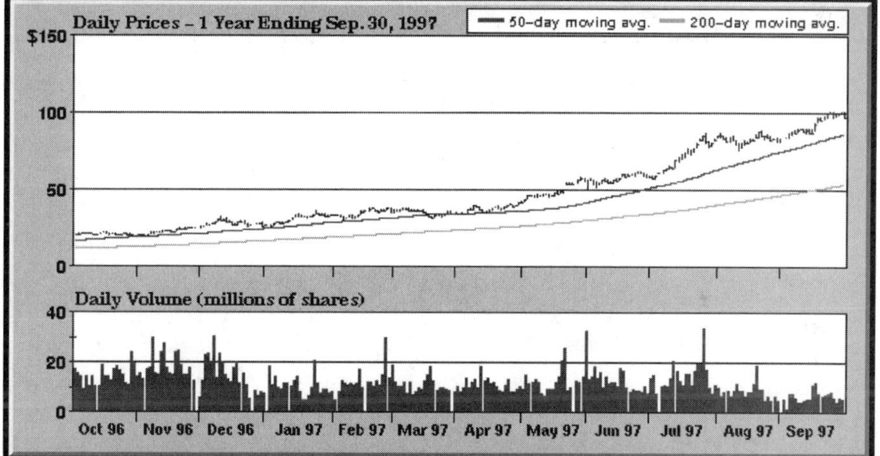

Latest Pricing Data (as of Sep. 30, 1997)		
Close (net change):	$96 7/8	(–3 1/2)
Day High & Low:	$100 7/8	$96 5/16
Volume & Avg. Volume:	5,417,000	13,421,751
52-Week High:	$101 1/4	Sep. 29, 1997
52-Week Low:	$18 29/32	Oct. 29, 1996
Latest Dividend:	$0.00	
Ind. Ann. Div. & Yield:	$0.00	N.A.
12 Month EPS:	$2.02	July 31, 1997
P/E Ratio & Beta Factor:	47.96	1.598
Shares Outstanding:	331.348 million	
Market Value:	$32.099 billion	
Institutional Holdings:	57.23%	
Number of Institutions:	678	
Primary Market:	Nasdaq NMS	
Component of:	S&P 500	

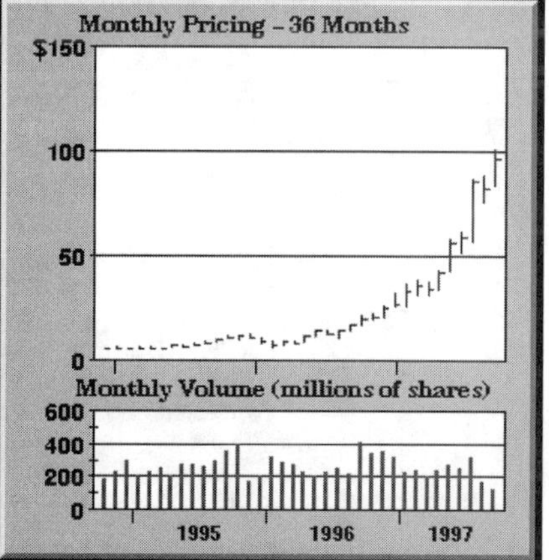

Currency: U.S. Dollars.

Source: IDD Information Services

Dell Computer Corporation
Symbol: DELL

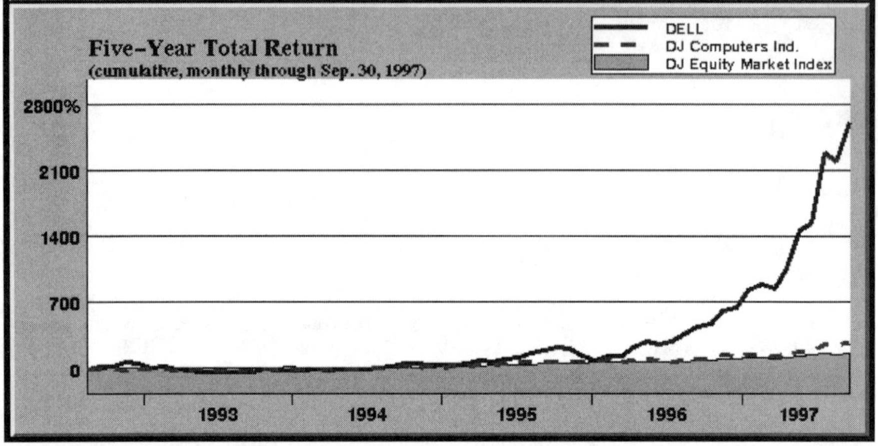

SELECTED INCOME STATEMENT AND BALANCE SHEET ITEMS

INCOME STATEMENT	1/29/93	1/31/94	1/31/95	1/31/96	1/31/97	LTM
Sales/Revenues	2,013.9	2,873.2	3,475.3	5,296.0	7,759.0	9,833.0
Cost of Goods Sold	1,544.9	2,409.7	2,704.2	4,191.0	6,046.0	7,621.0
Pre-tax Margin (%)	7.10	(1.40)	6.10	7.20	9.60	10.85
Operating Income	139.10	(38.900)	249.20	377.00	714.00	1,025.0
Net Income before Extras	101.60	(35.900)	149.20	272.00	531.00	749.00
Reported Net Income	101.60	(35.900)	149.20	272.00	531.00	749.00
Depreciation & Amortization	19.600	30.600	33.100	38.000	47.000	56.000
EPS from Net Income (Primary)	0.330	(0.140)	0.430	0.670	1.390	2.020
EPS from Net Income (Fully Diluted)	0.330	(0.140)	0.400	0.670	1.390	2.020
Dividend per Common Share	0.000	0.000	0.000	0.000	0.000	0.000
Dividend Yield (%)	N.A.	N.A.	N.A.	N.A.	N.A.	N.A.
Payout Ratio	N.A.	N.A.	N.A.	N.A.	N.A.	N.A.

BALANCE SHEET					
ASSETS					
Cash & Cash Equivalents	14.900	3.400	43.000	55.000	115.00
Inventories	303.20	220.30	292.90	429.00	251.00
Total Current Assets	852.80	1,048.4	1,470.4	1,957.0	2,747.0
Total Assets	927.00	1,140.5	1,594.0	2,148.0	2,993.0
LIABILITIES & EQUITY					
Short Term Debt	0.000	0.000	0.000	0.000	0.000
Long Term Debt	48.400	100.00	113.40	113.00	18.000
Total Liabilities	557.80	669.40	942.20	1,175.0	2,187.0
Shares Outstanding	294.864	303.432	317.440	373.788	346.094
Common Stockholder Equity	369.20	471.10	651.70	973.00	806.00
Total Stockholder Equity	369.20	471.10	651.70	973.00	806.00

Note: Figures in Millions of $ except: per share items, margins, yields, and ratios.

Source: IDD Information Services

DEPARTMENT 56

Donald Yacktman
Yacktman Asset Management

Company Profile

Chances are you own some of the ceramic lighted pieces from the Original Snow Village or Heritage Village collections put out by Department 56. These charming figurines are a common sight in most homes around Christmas. Or perhaps you're familiar with the company's Snowbabies and Snowbunnies products that have become so popular. In any case, Department 56 is a leading designer and marketer of lighted ceramic and porcelain houses and accessories, like those listed above. It also produces an extensive array of holiday and decorative products for the home, including Christmas tree ornaments. The company sells these products through gift, specialty, and department stores around the country. It retires a number of existing pieces each year to keep consumers interested in adding to their collections

"Department 56 designs these ceramic products, but they are made by hand in China and brought back here for distribution," notes Don Yacktman, president of Yacktman Asset Management and the company's largest shareholder. "It doesn't have any money tied up in fixed assets, and it makes enormous amounts of money. It nets about 20 cents on the dollar after tax on these things, yet the pieces are sold at reasonable prices and are collectibles."

The company's unit sales are growing at double digit rates, but that's not readily apparent from looking at its latest balance sheet. "What happened is a lot of the stores that sell these products were purchasing them at a faster rate than they were being bought by consumers," Yacktman explains. "So in 1996, the company began to slim down the marketing channels and reduce inventory levels. It also had people go into these stores and encourage buyers not to overstock since they could make better returns by being more conservative."

Nevertheless, with fewer reorders coming in, profits for the company went down. So did the price of its stock, from a high of $47 in 1994 to the mid-$20s at the end of 1996. But better days may be around the corner. That's why Yacktman is so enthusiastic. In fact, his firm has snapped up some 14.5 percent of the outstanding shares in anticipation of an upward reversal in sales and profits.

Reason for Recommendation

"Department 56 has taken many steps to turn this oversupply situation around and is meeting with reasonable success," he says. "One thing it did is move its production facilities from Taiwan to China, enabling it to get an eight-week turnaround, as opposed to several months. This allows stores to carry a smaller inventory, but they can get more product fast when they need it."

Retailers seem to be taking the company's advice to keep fewer collectibles on display. "Dealers are ordering smarter," says Department 56 president Susan Engel. "They are reordering less, ordering it later, and putting a greater emphasis on newly introduced products. They are substantially meeting consumer demand for older product with inventory they had accumulated over several years. At the same time, we have embarked on several marketing initiatives to increase demand." This includes a mix of collector shows, improved store displays, a Web site, more advertising, and the introduction of several new limited edition collectibles. In addition, the company is trying to open up several nontraditional marketing channels, such as incentive programs and the television shopping networks.

"You have a situation where you've shrunken the inventory in the channel, which means sales for Department 56 are slightly down," Yacktman explains. "But on the retail level, sales are still growing at double-digit rates." Yacktman maintains that the company should be able to grow by about 15 percent this year, and once the short-term trouble in earnings works itself out, he believes the stock will get a big boost. "The company should earn between $1.80 and $1.90 this year, with 20 cents of goodwill," he adds. "The company has enormous cash flows, generates excess money, and is virtually debt free. Management is also buying back stock." Yacktman contends the company sells for much less than it's worth, estimating the private market value of Department 56 to be around $40 per share.

There are several risks to consider: First, the company's sales are highly seasonal and dependent on the economy. If we get into a recession, people are likely to spend less on luxury items like porcelain collectibles. Also, there's no guarantee this problem of excess inventory will reverse itself quickly. It could take years. Furthermore, because all of the company's products are manufactured overseas, it has little control over quality and could find itself forced to pay higher labor costs. Finally, the market for gift items is highly competitive and someone else could come up with products that capture more public attention than those put out by Department 56.

Contact Information: Susan Engel
President and CEO
Department 56, Inc.
6436 City West Parkway
Eden Prairie, MN 55344
(612) 944-5600
http://www.d56.com

Department 56 Incorporated

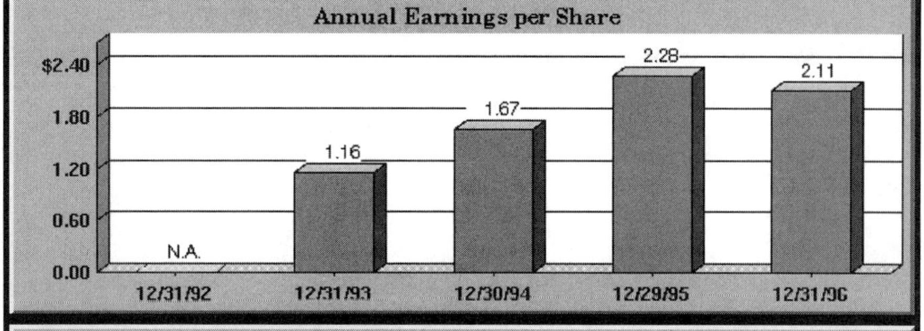

Department 56 Incorporated

Symbol: DFS Exchange: NYSE

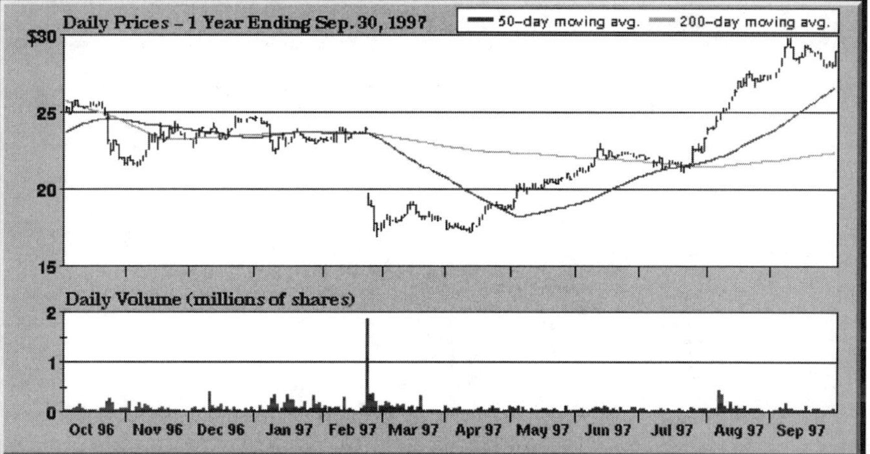

Latest Pricing Data (as of Sep. 30, 1997)		
Close (net change):	$28 15/16	(+7/8)
Day High & Low:	$29	$27 15/16
Volume & Avg. Volume:	50,400	157,351
52-Week High:	$29 13/16	Sep. 9, 1997
52-Week Low:	$16 7/8	Feb. 26, 1997
Latest Dividend:	$0.00	
Ind. Ann. Div. & Yield:	$0.00	N.A.
12 Month EPS:	$1.75	June 30, 1997
P/E Ratio & Beta Factor:	16.54	0.761
Shares Outstanding:	20.838 million	
Market Value:	$603 million	
Institutional Holdings:	79.94%	
Number of Institutions:	150	
Primary Market:	NYSE	

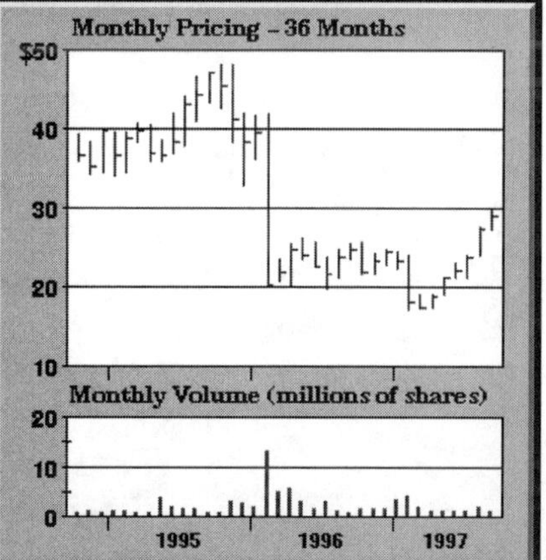

Currency: U.S. Dollars.

Source: IDD Information Services

Department 56 Incorporated
Symbol: DFS

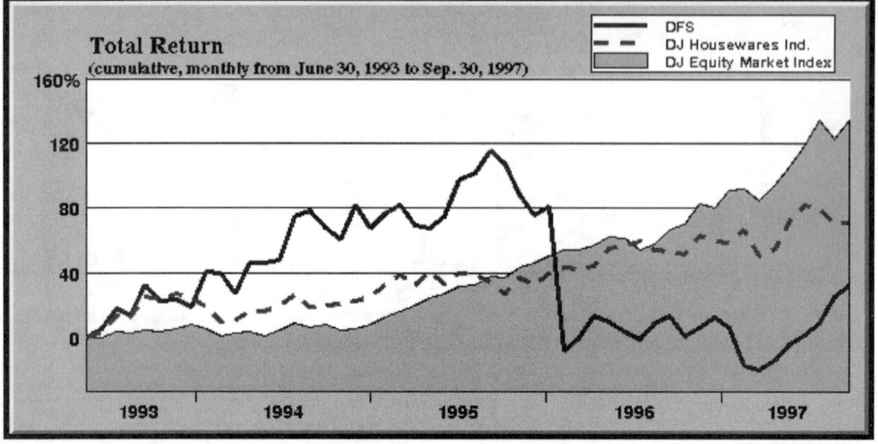

SELECTED INCOME STATEMENT AND BALANCE SHEET ITEMS

INCOME STATEMENT	12/31/92	12/31/93	12/30/94	12/29/95	12/31/96	LTM
Sales/Revenues	N.A.	184.40	217.90	252.00	228.80	198.80
Cost of Goods Sold	N.A.	85.600	96.500	108.40	93.500	81.100
Pre-tax Margin (%)	N.A.	23.20	28.10	33.10	33.10	29.67
Operating Income	N.A.	57.800	73.000	89.500	80.700	65.200
Net Income before Extras	N.A.	25.000	36.100	49.600	45.900	37.600
Reported Net Income	N.A.	25.000	36.100	49.600	45.900	37.600
Depreciation & Amortization	N.A.	6.300	6.600	6.200	6.300	6.200
EPS from Net Income (Primary)	N.A.	1.160	1.670	2.280	2.110	1.750
EPS from Net Income (Fully Diluted)	N.A.	1.160	1.670	2.280	2.110	1.750
Dividend per Common Share	N.A.	N.A.	N.A.	N.A.	N.A.	N.A.
Dividend Yield (%)	N.A.	N.A.	N.A.	N.A.	N.A.	N.A.
Payout Ratio	N.A.	N.A.	N.A.	N.A.	N.A.	N.A.

BALANCE SHEET					
ASSETS					
Cash & Cash Equivalents	N.A.	7.400	2.200	7.800	46.400
Inventories	N.A.	17.400	20.400	29.100	20.500
Total Current Assets	N.A.	44.600	52.400	77.700	109.30
Total Assets	N.A.	234.90	239.70	259.10	285.70
LIABILITIES & EQUITY					
Short Term Debt	N.A.	3.600	20.000	20.000	20.000
Long Term Debt	N.A.	148.00	93.000	60.000	40.000
Total Liabilities	N.A.	173.10	139.40	108.80	89.000
Shares Outstanding	N.A.	21.343	21.475	21.546	21.584
Common Stockholder Equity	N.A.	61.700	100.30	150.30	196.80
Total Stockholder Equity	N.A.	61.700	100.30	150.30	196.80

Note: Figures in Millions of $ except: per share items, margins, yields, and ratios.

Source: IDD Information Services

FANNIE MAE

David Dreman

Dreman Value Advisors

Company Profile

Fannie Mae might sound like the name of your sweet aunt who used to bake piping hot chocolate chip cookies served with a chilled glass of ice cold milk. In reality, however, this aunt looks more like your uncle — Uncle Sam, that is. That's because Fannie Mae (short for Federal National Mortgage Association) used to be part of the federal government. It was established by Congress in 1938 to bring stability to the U.S. housing market and make sure that mortgages were readily available to the public. Thirty years later, Fannie Mae became a private company and went public in 1970. The company no longer receives any government funding or backing. Instead, it is one of the country's biggest taxpayers.

"Fannie Mae is the nation's largest provider of residential mortgage funds," explains David Dreman of Dreman Value Advisors. "Its growth record has just been sensational over the years, yet it is attractively priced. It traded for around 40 times earnings back in the 1970s. Today, it's around 16 times earnings."

Fannie Mae doesn't lend money directly to homebuyers. Instead, it purchases mortgages from lenders like banks and savings and loans, thus giving them more funds to lend to other potential homebuyers. One in five home loans ultimately winds up in Fannie Mae's hands. The company then borrows money to buy these loans by issuing debt in the global capital markets. It profits from the spread between the yield of the mortgages and cost of this debt. "It might be getting an 8.5 percent return on money it borrowed for 7.5 percent," Dreman notes. "In this case, it makes the 1 percent spread, plus part of the servicing fees it charges."

Fannie Mae's other profit center, the mortgage-backed securities business, guarantees the timely payment of principal and interest on securities backed by pools of mortgages. "What it does is secure the loans," Dreman says. "In other words, it will package a whole group of these loans. Say it gets 500 or 1,000 loans. It will put them together in a package. Then it sells them off to investors. It's a very complex process. Fannie Mae promises to make good on the money if the loan package fails. It receives both a fee for putting the package together and a servicing fee." The company earned an incredible $2.7 billion in 1996 from these two activities and is now the largest corporation in the United States in terms of assets.

Fannie Mae is by far the leading owner of single-family American mortgages and the biggest financial services company in the world. Its book of business includes more than 10 million mortgages, and it has made a commitment to loan a total of $1 trillion by the end of the decade. The company has experienced consistent double-digit growth for the past decade, surviving various economic cycles and plummeting interest rates. "This is a very high-quality outfit that is dealing in a major market," Dreman says. "I expect growth to continue on the order of 12 to 15 percent a year. If this wasn't a financial company, and instead was called Fannie Internet, it would be trading a 300 times earnings given the kind of record it has."

Reason for Recommendation

Dreman calls Fannie Mae "about the closest thing you can find to owning part of the U.S. government." As previously mentioned, the company is no longer directly connected to any federal department, though it is on very friendly terms with both Congress and the White House. "Neither political party wants to attack the company since it makes loans in almost every county in the country," Dreman observes.

Two obvious risks to this stock are rising interest rates and the chance that the United States may hit hard times in 1998, which could cause an increase in the number of defaults on loans. But Dreman isn't worried. "Fannie Mae has very stringent standards," he points out. "It doesn't loan money for large homes, and always has very good collateral. The company has also become quite sophisticated. It matches its liabilities to its interest payments. In other words, if it puts out a heavy weighting of 30-year mortgages this year, it will make sure there are matching securities to protect against any swing in interest rates." Historically, the company's credit performance has been outstanding. Its credit loss ratio, which is the total credit losses as a percentage of mortgages outstanding, is a mere 0.05.

Dreman admits higher rates could hurt the stock in the short term. But, to him, this would be a buying opportunity for what he considers to be a long-term hold. The stock has certainly treated investors well in the past, averaging a compounded 30 percent annualized return over the past ten years. "This is a very well-managed, high-quality company," he adds. "As long as it continues to trade for a low PE ratio relative to the market, especially given the kind of growth it has had, I will be happy to own this stock."

Contact Information: James A. Johnson
Chairman and CEO
Fannie Mae
3900 Wisconsin Avenue
Washington, DC 20016
(800) 366-2968
http//www.fanniemae.com

Federal National Mortgage Association

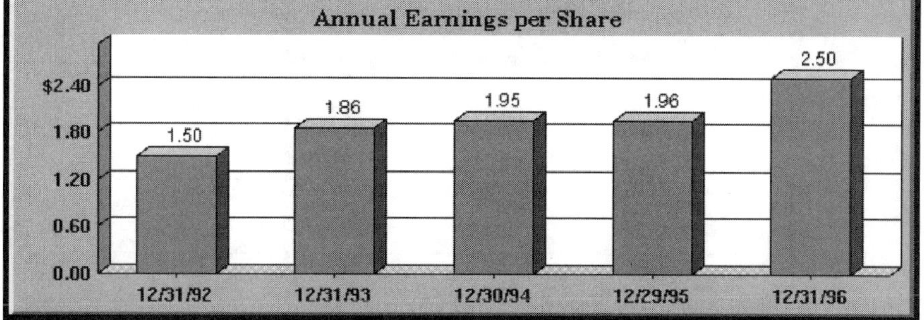

Federal National Mortgage Association

Symbol: FNM Exchange: NYSE

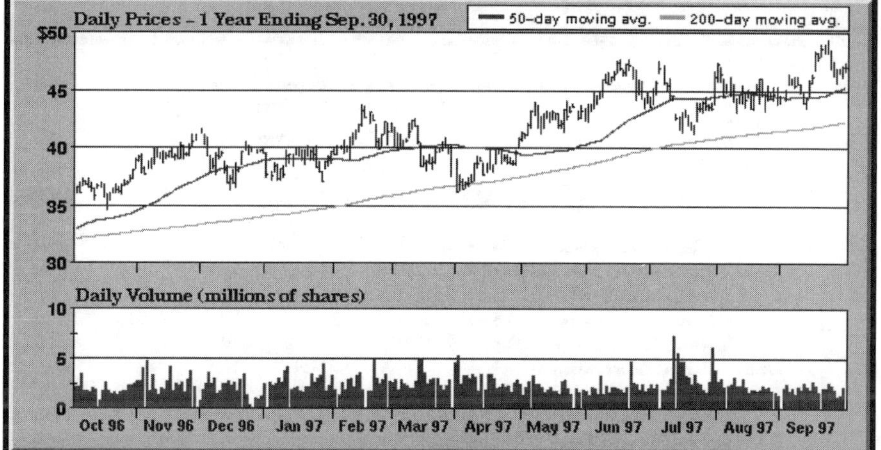

Latest Pricing Data (as of Sep. 30, 1997)		
Close (net change):	$47	(unch.)
Day High & Low:	$47 3/8	$46 1/2
Volume & Avg. Volume:	2,110,000	2,822,737
52-Week High:	$49 7/16	Sep. 22, 1997
52-Week Low:	$34 1/2	Oct. 16, 1996
Latest Dividend:	$0.21	July 29, 1997
Ind. Ann. Div. & Yield:	$0.84	1.79%
12 Month EPS:	$2.64	June 30, 1997
P/E Ratio & Beta Factor:	17.80	1.651
Shares Outstanding:	1.061 billion	
Market Value:	$49.867 billion	
Institutional Holdings:	80.12%	
Number of Institutions:	1704	
Primary Market:	NYSE	
Component of:	S&P 500	

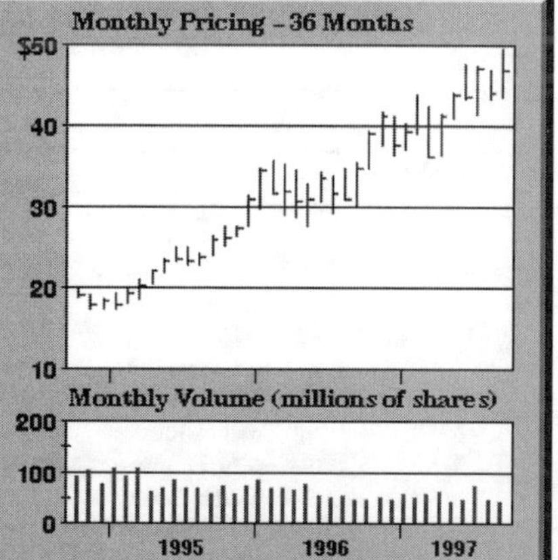

Currency: U.S. Dollars.

Source: IDD Information Services

Federal National Mortgage Association
Symbol: FNM

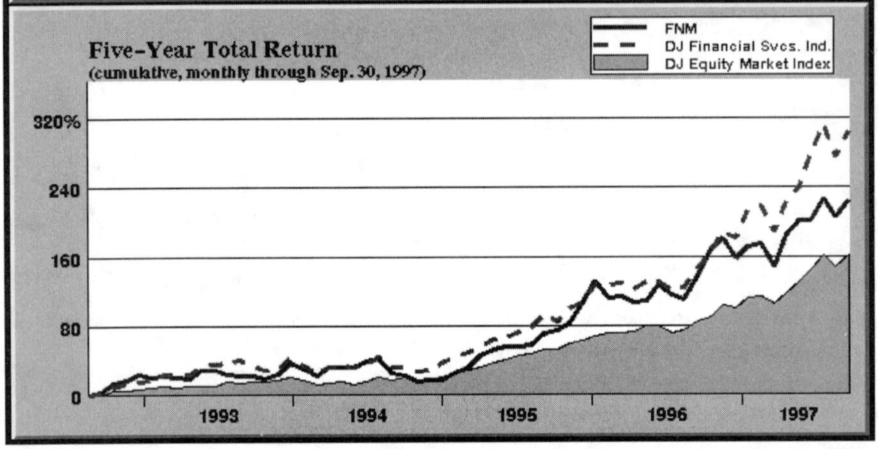

SELECTED INCOME STATEMENT AND BALANCE SHEET ITEMS

INCOME STATEMENT	12/31/92	12/31/93	12/30/94	12/29/95	12/31/96	LTM
Sales/Revenues	14,559	16,053	18,573	22,249	25,054	26,378
Cost of Goods Sold	N.A.	N.A.	N.A.	N.A.	N.A.	N.A.
Pre-tax Margin (%)	16.40	18.70	16.90	13.50	15.60	15.45
Operating Income	13,858	15,305	17,670	21,019	24,085	25,367
Net Income before Extras	1,649.0	2,042.0	2,141.0	2,155.6	2,753.6	2,888.9
Reported Net Income	1,649.0	2,042.0	2,141.0	2,155.6	2,753.6	2,888.9
Depreciation & Amortization	N.A.	N.A.	N.A.	N.A.	N.A.	N.A.
EPS from Net Income (Primary)	1.500	1.860	1.950	1.960	2.500	2.640
EPS from Net Income (Fully Diluted)	1.500	1.860	1.950	1.960	2.500	2.640
Dividend per Common Share	0.345	0.460	0.600	0.680	0.760	0.800
Dividend Yield (%)	1.81	2.34	3.29	2.20	2.02	1.83
Payout Ratio	0.23	0.25	0.31	0.35	0.30	0.30

BALANCE SHEET					
ASSETS					
Cash & Cash Equivalents	N.A.	N.A.	N.A.	N.A.	N.A.
Inventories	N.A.	N.A.	N.A.	N.A.	N.A.
Total Current Assets	N.A.	N.A.	N.A.	N.A.	N.A.
Total Assets	180,978	216,979	272,508	316,550	351,041
LIABILITIES & EQUITY					
Short Term Debt	56,404	71,950	112,602	146,153	159,900
Long Term Debt	109,896	129,162	144,628	153,021	171,370
Total Liabilities	174,204	208,927	262,967	305,591	338,268
Shares Outstanding	1,093.152	1,089.800	1,091.208	1,091.825	1,061.323
Common Stockholder Equity	6,774.0	8,052.0	9,541.0	10,959	11,773
Total Stockholder Equity	6,774.0	8,052.0	9,541.0	10,959	12,773

Note: Figures in Millions of $ except: per share items, margins, yields, and ratios.

Source: IDD Information Services

HARDING LAWSON ASSOCIATES

William Nasgovitz
Heartland Advisors

Company Profile

Things have literally been down in the dumps lately for Harding Lawson Associates. The company was founded in 1957 and offers engineering, consulting, and construction services related to the cleanup of contaminated waste sites. It provides site survey, construction management, and help with meeting government regulation and permitting requirements for companies throughout the United States, Australia, Latin America, and Asia. Unfortunately, revenues for the latest fiscal year have been on the decline due to a winding down of some large federal contracts and cutbacks in government spending. This has forced the company to restructure and put more focus on environmental construction projects in order to maintain profitability. Company president Donald L. Schreuder has vowed, "We have made, and will continue to make, significant changes in our management and operating systems to get the company back on track."

"In 1990, this stock sold for $26," notes Bill Nasgovitz of Heartland Advisors. "It has been in its own private bear market for seven years." The company has also fallen victim to a general dislike of environmental stocks on Wall Street. "Years back, everybody was excited about these companies and willing to pay 30 times earnings for them," Nasgovitz observes. "But an easing of environmental restrictions has caused many of these firms to experience hard times."

Harding Lawson works with clients through each stage of a project. In the beginning, it performs a site assessment and prepares planning reports on what needs to be done to comply with government regulations. It then provides risk assessment, engineering, and regulatory services to develop and negotiate cleanup standards and obtain the equipment necessary to do the job. Firms hire companies like Harding because federal and local environmental regulations are often complex and hard to understand. Therefore, they are forced to pay for outside expertise to make sure they are in proper compliance. Harding's client base is comprised of both the private sector (51 percent), federal government (31 percent) state and local governments (13 percent), and international organizations (5 percent).

As mentioned, changes in regulations and a decrease in government spending have forced the company to take some dramatic steps. President Donald Schreuder points out, "We have made solid progress in our strategy to transform the company from a specialty business heavily dependent on U.S.-based regulatory driven environmental programs to a multidisciplined firm providing environmental engineering, construction, and infrastructure services to growth markets in the United States and abroad."

The restructuring effort appears to be working. The company has won $80 million in new federal contracts over the past year. "Here's an example of what it is doing," Nasgovitz offers. "It just received a five-year $20 million contract to provide the U.S. Army with cleanup and monitoring support services for seven chemical biological defense command facilities in Alabama, Colorado, Kentucky, Indiana, Maryland, Oregon, and Utah. There are billions and billions of dollars worth of other activities like this that eventually must be done, and Harding is a major player."

Reason for Recommendation

Nasgovitz believes 1998 could be the year Harding starts to get the attention it deserves. "This company has a rock-solid balance sheet, with $7.11 per share in net working capital, which is current assets after subtracting current liabilities and all other long-term debts and liabilities," he says. "This means we're essentially getting the assets, plants, equipment, patents, goodwill, and management for free. We're buying a business for current assets after subtracting all debt. That's a real rarity and a low risk way to invest."

Harding has a book value of $9.25 and very little debt. It has also initiated a 500,000 share repurchase program. Furthermore, the stock has experienced strong insider buying. "Since the supply of stock is going down, even if the demand for this stock remains the same, the price is bound to go up," Nasgovitz insists. "I mean when you decrease the supply of anything, whether it be stock, popcorn or real estate, prices eventually rise."

Nasgovitz maintains that another catalyst that can drive the share price higher is improving profitability and a turnaround in environmental funding projects. "I think the company will earn 60 to 70 cents a share in 1998," he predicts. "So when the market gets excited about environmental stocks again somewhere down the road, I think this stock, because of its leadership position, strong balance sheet and history of success can easily double. And because it has been hit so hard, the downside risk is relatively low."

Contact Information: Donald L. Schreuder
President and CEO
Harding Lawson Associates Group, Inc.
7655 Redwood Boulevard
Novato, CA 94948
(415) 892-0821
http//www.harding.com

Harding Lawson Asscs Group Incorporated

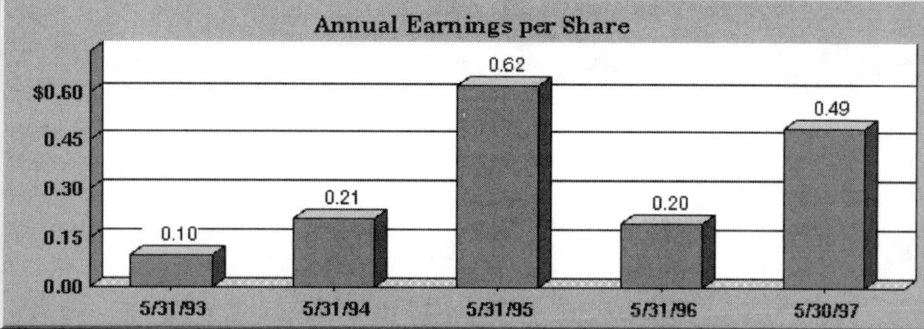

Harding Lawson Asscs Group Incorporated

Symbol: HRDG Exchange: Nasdaq NMS

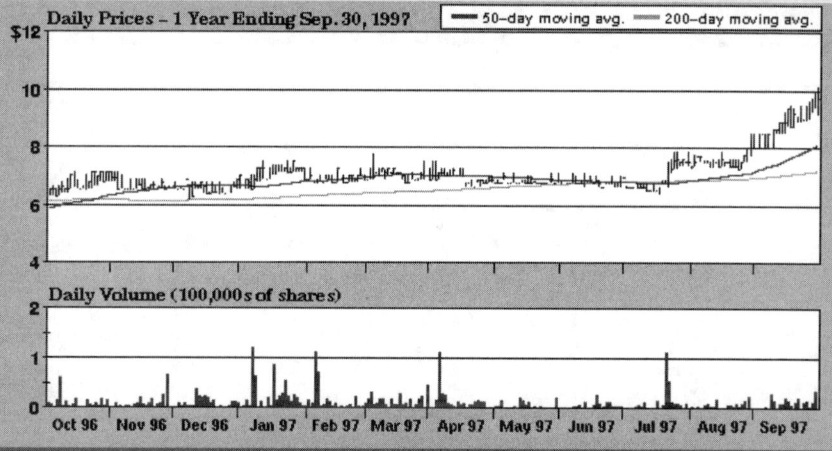

Latest Pricing Data (as of Sep. 30, 1997)		
Close (net change):	$9 3/4	(−1/4)
Day High & Low:	$10 1/8	$9 1/8
Volume & Avg. Volume:	34,900	12,664
52-Week High:	$10 1/8	Sep. 30, 1997
52-Week Low:	$6 1/8	Dec. 6, 1996
Latest Dividend:	$0.00	
Ind. Ann. Div. & Yield:	$0.00	N.A.
12 Month EPS:	$0.49	May 30, 1997
P/E Ratio & Beta Factor:	19.90	0.134
Shares Outstanding:	4.987 million	
Market Value:	$48.6 million	
Institutional Holdings:	56.59%	
Number of Institutions:	31	
Primary Market:	Nasdaq NMS	

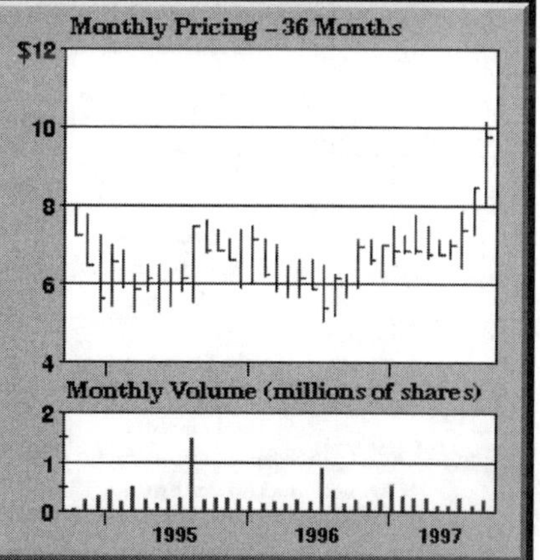

Currency: U.S. Dollars.

Source: IDD Information Services

Harding Lawson Asscs Group Incorporated
Symbol: HRDG

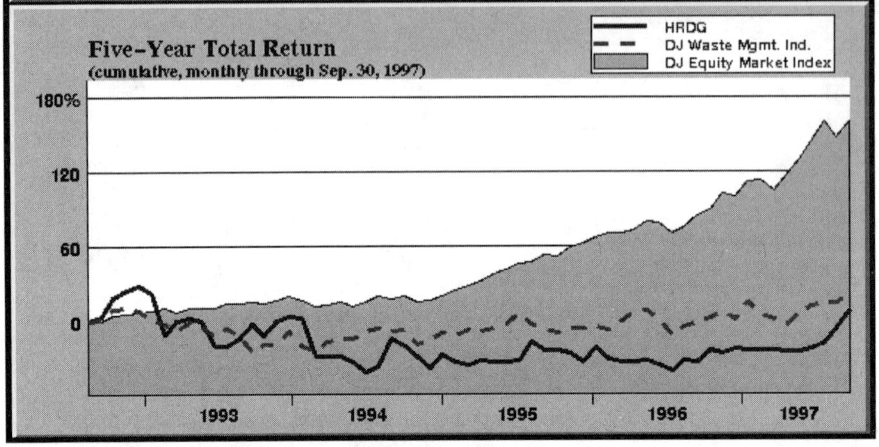

SELECTED INCOME STATEMENT AND BALANCE SHEET ITEMS

INCOME STATEMENT	5/31/93	5/31/94	5/31/95	5/31/96	5/30/97	LTM
Sales/Revenues	82.600	79.900	92.500	85.700	84.300	84.300
Cost of Goods Sold	(3.300)	(4.000)	(3.300)	(2.500)	(2.600)	(2.600)
Pre-tax Margin (%)	1.00	2.10	5.30	2.10	5.10	5.28
Operating Income	0.600	1.300	4.600	0.900	4.100	4.000
Net Income before Extras	0.500	1.000	3.000	1.000	2.400	2.500
Reported Net Income	0.500	1.000	3.000	1.000	2.400	2.500
Depreciation & Amortization	3.300	4.000	3.300	2.500	2.600	2.600
EPS from Net Income (Primary)	0.100	0.210	0.620	0.200	0.490	0.490
EPS from Net Income (Fully Diluted)	0.100	0.210	0.620	0.200	0.490	0.490
Dividend per Common Share	0.000	0.000	0.000	0.000	0.000	0.000
Dividend Yield (%)	N.A.	N.A.	N.A.	N.A.	N.A.	N.A.
Payout Ratio	N.A.	N.A.	N.A.	N.A.	N.A.	N.A.

BALANCE SHEET					
ASSETS					
Cash & Cash Equivalents	12.200	8.900	12.600	19.000	24.500
Inventories	0.000	0.000	0.000	0.000	0.000
Total Current Assets	47.900	49.200	49.500	49.300	56.000
Total Assets	59.800	61.500	60.800	60.400	66.400
LIABILITIES & EQUITY					
Short Term Debt	0.000	2.000	0.000	0.000	0.000
Long Term Debt	0.000	0.000	0.000	0.000	0.000
Total Liabilities	20.300	22.500	18.100	16.000	19.700
Shares Outstanding	4.808	4.603	4.719	4.845	4.865
Common Stockholder Equity	39.500	39.000	42.700	44.400	46.600
Total Stockholder Equity	39.500	39.000	42.700	44.400	46.600

Note: Figures in Millions of $ except: per share items, margins, yields, and ratios.

Source: IDD Information Services

HERMAN MILLER

Louis Navellier
Navellier & Associates

Company Profile

Attention Dilbert fans: If you've ever wondered where all those cubicles Dilbert and his cohorts work in are made, Louis Navellier has the answer. "They're built by Herman Miller," he says. "It's an office furniture manufacturer that makes cubes and all kinds of good stuff like that." In fact, it is the leader in building modular, free-standing office partition systems. Most of its products are coordinated in design and can be used interchangeably.

The company is headquartered in Zeeland, Michigan, which it calls "a small community with 20 churches and no bars." It was founded in 1923, when D.J. DePree bought the Star Furniture Company. DePree renamed the business after his father-in-law and major shareholder, Herman Miller. By 1960, the company introduced what was then a radical concept known as systems furniture. Its Action Office product has since changed the way people work. More than 30 percent of all businesses currently use open-plan office furniture. That's a nice way of saying "cubicles" or "cubes." Herman Miller is the largest producer of these products in the industry. It also makes chairs, free-standing furniture (like desks), storage cabinets, and furniture for the home office. Most recently, it introduced a line of ergonomic seating and materials handling systems for hospitals and factories.

In addition to its Zeeland location, Herman Miller operates six other manufacturing plants in Michigan and has additional facilities in California, Georgia, England, and Mexico.

"The company's products are designed to make businesses and offices more efficient," Navellier observes. "General Motors just moved into a new headquarters in downtown Detroit and awarded Herman Miller the entire $50 million contract to furnish the building."

Herman Miller took a giant leap forward in terms of financial performance during 1996. After a year of slumping profitability, the company posted record orders, sales, and earnings per share. Sales reached $1.28 billion, which was an increase of 18.5 percent from the previous year. The company has a relatively new and young president, Michael Volkema, who recently implemented a turnaround plan to keep this impressive progress moving forward. "Herman Miller is beginning to adopt a new financial measurement called Economic Value Added, which is a financial framework used by several leading corporations," Volkema says. "We plan to evaluate all investments based on our ability to create economic value." The approach appears to be working. *Fortune* magazine recently selected Herman Miller as America's most admired furniture company.

Reason for Recommendation

"The bottom line is that business is booming," Navellier exclaims. "The company's sales are quite phenomenal, and I'm very excited about this stock. Sales are up a little more than 16 percent in the last year, earnings have grown even faster than that because of margin expansion, the analyst community has been aggressively revising earnings estimates higher, operating margins have gone from 3.6 percent to as high as 8.8 percent in the latest quarter, and the company has a good history of positive earnings surprises."

Beyond that, Navellier is convinced the strong demand for Herman Miller's products will continue through the next century. "Corporate America continues to restructure and is buying more and more cubes," he notes. "Herman Miller will profit as companies become efficient and use more cubes and less office space. When I moved my company from Tahoe to Reno last year, I put more cubes in my office."

Navellier believes the stock is running on all cylinders right now, with higher earnings and expanding profit margins. He also points out that, in his mind, the company has relatively little downside exposure. "This is a pretty moderate-risk pick for me," he admits. "But at this time in the market, I really feel that it's hard to hit a home run. So I'd rather have somebody stick with a smooth, steady grower like this right now."

It goes without saying that there's plenty of competition in the furniture business, and there's no guarantee the company will stay on top. After all, even the corner office supply superstores are starting to sell cubicles. However, Herman Miller's quality is not easily surpassed. Furthermore, even if the economy slows down, that could have a positive impact on the company. That's because corporate America would presumably shrink its workforce and office space, opting instead to buy more cube products from Herman Miller. For all of these reasons, Navellier is enthusiastic about the company's prospects. "I would be disappointed if this stock didn't hit $50 a share this year," he adds.

Contact Information: Michael A. Volkema
President and CEO
Herman Miller, Inc.
855 Main Avenue, P.O. Box 302
Zeeland, MI 49464-0302
(616) 654-3000
http://www.hermanmiller.com

Miller Herman Incorporated

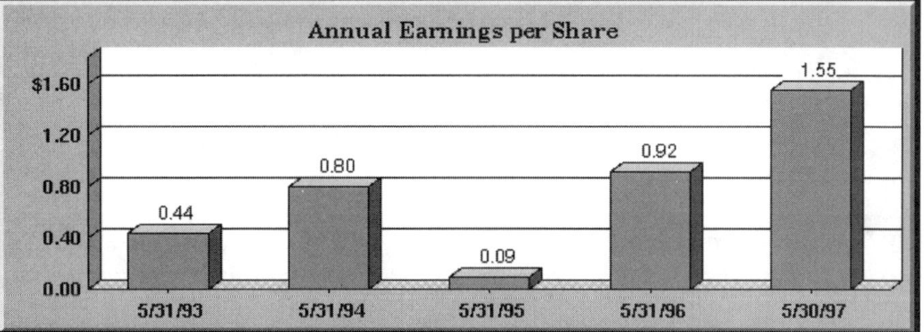

Miller Herman Incorporated

Symbol: MLHR Exchange: Nasdaq NMS

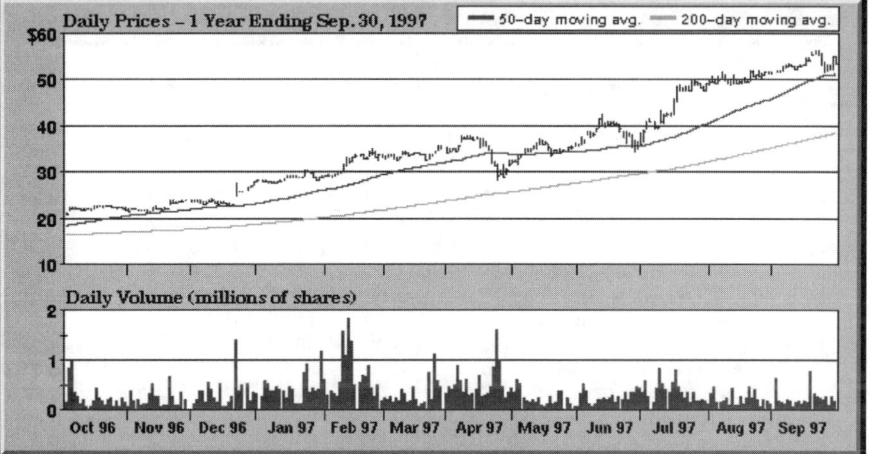

Latest Pricing Data (as of Sep. 30, 1997)		
Close (net change):	$53 1/2	(–1 15/32)
Day High & Low:	$55 1/8	$53 1/2
Volume & Avg. Volume:	174,000	309,117
52-Week High:	$56 3/8	Sep. 22, 1997
52-Week Low:	$20 11/16	Oct. 2, 1996
Latest Dividend:	$0.07	Aug. 27, 1997
Ind. Ann. Div. & Yield:	$0.29	0.54%
12 Month EPS:	$1.54	May 30, 1997
P/E Ratio & Beta Factor:	34.74	0.569
Shares Outstanding:	46.114 million	
Market Value:	$2.467 billion	
Institutional Holdings:	62.46%	
Number of Institutions:	287	
Primary Market:	Nasdaq NMS	

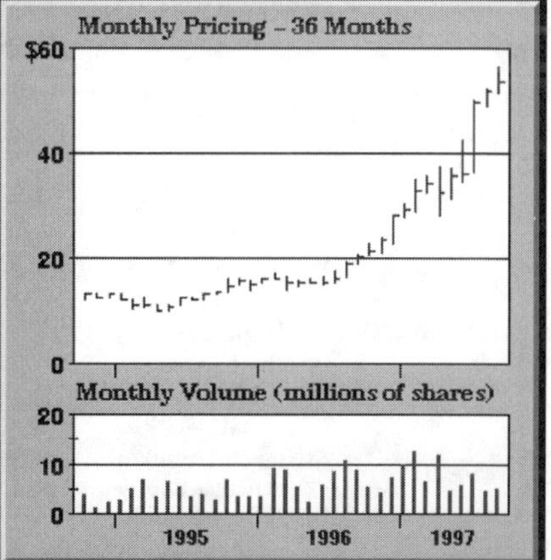

Currency: U.S. Dollars.

Source: IDD Information Services

Miller Herman Incorporated
Symbol: MLHR

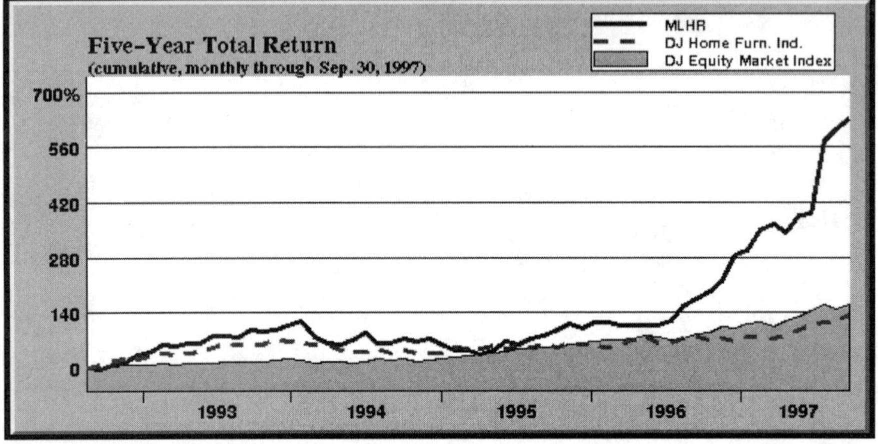

SELECTED INCOME STATEMENT AND BALANCE SHEET ITEMS

INCOME STATEMENT	5/31/93	5/31/94	5/31/95	5/31/96	5/30/97	LTM
Sales/Revenues	855.70	953.20	1,083.1	1,283.9	1,495.9	1,495.9
Cost of Goods Sold	525.60	582.90	665.10	804.00	914.00	919.40
Pre-tax Margin (%)	5.00	6.70	0.40	5.50	8.40	8.30
Operating Income	43.800	61.800	9.100	74.900	130.70	130.80
Net Income before Extras	22.100	40.400	4.300	45.900	74.400	74.400
Reported Net Income	22.100	40.400	4.300	45.900	74.400	74.400
Depreciation & Amortization	31.600	33.200	39.700	45.000	48.000	48.000
EPS from Net Income (Primary)	0.440	0.800	0.090	0.920	1.550	1.540
EPS from Net Income (Fully Diluted)	0.440	0.800	0.090	0.920	1.550	1.540
Dividend per Common Share	0.260	0.260	0.260	0.260	0.267	0.267
Dividend Yield (%)	2.03	2.12	2.40	1.68	0.75	0.75
Payout Ratio	0.59	0.32	2.89	0.28	0.17	0.17
BALANCE SHEET						
ASSETS						
Cash & Cash Equivalents	16.500	22.700	16.500	57.100	106.20	
Inventories	56.000	59.800	71.100	65.700	53.900	
Total Current Assets	207.60	228.70	297.10	334.90	385.90	
Total Assets	484.30	533.70	659.00	694.90	755.60	
LIABILITIES & EQUITY						
Short Term Debt	18.700	49.400	84.000	24.300	43.000	
Long Term Debt	21.100	20.600	60.100	110.20	110.10	
Total Liabilities	200.40	237.40	372.00	386.60	468.50	
Shares Outstanding	50.008	49.180	49.672	49.398	46.031	
Common Stockholder Equity	283.90	296.30	286.90	308.10	287.10	
Total Stockholder Equity	283.90	296.30	286.90	308.10	287.10	

Note: Figures in Millions of $ except: per share items, margins, yields, and ratios.

Source: IDD Information Services

INTERNATIONAL PAPER

James O'Shaughnessy
O'Shaughnessy Capital Management

Company Profile

International Paper is one of the world's preeminent manufacturers of printing papers, packaging materials, forest products and specialty items. It operates more than six million acres of forestland and manages production plants in more than 30 different countries. Its white and colored papers are marketed under the Hammermill, Strathmore, Beckett, and Springhill brand names. Its coated papers are used by a variety of magazine publishers, including *Forbes* and *Parents*, and its forestry products are turned into everything from kitchen cabinets to entire homes. Clearly, the items manufactured by International Paper are used by most of us on a daily basis.

However, lower demand for pulp, paper and packaging products caused by excess inventories throughout the industry led to lower earnings for the company in 1996. This followed a banner year, in which earnings reached a record $4.50 per share. The outlook is much brighter now. Demand for paper products is increasing and inventories are approaching more normal levels, which should translate into impressive gains this year. In addition, the company's merger with Federal Paper Board is complete, and it has just executed one of the largest internal expansion programs in its nearly 100-year history.

But James O'Shaughnessy of O'Shaughnessy Capital Management could care less about all of this. It's of no concern to him that the company has a new chairman, or that employees are being given more management responsibility than ever before. He's not even impressed by the fact that the company is positioned to prosper in areas of the world, including Asia and South America, where economic growth rates and the demand for its products outpace that of the United States.

Instead, O'Shaughnessy chose International Paper as his top pick for 1998 because it presently fits his strategy of buying the second-lowest priced of the top ten yielding stocks in the Dow Jones Industrial Average. It's yet another version of the increasingly popular "Dogs of the Dow" technique. "I tested this strategy back to 1928 and found that while it is considerably more volatile than the traditional Dogs of the Dow approach, the returns it generates are outstanding," he says. "It has averaged about 26 percent annually going back over 60 years."

The premise behind this strategy is simple. The high yield is a sign the stock is out of favor. "Essentially, you're buying a well-known blue chip company when it is under some degree of distress and/or is unloved or misunderstood on Wall Street," he explains. "The fact is, if you were to do additional fundamental research on these companies, you would probably find a reason not to invest in them. This strategy works because it forces you to buy Union Carbide after it has blown up India, or Exxon when the oil is still glistening on the bay, or Philip Morris as 18 other states sue it for reimbursement. If you do additional outside research, you will be absolutely certain this is the one stock you don't want to buy."

It doesn't matter when you purchase the stock, but you must hold on to it for exactly one year at which time you go through the whole process again to see whether it is still the second-lowest priced high yielder, or whether it should be replaced by another company. "I have found the best time to buy the 'Dogs' is at the end of the year," O'Shaughnessy adds. "But there's not a huge difference. Anyone who starts now or next month is generally going to be very happy five years from now."

Reason for Recommendation

As previously mentioned, O'Shaughnessy only likes this stock because it fits into his strategy at the time this book was being written. In fact, by the time you read this, the company matching this profile might have changed. Therefore, you should sit down, jot down a list of the ten highest yielding Dow stocks, which are listed in the *Wall Street Journal* each month, and see which one has the second-lowest price. If it's still International Paper, that's the stock to buy. If it's another company, put your money in that one instead.

The underlying theory behind this strategy is that these out of favor stocks are so strong and mighty they will eventually get their acts together and turn around. "These are not brand new babies," O'Shaughnessy explains. "They're wise old guys. They've been around the block a million times and can weather virtually any downturn. If the movie 'Independence Day' comes true, these companies will still be around."

It's also important to point out that this is a technique for buying one stock to add to your overall portfolio. You should never put all of your money into a single holding. O'Shaughnessy recommends you own at least ten and preferably 25 different companies for proper diversification.

Contact Information: John T. Dillon
Chairman and CEO
International Paper Company
Two Manhattanville Road
Purchase, NY 10577
(914) 397-1500
http://www.ipaper.com

International Paper Company

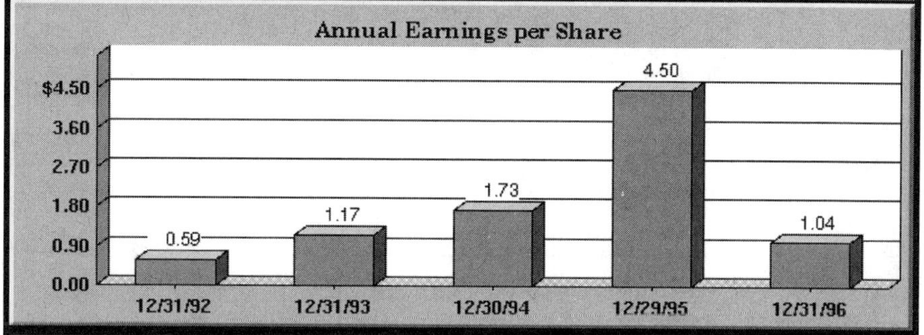

International Paper Company

Symbol: IP Exchange: NYSE

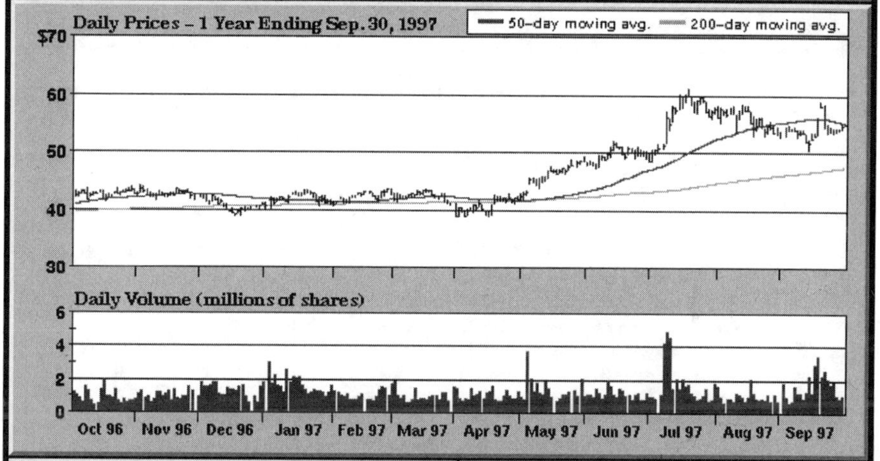

Latest Pricing Data (as of Sep. 30, 1997)		
Close (net change):	$55	(+3/16)
Day High & Low:	$55 3/16	$54 3/4
Volume & Avg. Volume:	1,036,900	1,365,467
52-Week High:	$61	July 17, 1997
52-Week Low:	$38 5/8	Apr. 3, 1997
Latest Dividend:	$0.25	Aug. 20, 1997
Ind. Ann. Div. & Yield:	$1.00	1.82%
12 Month EPS:	($0.93)	June 30, 1997
P/E Ratio & Beta Factor:	N.A.	0.661
Shares Outstanding:	300.852 million	
Market Value:	$16.547 billion	
Institutional Holdings:	67.55%	
Number of Institutions:	851	
Primary Market:	NYSE	
Component of:	DJIA, S&P 500	

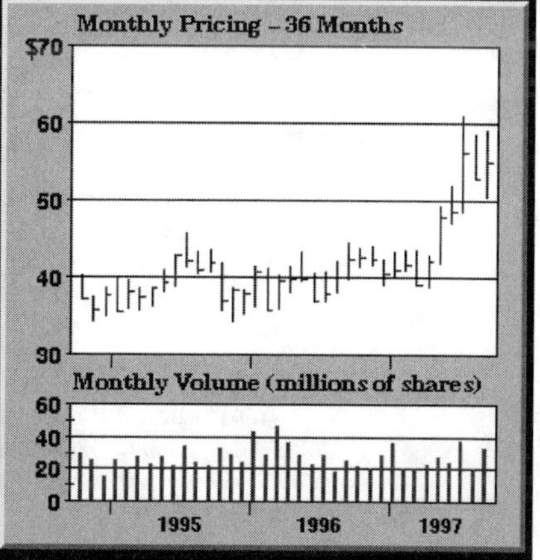

Currency: U.S. Dollars.

Source: IDD Information Services

International Paper Company
Symbol: IP

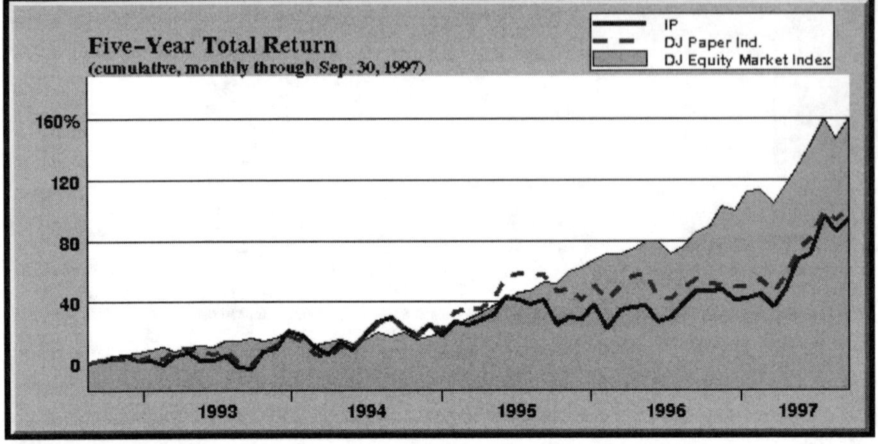

SELECTED INCOME STATEMENT AND BALANCE SHEET ITEMS

INCOME STATEMENT	12/31/92	12/31/93	12/30/94	12/29/95	12/31/96	LTM
Sales/Revenues	13,598	13,685	14,966	19,797	20,143	20,104
Cost of Goods Sold	10,137	10,191	11,143	13,896	14,901	14,996
Pre-tax Margin (%)	1.50	3.70	4.40	9.50	3.10	(1.58)
Operating Income	453.00	810.00	1,013.0	2,521.0	1,420.0	1,129.0
Net Income before Extras	142.00	289.00	432.00	1,153.0	303.00	(279.00)
Reported Net Income	142.00	289.00	432.00	1,153.0	303.00	(279.00)
Depreciation & Amortization	850.00	898.00	885.00	1,031.0	1,194.0	1,267.0
EPS from Net Income (Primary)	0.590	1.170	1.730	4.500	1.040	(0.930)
EPS from Net Income (Fully Diluted)	0.590	1.170	1.730	4.500	1.040	(0.930)
Dividend per Common Share	0.840	0.840	0.840	0.920	1.000	1.000
Dividend Yield (%)	2.52	2.48	2.23	2.43	2.47	2.06
Payout Ratio	1.42	0.72	0.49	0.20	0.96	N.A.
BALANCE SHEET						
ASSETS						
Cash & Cash Equivalents	225.00	242.00	270.00	312.00	352.00	
Inventories	1,938.0	2,024.0	2,075.0	2,784.0	2,840.0	
Total Current Assets	4,366.0	4,401.0	4,830.0	5,873.0	5,998.0	
Total Assets	16,459	16,631	17,836	23,977	28,252	
LIABILITIES & EQUITY						
Short Term Debt	2,356.0	2,089.0	2,083.0	2,283.0	3,296.0	
Long Term Debt	3,096.0	3,601.0	4,464.0	5,946.0	6,691.0	
Total Liabilities	10,270	10,406	11,322	15,730	18,458	
Shares Outstanding	245.400	247.800	251.800	261.000	300.200	
Common Stockholder Equity	6,189.0	6,225.0	6,514.0	7,797.0	9,344.0	
Total Stockholder Equity	6,189.0	6,225.0	6,514.0	8,247.0	9,794.0	

Note: Figures in Millions of $ except: per share items, margins, yields, and ratios.

Source: IDD Information Services

ISIS PHARMACEUTICALS

Michael Murphy

California Technology Stock Letter

Company Profile

Isis Pharmaceuticals is a biotechnology company focused on converting antisense technology into therapeutically and commercially valuable drugs. If that makes little or no sense to you, don't feel bad. This is an extremely sophisticated operation run by a team of highly educated scientists. Right now, Isis doesn't have any FDA-approved drugs. But it is working on several different ones, and if any prove to be successful, Michael Murphy of the *California Technology Stock Letter* says investors could be richly rewarded.

First, let's define the term "antisense." This is a novel drug discovery method that works at the genetic level to interrupt the process by which disease-causing proteins are produced. "Isis is what we call an inside-the-cell company," Murphy explains. "What it does is figure out the sequence of the DNA or messenger RNA in question. Then it creates a chain of the exact opposite sequence for it to bind to, thus blocking it from replicating. It's a very powerful technology that can obviously spin off lots of drugs."

Almost all human diseases are the result of improper protein production. Traditional drugs are designed to interact with protein molecules through the body that either support or cause disease. Antisense drugs, on the other hand, are designed to actually inhibit the production of these disease-causing proteins in the first place. They can be used to treat a wide array of infectious, inflammatory and cardiovascular diseases, and cancers, and are much more effective and selective than traditional medications.

One of the more notable drugs Isis is working on is one called Fomivirsen, which is presently undergoing trials in Europe, Latin America, Canada, and Australia. "This is for people who have AIDS," Murphy says. "It blocks the CMV retinitis protein, which causes patients to go blind. This drug is in phase three right now (the final phase before FDA approval), and Isis owns all the rights to it."

While promising, the drug did run into a potentially fatal roadblock. "About three years ago, it was doing a trial with a couple of people who looked like they were having retinal detachment while taking this drug," Murphy shares. "Isis was forced to stop testing it for awhile, before going back through the pharmacology on the whole thing and restarting the trials. There has never been a recurrence of this since. It was concluded that it was random chance, and these folks would have had adverse retinal events with or without the drug."

Fomivirsen has been very well tolerated by patients with few side effects. It can also be used safely in conjunction with other medications. "Eighty percent of the people who take this drug don't go blind for as long as a year-and-a-half, compared to just ten days to two weeks without it," Murphy adds. If the trials continue to produce positive results, Murphy expects Isis to get FDA approval for Fomiversen sometime in 1998.

Another product being developed by Isis is an anti-inflammation drug called ICAM-1. CAM is an acronym for cellular adhesion molecules. CAM's are on the surface of virtually every cell in your body and play a critical role in such functions as wound healing and organ/tissue development. "ICAM-1 blocks the initiation of cells that cause inflammation," Murphy notes. "Inflammation is often part of the normal healing process. But when it gets out of control, it causes a host of other problems. This drug is useful for combatting many kinds of inflammation and is currently in several different clinical trials." Among other things, ICAM-1 is designed to be used in patients with colitis, rheumatoid arthritis, psoriasis, and Crohn's Disease, which is an inflammatory disease of the small and large intestine. "The drug had a 50 percent response with Crohn's Disease, while the placebo had basically zero," Murphy adds. "Those who responded were in good shape five months later." This could be very promising, since the cause of Crohn's Disease is still unknown.

Reason for Recommendation

Murphy believes Isis will start to get FDA approval for its many drugs beginning in 1998, bringing it to profitability for the first time. "There are a number of good things happening for the company this year, in terms of clinical trials beginning and ending," Murphy says. "It is also really attractive on a valuation basis. The company has spent $121 million on research and development in the last five years, and the total market capitalization is only three times that amount."

Once Isis does get its first FDA approval, Murphy expects the stock to trade for around $125 per share. "I know this sounds like a bizarre jump from where it's at," he admits. "But the truth is, if it has an approved drug, the $125 price would reflect a total market capitalization on the whole company of less than $4 billion, and we've seen that happen already to so many companies, like Biogen and Amgen."

Contact Information: Stanley T. Crooke, M.D., Ph.D.
Chairman and CEO
Isis Pharmaceuticals, Inc.
2292 Faraday Avenue
Carlsbad, CA 92008
(619) 931-9200
http://www.isip.com

Isis Pharmaceuticals Inc.

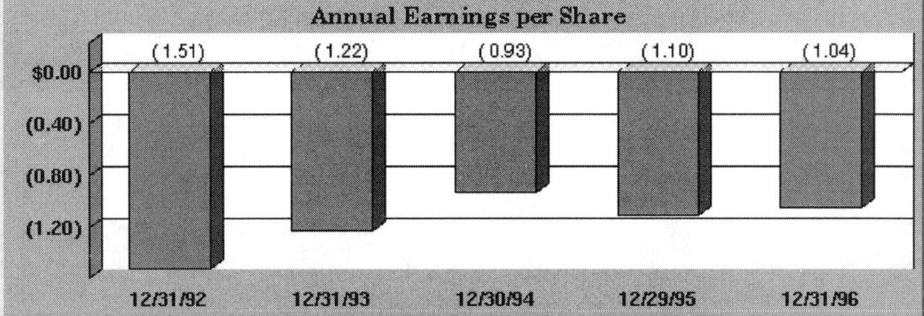

Isis Pharmaceuticals Inc.

Symbol: ISIP Exchange: Nasdaq NMS

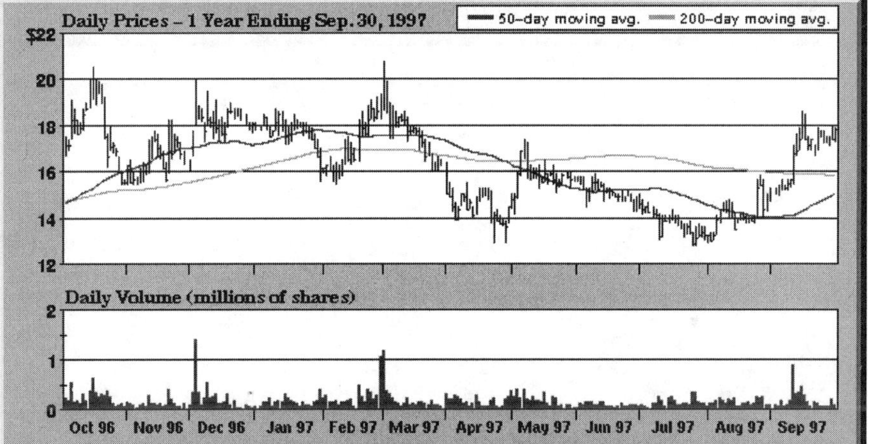

Latest Pricing Data (as of Sep. 30, 1997)		
Close (net change):	$17 13/16	(+7/16)
Day High & Low:	$17 7/8	$17 1/4
Volume & Avg. Volume:	94,100	256,662
52-Week High:	$20 3/4	Feb. 28, 1997
52-Week Low:	$12 3/4	July 25, 1997
Latest Dividend:	$0.00	
Ind. Ann. Div. & Yield:	$0.00	N.A.
12 Month EPS:	($1.24)	June 30, 1997
P/E Ratio & Beta Factor:	N.A.	0.657
Shares Outstanding:	26.353 million	
Market Value:	$469 million	
Institutional Holdings:	24.65%	
Number of Institutions:	85	
Primary Market:	Nasdaq NMS	

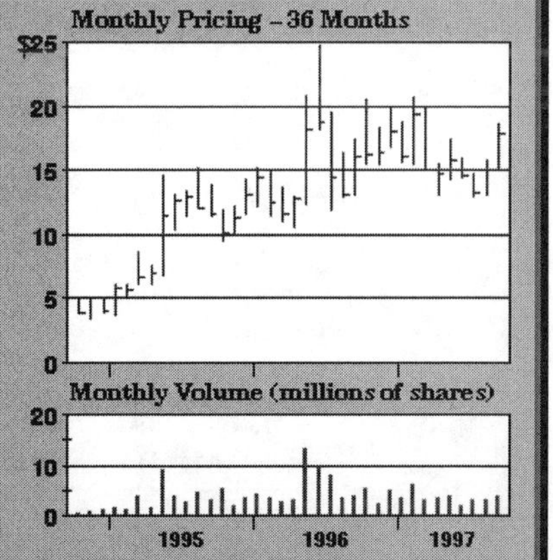

Currency: U.S. Dollars.

Source: IDD Information Services

Isis Pharmaceuticals Inc.
Symbol: ISIP

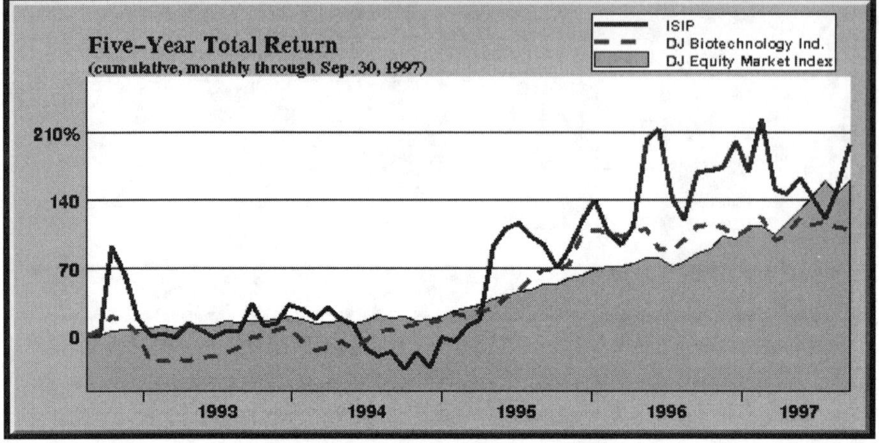

SELECTED INCOME STATEMENT AND BALANCE SHEET ITEMS

INCOME STATEMENT	12/31/92	12/31/93	12/30/94	12/29/95	12/31/96	LTM
Sales/Revenues	8.700	12.100	10.100	13.000	22.600	23.900
Cost of Goods Sold	(2.000)	22.400	(3.900)	(2.800)	(2.600)	(23.600)
Pre-tax Margin (%)	N.A.	N.A.	N.A.	N.A.	N.A.	N.A.
Operating Income	(21.600)	(18.300)	(22.300)	(25.600)	(29.200)	(32.900)
Net Income before Extras	(19.500)	(19.100)	(18.200)	(23.700)	(26.500)	(32.200)
Reported Net Income	(19.500)	(19.100)	(18.200)	(23.700)	(26.500)	(32.200)
Depreciation & Amortization	2.000	3.200	3.900	2.800	2.600	2.600
EPS from Net Income (Primary)	(1.510)	(1.220)	(0.930)	(1.100)	(1.040)	(1.240)
EPS from Net Income (Fully Diluted)	(1.510)	(1.220)	(0.930)	(1.100)	(1.040)	(1.240)
Dividend per Common Share	N.A.	N.A.	N.A.	N.A.	N.A.	N.A.
Dividend Yield (%)	N.A.	N.A.	N.A.	N.A.	N.A.	N.A.
Payout Ratio	N.A.	N.A.	N.A.	N.A.	N.A.	N.A.
BALANCE SHEET						
ASSETS						
Cash & Cash Equivalents	16.500	33.700	12.900	46.500	37.100	
Inventories	0.000	0.000	0.000	0.000	0.000	
Total Current Assets	38.500	55.600	45.000	79.000	79.400	
Total Assets	55.500	78.800	66.600	99.600	101.30	
LIABILITIES & EQUITY						
Short Term Debt	6.100	4.900	2.400	5.000	6.200	
Long Term Debt	6.700	8.800	9.300	4.700	19.900	
Total Liabilities	15.700	20.300	20.600	23.700	43.000	
Shares Outstanding	13.032	18.773	19.716	25.249	26.201	
Common Stockholder Equity	39.800	58.500	46.000	75.900	58.400	
Total Stockholder Equity	39.800	58.500	46.000	75.900	58.400	

Note: Figures in Millions of $ except: per share items, margins, yields, and ratios.

Source: IDD Information Services

MANPOWER

Jean-Marie Eveillard
SoGen Funds

Company Profile

Companies around the globe are increasingly using temporary workers as a way to save money and increase flexibility. Manpower, the world's largest employment services organization, is clearly benefiting from this trend.

"It pioneered the temporary employment agency business more than 50 years ago," notes Jean-Marie Eveillard, president and portfolio manager of the SoGen International Fund. "Today, it's the leader in this industry, although it has less than a 10 percent market share in the United States. We're talking about a business that remains extremely fragmented both here and abroad. Accordingly, there are opportunities for Manpower to significantly increase its market share in virtually every area it serves."

The company is clearly an international powerhouse, with roughly two-thirds of its business coming from outside the United States It has 2,500 offices in 43 countries, with its largest operations being in the United States, France, and the United Kingdom.

Manpower provides both temporary and permanent workers to a wide variety of customers. It also offers training classes for its employees and sells franchises in select locations. During 1996, approximately 39 percent of the company's United States temporary-help revenues came from placing office workers, with 41 percent from filling industrial positions, and 20 percent from finding technical and other employees for both small and large corporations.

Internationally, Manpower is the leading temporary employment service provider in the United Kingdom and the second largest in France. It operates 244 branch offices and 51 franchises in other European countries as well, including Belgium, Denmark, Germany, Spain, Switzerland, Sweden, and the Netherlands.

"Manpower generates more than 50 percent of its revenue in Europe and is the number two firm in Japan," Eveillard points out. "The temporary employment business is not a mature market. It's still growing worldwide. In the United States, for instance, just 2 percent of the labor force is currently comprised of temporary employees. In Europe, that number is less than 1 percent. In Italy it's zero right now because temporary employment is illegal there. In Japan, it's around 0.2 percent."

Reason for Recommendation

According to the Bureau of Labor Statistics, roughly 90 percent of all U.S. businesses use temporary workers. This means employment staffing should remain one of the top growth industries in 1998 and beyond. What's more, while the temporary staffing industry in general is growing at approximately 10 to 12 percent a year, Manpower has experienced growth in excess of 15 percent for the past several years.

"Corporations want temporary employment, and labor laws are changing around the world to make it more available," Eveillard contends. "It's a growing market globally. Plus, because it's a service business, it's not really capital intensive. The big item that has to be financed is receivables. But there are no inventories to speak of and no fixed assets. Accordingly, the business tends to generate excess cash and, if run properly, it provides a high return on equity." In the case of Manpower, ROE in 1996 was 34 percent, which is double that of the average American company.

"I would characterize Manpower as a good business at a fair price," Eveillard says. "Admittedly, the stock is not extraordinarily cheap on an absolute basis. But on a relative basis, compared to other multinationals, it is."

There are three negatives staring Manpower in the face that prudent investors should note. To begin with, the temporary staffing business is cyclical. Right now, the U.S. and European economies are relatively strong. If we enter a recession, that could hurt its business. "However, Manpower operates in more than 40 countries, so as long as there is not a worldwide recession, it shouldn't be a major problem," Eveillard maintains.

In addition, large temporary agencies are increasingly signing contracts with the major Fortune 500 companies to provide employment for reduced rates throughout the world. "Sometimes these large contracts provide lower gross margins, although they also require fewer expenses," Eveillard notes. "But that's something to watch when two big companies are negotiating with each other." Finally, because Manpower operates in many foreign countries, it is impacted by currency fluctuations.

Even though the company has been growing organically, as opposed to buying up smaller agencies, Eveillard thinks more mergers and consolidations may be in store this year and beyond. "I suspect the big employment agencies like Manpower will gain market share over their smaller rivals, because the major corporations only want to sign long-term contracts with the established multinationals," he adds.

Contact Information: Mitchell S. Fromstein
Chairman, President and CEO
Manpower, Inc.
5301 North Ironwood Road
Milwaukee, WI 53217
(414) 961-1000
http://www.manpower.com

Manpower Incorporated Wisconsin

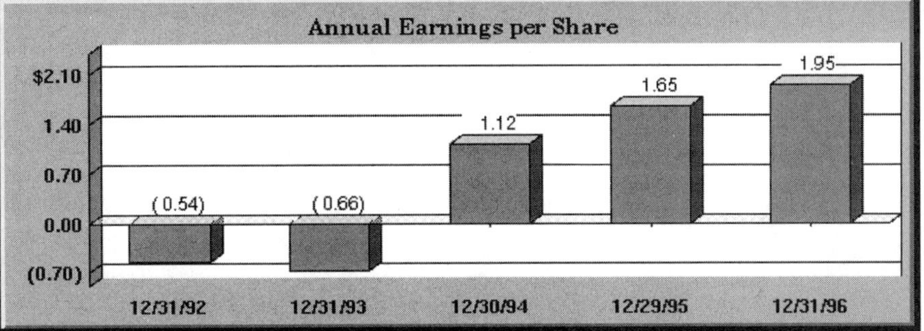

Manpower Incorporated Wisconsin

Symbol: MAN Exchange: NYSE

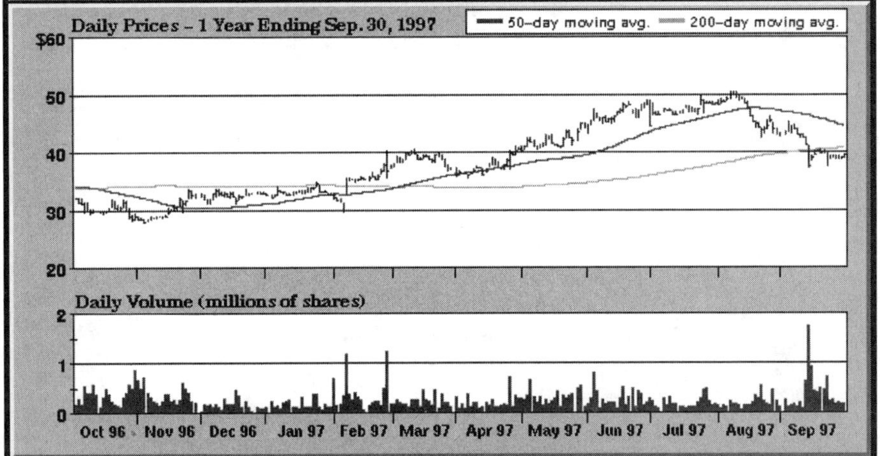

Latest Pricing Data (as of Sep. 30, 1997)		
Close (net change):	$39 1/2	(+9/16)
Day High & Low:	$39 5/8	$38 3/4
Volume & Avg. Volume:	179,500	344,423
52-Week High:	$50 3/8	Aug. 7, 1997
52-Week Low:	$27 7/8	Nov. 4, 1996
Latest Dividend:	$0.08	May 23, 1997
Ind. Ann. Div. & Yield:	$0.16	0.41%
12 Month EPS:	$2.02	June 30, 1997
P/E Ratio & Beta Factor:	19.55	0.791
Shares Outstanding:	83.119 million	
Market Value:	$3.283 billion	
Institutional Holdings:	82.11%	
Number of Institutions:	338	
Primary Market:	NYSE	

Currency: U.S. Dollars.

Source: IDD Information Services

Manpower Incorporated Wisconsin
Symbol: MAN

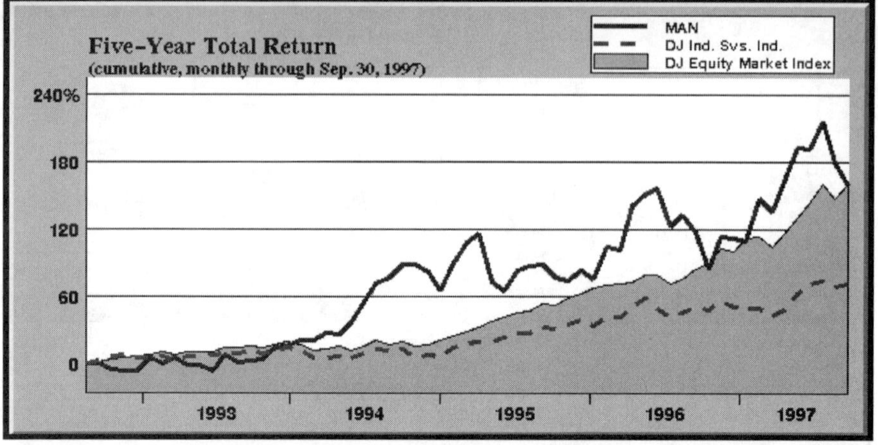

SELECTED INCOME STATEMENT AND BALANCE SHEET ITEMS

INCOME STATEMENT	12/31/92	12/31/93	12/30/94	12/29/95	12/31/96	LTM
Sales/Revenues	3,186.6	3,180.4	4,296.4	5,484.2	6,079.9	6,623.3
Cost of Goods Sold	2,520.0	2,536.5	3,479.0	4,455.5	4,896.3	5,354.7
Pre-tax Margin (%)	(0.40)	(0.90)	3.20	3.70	4.00	3.72
Operating Income	1.100	(15.200)	151.80	211.70	227.00	243.40
Net Income before Extras	(39.700)	(48.900)	83.900	128.00	162.30	168.00
Reported Net Income	(39.700)	(48.900)	83.900	128.00	162.30	168.00
Depreciation & Amortization	22.300	96.800	27.700	27.800	35.600	38.700
EPS from Net Income (Primary)	(0.540)	(0.660)	1.120	1.650	1.950	2.020
EPS from Net Income (Fully Diluted)	(0.540)	(0.660)	1.120	1.650	1.950	2.020
Dividend per Common Share	0.000	0.000	0.110	0.130	0.150	0.160
Dividend Yield (%)	N.A.	N.A.	0.39	0.46	0.46	0.36
Payout Ratio	N.A.	N.A.	0.10	0.08	0.08	0.08

BALANCE SHEET					
ASSETS					
Cash & Cash Equivalents	50.600	63.300	82.000	142.80	180.60
Inventories	0.000	0.000	0.000	0.000	0.000
Total Current Assets	670.90	651.30	1,007.3	1,277.3	1,439.1
Total Assets	922.40	833.30	1,203.7	1,517.8	1,752.3
LIABILITIES & EQUITY					
Short Term Debt	46.500	41.800	56.300	39.000	27.400
Long Term Debt	203.10	130.00	130.90	61.800	100.80
Total Liabilities	762.80	730.60	1,000.1	1,062.9	1,151.5
Shares Outstanding	73.449	73.677	74.289	81.153	82.206
Common Stockholder Equity	159.60	102.70	203.50	455.00	600.70
Total Stockholder Equity	159.60	102.70	203.50	455.00	600.70

Note: Figures in Millions of $ except: per share items, margins, yields, and ratios.

Source: IDD Information Services

McDONALD'S

Elaine Garzarelli
Garzarelli Investment Management

Company Profile

I realize Elaine Garzarelli selected McDonald's as her favorite pick for 1997, but she insists this is still her top idea for 1998 as well. "I can't think of any other stock I like better right now," she says. "The demographics are with us and more and more folks are eating out as their schedules get busier. I also think there are tons of opportunities for this company in China, the Soviet Union, Mexico, Argentina, Chile, and many other places around the world."

McDonald's is by far the largest and most recognized food service company in the world, boasting some 21,000 restaurants in 101 different countries. The breakdown looks something like this: There are roughly 12,000 restaurants in the United States; 3,500 in Europe, Africa, and the Middle East; 1,000 in Canada; 3,600 in Asia, and 850 in Latin America. Still, on any given day, McDonald's serves less than 1 percent of the global population, which shows its enormous potential for the kind of growth Garzarelli envisions. In fact, although just 38 percent of the chain's current restaurants are located outside the United States, they account for 47 percent of systemwide sales and 54 percent of operating income. The company plans to grow by adding between 2,400 and 2,800 restaurants this year, more than 70 percent of which will be located abroad.

While building new McDonald's restaurants continues to be the primary means of expansion, the company is always open to new opportunities. For example, it recently purchased about 80 restaurants in Italy from Burghy, Italy's largest burger chain.

McDonald's is constantly changing its menu here in the United States to keep up with the tastes of an aging population. Its Arch Deluxe has met with only mild success, but it has also added the Crispy Chicken Deluxe, Grilled Chicken Deluxe, and Fish Filet Deluxe sandwiches. Most of its domestic business is conducted through drive-thrus, which account for 54 percent of total sales. That's why the company is developing tools to help shorten the time people wait for their orders, while increasing the capacity to move more cars through without making any new investments.

The fast-food chain has reduced the cost of building a new location by 26 percent over the past six years through improved construction methods and more efficient building designs, allowing some stores to be erected in less than nine hours. Roughly one-third of all new restaurants are nontraditional satellite locations inside places like service stations, hospitals, zoos, airports, and retail establishments, such as Wal-Mart, The Home Depot, and Incredible Universe. The company's goal in the United States is to increase sales to existing customers while continuing to penetrate that portion of the market it doesn't already serve. Internationally, McDonald's wants to establish itself as a leader in untapped regions before competitors even have a chance to enter. The company's main challenge overseas may be keeping up with the strong demand.

Reason for Recommendation

While the fundamentals certainly look promising, Garzarelli is more interested in the company from a technical standpoint. She specializes in sector analysis. In other words, she looks for areas of the market that are undervalued and poised to significantly outperform. "The restaurant industry is a group that has historically traded at a valuation multiple substantially higher than the average for the overall market," she observes. "Based on my earnings outlook and current prices, this group is trading at a relative PE multiple near its historic low of a 4 percent premium to the S&P 500, compared to its norm of 40 percent. I foresee strong upside outperformance potential from this stock." Even though Garzarelli likes restaurant stocks in general, McDonald's comprises 89 percent of the entire sector, so it's her number one favorite.

But what about all of McDonald's recent troubles, you might ask? First off, expansion plans have been behind schedule over the past 18 months. Then there was that failed campaign to offer Big Macs and other sandwiches for 55 cents in early 1997. Garzarelli insists the company's recent problems don't have anything to do with her belief that the stock is undervalued. "There are so many other factors that go into my model," she says. "When I examine an industry, I don't look at individual companies. I look at the economic factors that go into the industry. I examine where it is now, compared to its normal relative PE. The fact that McDonald's is having short-term problems doesn't matter. I'm looking strictly at economic factors, and based on what I see, this stock is a great buy."

Garzarelli is also quick to point out that others are starting to agree with her. "Analysts who follow the stock have begun to upgrade their opinions on McDonald's," she says. "So I'm not the only one who's optimistic about its prospects."

Contact Information: Michael R. Quinlan
Chairman and CEO
McDonald's Corporation
One Kroc Drive
Oak Brook, IL 60521
(630) 623-3000
http://www.mcdonalds.com

McDonalds Corporation

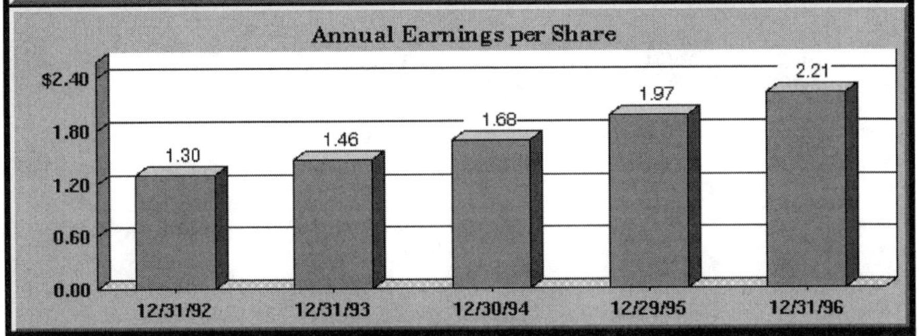

McDonalds Corporation

Symbol: MCD Exchange: NYSE

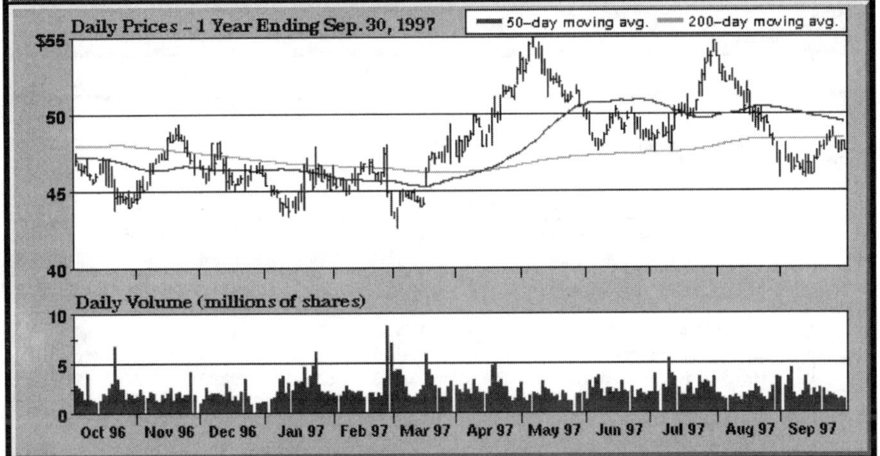

Latest Pricing Data (as of Sep. 30, 1997)		
Close (net change):	$47 5/8	(-1/2)
Day High & Low:	$48 1/8	$47 1/2
Volume & Avg. Volume:	1,324,500	1,951,927
52-Week High:	$54 7/8	May 6, 1997
52-Week Low:	$42 1/2	Mar. 3, 1997
Latest Dividend:	$0.08	Aug. 27, 1997
Ind. Ann. Div. & Yield:	$0.33	0.69%
12 Month EPS:	$2.32	June 30, 1997
P/E Ratio & Beta Factor:	20.53	0.721
Shares Outstanding:	688.017 million	
Market Value:	$32.767 billion	
Institutional Holdings:	51.56%	
Number of Institutions:	1229	
Primary Market:	NYSE	
Component of:	DJIA, S&P 500	

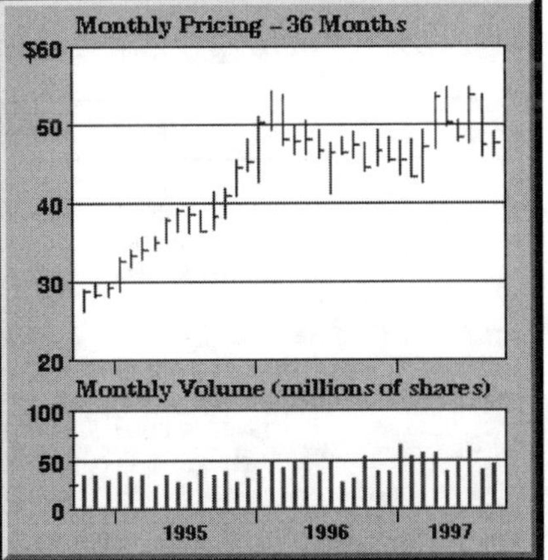

Currency: U.S. Dollars.

Source: IDD Information Services

McDonalds Corporation
Symbol: MCD

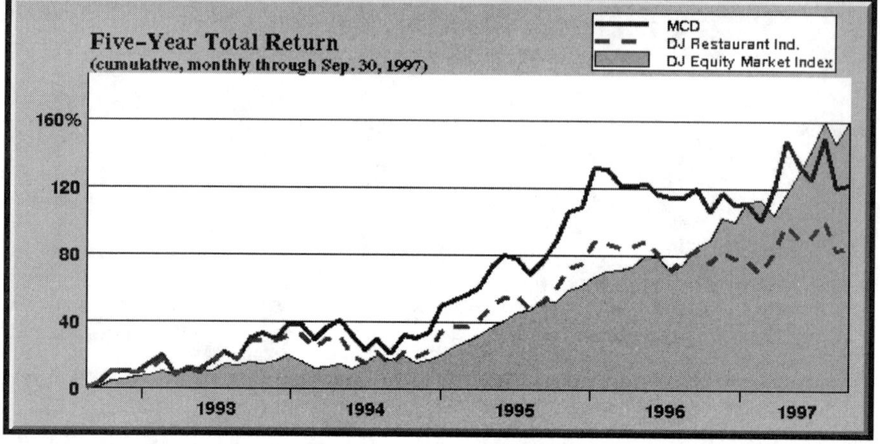

SELECTED INCOME STATEMENT AND BALANCE SHEET ITEMS

INCOME STATEMENT	12/31/92	12/31/93	12/30/94	12/29/95	12/31/96	LTM
Sales/Revenues	7,133.3	7,408.1	8,320.8	9,794.5	10,686	11,046
Cost of Goods Sold	1,133.9	1,166.7	1,305.6	1,610.4	1,803.7	2,312.9
Pre-tax Margin (%)	20.30	22.60	22.70	22.10	21.10	21.10
Operating Income	1,797.6	1,922.0	2,157.3	2,495.6	2,586.8	2,655.9
Net Income before Extras	958.60	1,082.5	1,224.4	1,427.3	1,572.6	1,633.3
Reported Net Income	958.60	1,082.5	1,224.4	1,427.3	1,572.6	1,633.3
Depreciation & Amortization	554.90	568.40	628.60	709.00	742.90	757.90
EPS from Net Income (Primary)	1.300	1.460	1.680	1.970	2.210	2.320
EPS from Net Income (Fully Diluted)	1.300	1.460	1.680	1.970	2.210	2.320
Dividend per Common Share	0.196	0.211	0.234	0.263	0.293	0.308
Dividend Yield (%)	0.81	0.74	0.80	0.58	0.64	0.64
Payout Ratio	0.15	0.14	0.14	0.13	0.13	0.13

BALANCE SHEET					
ASSETS					
Cash & Cash Equivalents	436.50	185.80	179.90	334.80	329.90
Inventories	43.500	43.500	50.500	58.000	69.600
Total Current Assets	864.70	662.80	740.70	955.80	1,102.5
Total Assets	11,681	12,035	13,592	15,415	17,386
LIABILITIES & EQUITY					
Short Term Debt	680.40	223.30	1,046.9	578.20	693.30
Long Term Debt	3,176.4	3,489.4	2,935.4	4,257.8	4,830.1
Total Liabilities	5,788.8	5,761.1	6,706.5	7,553.3	8,667.8
Shares Outstanding	727.048	707.400	693.700	699.700	694.600
Common Stockholder Equity	5,212.2	5,596.8	6,211.2	7,503.3	8,360.2
Total Stockholder Equity	5,892.4	6,274.1	6,885.4	7,861.3	8,718.2

Note: Figures in Millions of $ except: per share items, margins, yields, and ratios.

Source: IDD Information Services

MEMTEC

Vivian Lewis

Global Investing

Company Profile

Vivian Lewis says her favorite stock for 1998 is admittedly a bit "off the wall." Nevertheless, it's profitable and serves an area that is essential to all of us. The company is an Australian-based concern called Memtec. It's involved in the membrane technology business. "It makes modular filters for water treatment," Lewis explains. "What modular means is if you need to filter more water, you snap on another one. The filters are used for treating not only water, but also other fluids."

Memtec is divided into four different divisions. Filterite, which is headquartered in Timonium, Maryland, manufactures a wide range of filters used to clear water of paints, inks, dyes, and other chemicals for the electronics industry. Customers of this unit include IBM, Texas Instruments, Motorola, Sanyo, and Polaroid. Fluid Dynamics, the second division, is located in DeLand, Florida and produces filters and filtration systems composed of nonwoven fine metallic fiber structures. These devices are used by companies like 3M, DuPont, and Eastman Kodak, which work on projects involving high temperatures and corrosion. The metallic filtration material is also sold to be used for making air bags, disposable ink jet print cartridges, and devices to shield computers from high frequency radio waves.

Memcor is a Memtec division headquartered in Windsor, New South Wales. It offers large-volume self-cleaning membrane-based systems used to filter municipal drinking and waste water. These systems employ Memtec's proprietary continuous microfiltration long life systems instead of disposable filters. Finally, its Seitz division in Bad Krueznach, Germany is the latest addition to the Memtec family. Seitz produces a plethora of depth filters, cartridges, and proprietary membrane filters for the food and beverage market, as well as the pharmaceutical industry. Seitz products are used by such companies as Avon, Nestlé, and Revlon.

"The equipment Memtec makes is used for treating drinking water, water for industrial plants, sewage, and industrial fluid waste," Lewis shares. "Industries that make polymers, semiconductors, food, and drugs are big users of this stuff." The Memcor and Fluid Dynamics units have been growing the fastest, in terms of booking an increased backlog. Still, net income rose 5.7 percent in the latest fiscal year, which is slightly below the industry average. Company chairman Denis M. Hanley vows to get those numbers up. "We now have a long history of strong earnings growth, a history of successful acquisitions, the expanding market potential of drinking and waste water, health care, power generation, and airbags," he says. "This all indicates, particularly in the form of our backlog, that our future will be every bit as exciting as our past."

Reason for Recommendation

Why does Lewis like this rather mundane and unglamorous company so much? "First of all, I think water is hot," she exclaims. "As we move into the 21st century, there's not going to be an energy or population crisis, but there is going to be a water crisis. People need water not only to drink but also to grow food, and treating water is the way to go. Starting in Australia, which is a dry place, we're going to learn about technologies that enable us to use water more effectively than we are right now. That's the way the world is going."

Lewis notes that Memtec is well-positioned to capitalize on this opportunity. "Its systems are used all around the world, from California to China, all along the Pacific Rim and even in Wales," she says. What's more, Lewis emphasizes that Memtec products are used to treat water for brewing beer. "This may not seem like much, but beer is big," she insists. "As the world becomes more prosperous, more people want a beer or Coke."

Memtec's net sales grew by 20 percent during the latest fiscal year to $175 million. It would have been slightly higher, were it not for negative currency fluctuations. There are other companies making products like Memtec, but Lewis isn't concerned. "The competition doesn't manufacture the same kinds of filtration systems," she says. "The scale on Memtec's stuff is pretty huge. We're talking about major systems that are hard to duplicate."

Memtec stock is available on the Nasdaq exchange, but is not widely followed on Wall Street, which is something Lewis likes. It is owned by such major investment companies as Putnam Investments, Fidelity, and Farmers Group. Lewis adds that the stock is highly liquid, unlike some foreign securities, and expects it to trade for around $50 by the end of the year.

Contact Information: Denis M. Hanley
Chairman
Memtec Limited
1 Memtec Parkway
Windsor, NSW 2756 Australia
011 61 45 77 6800

U.S. Contact—Bank of New York
101 Barclay Street, 22nd Floor
New York, NY 10015
(212) 815-2009

Memtec Limited
Symbol: MEMA F

Annual Earnings per Share

Memtec Limited
Symbol: MEMA F

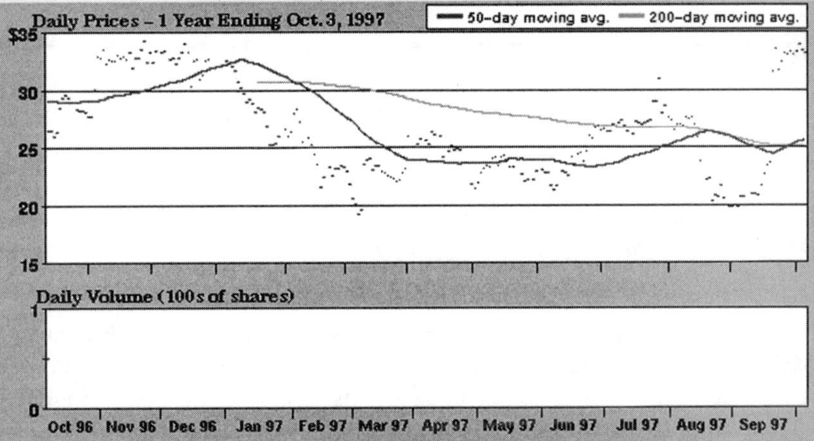

Latest Pricing Data (as of Oct. 6, 1997)		
Close (net change):	$34 5/16	(+1/2)
Day High & Low:	$34 5/16	$33 1/8
Volume & Avg. Volume:	N.A.	N.A.
52-Week High:	$34 5/16	
52-Week Low:	$19 1/4	Mar. 4, 1997
Latest Dividend:	$0.10	Nov. 22, 1996
Ind. Ann. Div. & Yield:	$0.00	N.A.
12 Month EPS:	N.A.	
P/E Ratio & Beta Factor:	N.A.	0.466
Shares Outstanding:	10.336 million	
Market Value:	$342 million	
Institutional Holdings:	N.A.	
Number of Institutions:	N.A.	
Primary Market:		
Component of:	N.A.	

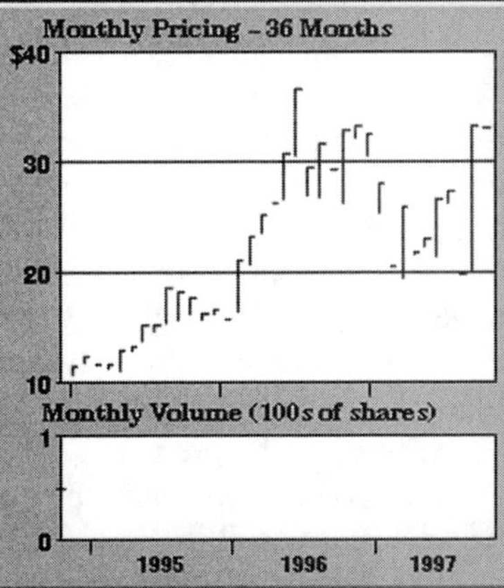

Currency: U.S. Dollars.

Source: IDD Information Services

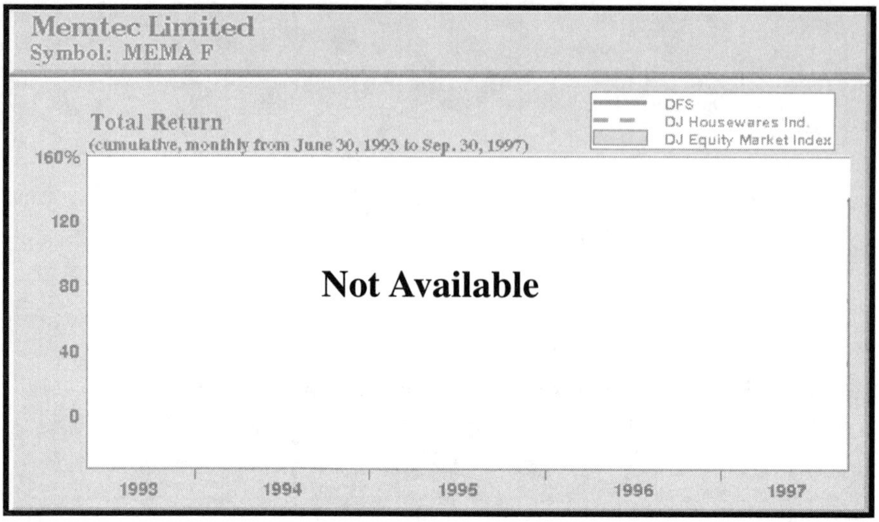

Special Update on Memtec:

On September 17, 1997, U.S. Filter Corp. made an unsolicited offer to buy Memtec for $30 per share. U.S. Filter chairman Richard Heckman said Memtec's strong water-treatment, filtration and membrane technologies would fit in well with U.S. Filter's existing operations, especially globally. Memtec's board came out two weeks later and strongly advised its shareholders to reject the offer. The board concluded the offer was "opportunistic, and it fundamentally undervalued Memtec's current and future opportunities." The board also noted that Memtec's shares have traded above $30 several times in the past, which it continued to do at press time. Nevertheless, on the day U.S. Filter's offer was announced, Memtec shares were selling below $24 a share. By the end of the session, they had jumped by more than 34 percent.

As this book went to print, the U.S. Filter buyout offer was still on the table. It's possible that this $30 bid will be sweetened or that another interested buyer will come along. Alternatively, Memtec could continue to operate independently.

Therefore, before purchasing Memtec stock, be sure to find out how this unexpected development is progressing. Purchasing takeover candidates can be tricky, especially when you get involved after an announcement has already been made.

NORTHERN TRUST

John Rogers
Ariel Capital Management

Company Profile

Northern Trust is a company right in John Rogers's backyard. "It is a preeminent, well-known bank in Chicago," says the president of Ariel Capital Management, which is also located in the Windy City. "But the real story is it has an extraordinary franchise when it comes to the master trust business for large pension plans and wealthy individuals." At last count, Northern Trust had some $694 billion in assets under administration on behalf of large U.S. companies, institutions, and retirement funds. "It has all the systems in place to keep track of assets and performance, all the bells and whistles that are necessary for that business," Rogers explains. "So instead of being a typical bank, where success is based on lending money, it makes the bulk of its profits each year on a fee-based, recurring revenue stream."

That is particularly important to Rogers, because banks often have a hard time when inflation creeps up and interest rates rise. He expects both of these things to happen in 1998. "In situations like this, people have a harder time paying back their debts, and business becomes more volatile," he says. "The master trust business, on the other hand, is very predictable and consistent. It's one of those wonderful businesses that can grab more assets and market share regardless of what happens."

While Northern Trust is headquartered in Chicago, it has offices around the country, including Florida, Arizona, Texas, and California. The bank was founded by Byron L. Smith in 1889 and has grown into the nation's 33rd largest bank based on assets. The company also has several nonbank subsidiaries, including Northern Trust Securities, which provides full brokerage services and underwrites general obligation municipal securities.

Its main business units can be divided into five different categories: corporate and institutional services, personal financial services, worldwide operations and technology, investment services, and risk management. The corporate and institutional services unit provides trust, commercial banking, and treasury management services to a broad array of clients. This includes custody services for securities, asset management, and the master trust product.

The personal financial services unit encompasses personal trusts, real estate administration, personal banking, mortgage lending, and investment management. Most of these services are targeted to high net worth individuals. Its national wealth management business now serves 140 families with assets in excess of $100 million each. "Wealthy individuals know this is the place to have their money managed," Rogers says. Northern Trust is also experimenting with a product called Private Passport, which allows individuals to bank using a personal computer.

Worldwide operations and technology help the above units deliver more effective products and services to clients, while the $4.7 billion Northern Funds group of no-load funds is part of the company's investment services unit. This division provides portfolio management, along with equity and fixed-income research, to institutional and individual investors alike. Finally, the risk management unit writes the bank's credit policy and is responsible for managing the bank's wholesale funding and interest rate risk.

Reason for Recommendation

You can see by now that Northern Trust is not your average bank. Its true area of expertise is managing money for the wealthy and offering the master trust service that so intrigues Rogers. "This bank has a very solid management team that has been around for a long time helping to build the brand name," he observes. "It is working hard to cut costs and run the business more effectively. The stock is also very cheap relative to the market in general, its growth rate, and the expectations that I have for it going forward."

As previously mentioned, the master trust division should provide reliable cash flow, regardless of what happens with the economy. But if interest rates do go up, Rogers admits this stock will likely get hit, even though it won't be impacted as much as some competitors. "Everyone wants to paint Northern Trust with the same brush as other financial institutions," he reasons. "I think that when people ultimately get more discriminating and do their homework, they'll realize this is a preeminent company. This stock really fits our strategy of finding a company that's in a consistent industry with predictable earnings and revenues, and where it's hard for other people to come in and compete." Rogers adds that Northern Trust also passes his strict social screens. "It just opened a branch in the inner-city of Chicago," he notes. "It has a talented and diverse group of senior managers who are very active in the community." Rogers expects the company to earn $2.50 a share over the next 12 months and feels the stock is worth around $60.

Contact Information: William A. Osborn
Chairman and CEO
Northern Trust Corporation
50 South LaSalle Street
Chicago, IL 60675
(312) 630-6000
http://www.ntrs.com

Northern Trust Corporation

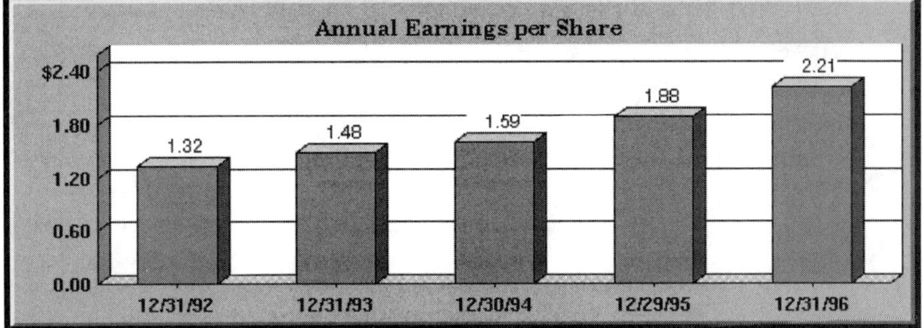

Northern Trust Corporation

Symbol: NTRS Exchange: Nasdaq NMS

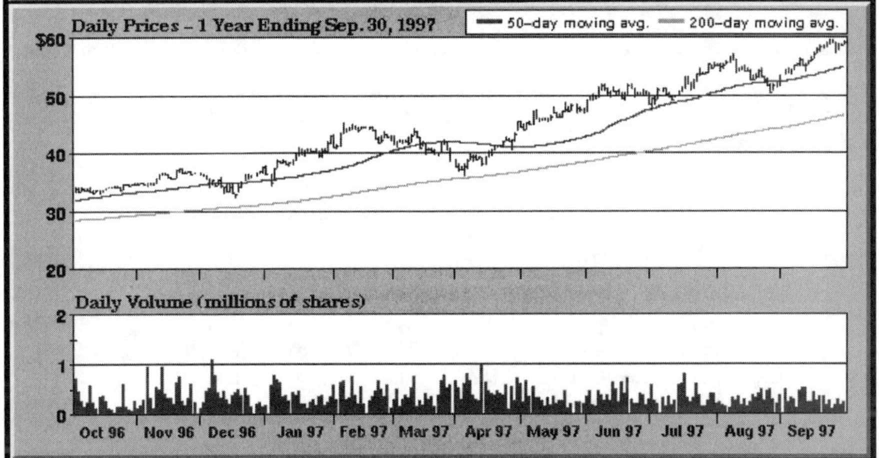

Latest Pricing Data (as of Sep. 30, 1997)		
Close (net change):	$59 1/8	(+9/16)
Day High & Low:	$59 1/4	$58 5/8
Volume & Avg. Volume:	219,300	346,343
52-Week High:	$59 1/2	Sep. 24, 1997
52-Week Low:	$32	Dec. 17, 1996
Latest Dividend:	$0.18	Sep. 8, 1997
Ind. Ann. Div. & Yield:	$0.72	1.22%
12 Month EPS:	$2.42	June 30, 1997
P/E Ratio & Beta Factor:	24.43	0.887
Shares Outstanding:	111.679 million	
Market Value:	$6.603 billion	
Institutional Holdings:	62.41%	
Number of Institutions:	393	
Primary Market:	Nasdaq NMS	

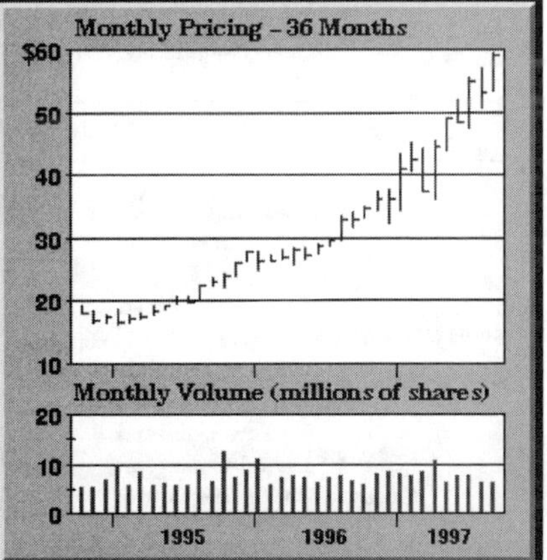

Currency: U.S. Dollars.

Source: IDD Information Services

Northern Trust Corporation
Symbol: NTRS

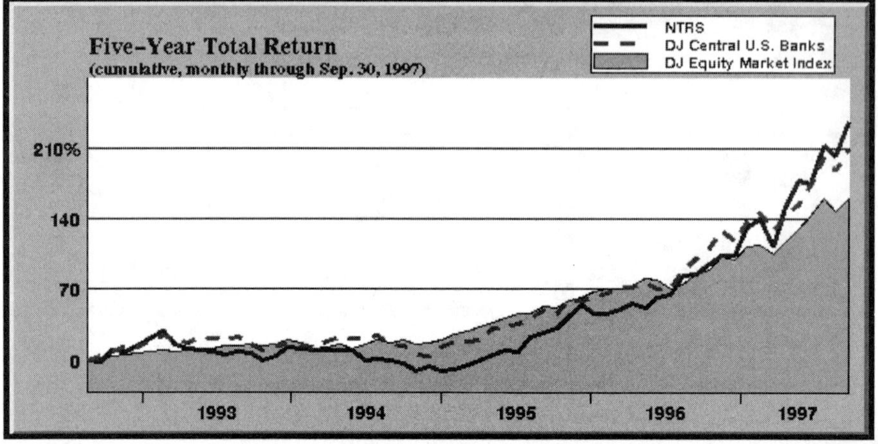

SELECTED INCOME STATEMENT AND BALANCE SHEET ITEMS

INCOME STATEMENT	12/31/92	12/31/93	12/30/94	12/29/95	12/31/96	LTM
Sales/Revenues	1,231.3	1,258.8	1,478.5	1,782.1	1,929.4	2,039.2
Cost of Goods Sold	N.A.	N.A.	N.A.	N.A.	N.A.	N.A.
Pre-tax Margin (%)	16.80	18.60	17.70	18.00	20.10	20.75
Operating Income	617.20	611.10	772.00	1,066.9	1,150.6	1,221.1
Net Income before Extras	149.50	167.90	182.20	220.00	258.80	281.00
Reported Net Income	149.50	167.90	182.20	220.00	258.80	281.00
Depreciation & Amortization	N.A.	N.A.	N.A.	N.A.	N.A.	N.A.
EPS from Net Income (Primary)	1.320	1.480	1.590	1.880	2.210	2.420
EPS from Net Income (Fully Diluted)	1.320	1.480	1.580	1.850	2.200	2.420
Dividend per Common Share	0.302	0.388	0.460	0.545	0.555	0.605
Dividend Yield (%)	1.44	1.96	2.63	1.95	1.53	1.25
Payout Ratio	0.23	0.26	0.29	0.29	0.25	0.25

BALANCE SHEET					
ASSETS					
Cash & Cash Equivalents	N.A.	N.A.	N.A.	N.A.	N.A.
Inventories	N.A.	N.A.	N.A.	N.A.	N.A.
Total Current Assets	N.A.	N.A.	N.A.	N.A.	N.A.
Total Assets	14,960	16,903	18,562	19,934	21,608
LIABILITIES & EQUITY					
Short Term Debt	799.80	2,125.3	957.40	1,022.6	3,291.1
Long Term Debt	545.20	1,143.8	791.80	351.60	732.80
Total Liabilities	13,949	15,751	17,281	18,481	20,064
Shares Outstanding	105.664	106.586	108.178	111.328	111.248
Common Stockholder Equity	840.50	981.70	1,110.7	1,282.6	1,424.1
Total Stockholder Equity	1,010.5	1,151.7	1,280.7	1,452.6	1,544.1

Note: Figures in Millions of $ except: per share items, margins, yields, and ratios.

Source: IDD Information Services

PHILIP MORRIS

Robert Sanborn
The Oakmark Fund

Company Profile

"The market looks at this company and focuses on every little legal case and the stock goes up and down based on the sentiment of the day," says Robert Sanborn, portfolio manager of The Oakmark Fund. "I don't pay attention to that at all." Instead Sanborn concentrates on how Philip Morris is the world's largest producer and marketer of consumer packaged goods, and how much money it continues to make. In 1996 alone, earnings per share climbed 18 percent driven by strong growth in its worldwide tobacco and domestic food businesses. Operating revenues jumped 8.1 percent, a record 891 billion cigarettes were shipped around the world, and the quarterly dividend was raised 20 percent. The company also bought back 28.6 million shares of its own stock.

Despite all of the controversy, people continue to smoke. The company's flagship Marlboro brand has captured 33.3 percent of the domestic retail market, and international tobacco sales are growing in excess of 11 percent a year. But Philip Morris stock seems to remain under constant pressure due to uncertainty about how a plethora of legal cases by smokers will ultimately impact the bottom lines of tobacco companies.

"I look at the litigation issue in the following way," Sanborn offers. "If there was no litigation exposure whatsoever, I suggest this stock would trade at the same valuation as the other real dominant brand name companies, like Coca-Cola and Gillette. Actually, in the past ten years, Philip Morris has outperformed both of those companies as businesses. To be perfectly honest, I think it will continue to do so for a long time, because the Marlboro brand name is probably stronger than any of them. More importantly, it competes against weak competitors, which means Philip Morris has tremendous growth potential for years to come."

Still, Sanborn says he's more concerned about the litigation issue now than ever before, because he fears jurors in these cases may start acting with their emotions instead of the facts, although up until now, this certainly hasn't been the case. "My biggest concern is jury nullification in the tobacco area," he explains. "Juries have always looked at the law and concluded that the smoker was responsible for his or her decision. I'm worried they'll begin to say, 'Yes, that's the law, but these are bad guys so let's get them.' But even with that, in the long run, the liability is not as much as the market is discounting." Nevertheless, several states have filed class-action lawsuits, both here and abroad, with one case pending in Canada and another in Brazil. As for talks of a possible settlement, Sanborn says he'd welcome one, as long as it was good for the company.

It's also important to remember that Philip Morris is more than just a lot of smoke. Roughly a third of the company's operating income comes from domestic tobacco sales, another third from international tobacco sales, and the final third from its food-related businesses. The company has 68 brands that generate annual revenues of more than $100 million each, plus five principal operating companies: Kraft Foods, Miller Brewing Company, Philip Morris International, Philip Morris USA, and Philip Morris Capital Corporation. Among the most popular food items it puts out are Jell-O, Oscar Meyer, Maxwell House, Cool Whip, Stove Top, Altoids, Miracle Whip, DiGiorno's Pizza, Kool-Aid, Country Time, Breyers, Miller Lite, and Post cereals.

Reason for Recommendation

The lingering litigation has put Philip Morris stock on sale, according to Sanborn. "If it traded in sync with other companies of its caliber, its market cap would rise from $100 billion to $350 billion, which implies a current litigation penalty of $250 billion," he calculates. "My conclusion is it will never have to pay anything like that to get this legal stuff behind it." Sanborn also questions whether any lawyer will be able to legitimately prove that smoking is addictive. "If you accept the scientific definition, cigarette smoking is not addictive," he argues. "It's a matter of opinion."

But almost everyone agrees the company will be forced to pay something at one point or another. Doesn't that create a great risk for this stock? Not necessarily, says Sanborn, because the company can simply pass those added costs on to consumers in the form of higher prices. "My bottom line is that the market is overdiscounting what the likely litigation is going to be," he concludes. "As long as that gap is so large, I like the stock." In addition, 1998 could be a turning point for this company, if an acceptable settlement to the pending litigation is finally reached.

As for the company's leadership, Sanborn is impressed. "I personally think Philip Morris management is about as good as any team I've run across because of the way they've run their business for the past 15 years," he maintains. "I look for the stock to reach around $67 sometime this year."

Contact Information: Geoffrey C. Bible
Chairman and CEO
Philip Morris Companies, Inc.
120 Park Avenue
New York, NY 10017
(212) 880-5000

Philip Morris Companies Incorporated

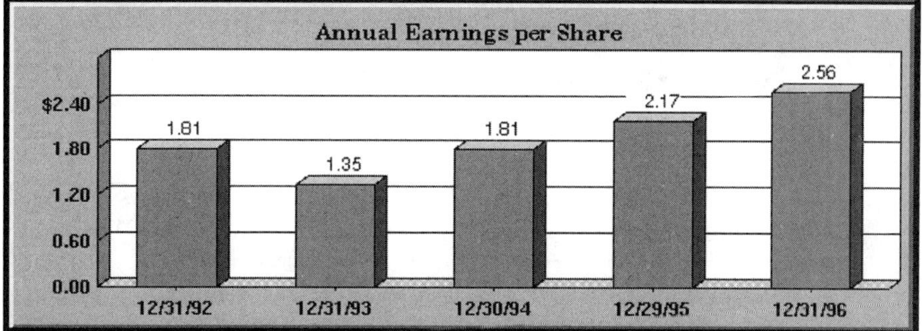

Philip Morris Companies Incorporated

Symbol: MO Exchange: NYSE

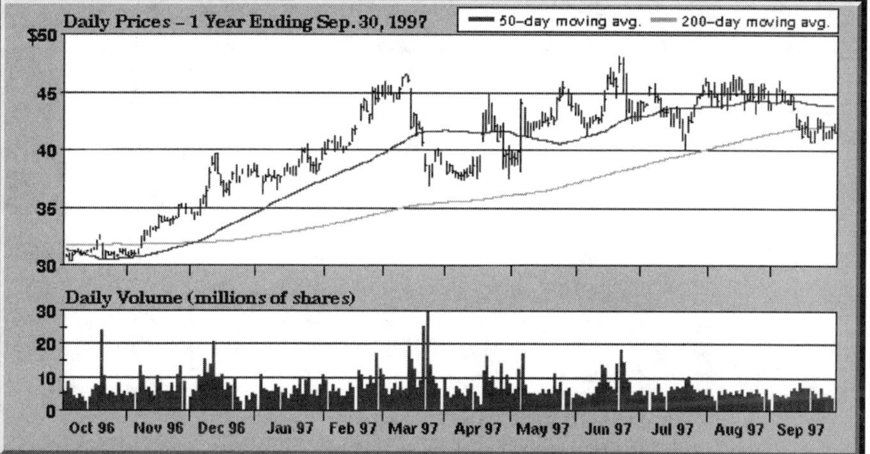

Latest Pricing Data (as of Sep. 30, 1997)		
Close (net change):	$41 9/16	(–5/16)
Day High & Low:	$42 5/16	$41 1/2
Volume & Avg. Volume:	4,003,000	7,959,578
52-Week High:	$48 1/8	June 19, 1997
52-Week Low:	$30 13/64	Oct. 3, 1996
Latest Dividend:	$0.40	Sep. 11, 1997
Ind. Ann. Div. & Yield:	$1.60	3.85%
12 Month EPS:	$2.76	June 30, 1997
P/E Ratio & Beta Factor:	15.06	0.955
Shares Outstanding:	2.423 billion	
Market Value:	$100.705 billion	
Institutional Holdings:	60.93%	
Number of Institutions:	2102	
Primary Market:	NYSE	
Component of:	DJIA, S&P 500	

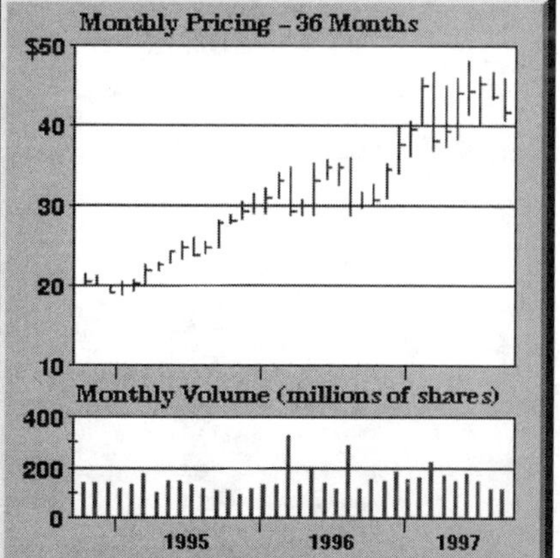

Currency: U.S. Dollars.

Source: IDD Information Services

Philip Morris Companies Incorporated
Symbol: MO

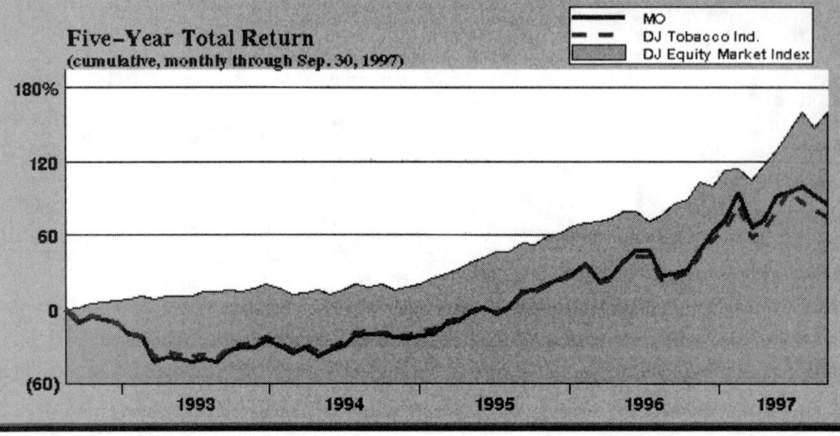

SELECTED INCOME STATEMENT AND BALANCE SHEET ITEMS

INCOME STATEMENT	12/31/92	12/31/93	12/30/94	12/29/95	12/31/96	LTM
Sales/Revenues	59,131	60,901	65,125	66,071	69,204	70,834
Cost of Goods Sold	24,540	25,152	26,629	25,605	25,463	25,446
Pre-tax Margin (%)	14.60	10.20	12.60	14.10	15.40	16.00
Operating Income	10,059	7,587.0	9,449.0	10,526	11,769	12,456
Net Income before Extras	4,939.0	3,568.0	4,725.0	5,478.0	6,303.0	6,726.0
Reported Net Income	4,939.0	3,568.0	4,725.0	5,478.0	6,303.0	6,726.0
Depreciation & Amortization	1,542.0	1,619.0	2,326.0	1,671.0	1,691.0	1,713.0
EPS from Net Income (Primary)	1.810	1.350	1.810	2.170	2.560	2.760
EPS from Net Income (Fully Diluted)	1.810	1.350	1.810	2.170	2.560	2.760
Dividend per Common Share	0.783	0.867	1.010	1.220	1.467	1.600
Dividend Yield (%)	3.05	4.67	5.27	4.06	3.89	3.62
Payout Ratio	0.43	0.64	0.56	0.56	0.57	0.58
BALANCE SHEET						
ASSETS						
Cash & Cash Equivalents	1,021.0	182.00	184.00	1,138.0	240.00	
Inventories	7,785.0	7,358.0	7,987.0	7,862.0	9,002.0	
Total Current Assets	13,906	12,808	13,908	14,879	15,190	
Total Assets	50,014	51,205	52,649	53,811	54,871	
LIABILITIES & EQUITY						
Short Term Debt	2,862.0	2,935.0	1,497.0	2,719.0	2,279.0	
Long Term Debt	14,583	15,221	14,975	13,107	12,961	
Total Liabilities	37,451	39,578	39,863	39,826	40,653	
Shares Outstanding	2,680.952	2,633.907	2,561.138	2,496.006	2,433.781	
Common Stockholder Equity	12,563	11,627	12,786	13,985	14,218	
Total Stockholder Equity	12,563	11,627	12,786	13,985	14,218	

Note: Figures in Millions of $ except: per share items, margins, yields, and ratios.

Source: IDD Information Services

PLAYTEX

Cappy McGarr
McGarr Capital Management

Company Profile

Although Playtex is known primarily for its various tampon products, the company is involved in much more than that. Its sun care division sells the Banana Boat tanning line, its household products arm manufactures disposable gloves and Woolite carpet cleaner, and its infant care unit makes an array of spill-proof cups and disposable bottles. But the company has been in the dog house for several years, as far as Wall Street is concerned, thanks to lackluster sales growth and a slide in profitability. "I heard one analyst call it a 'show me' stock, as in 'show me the money' before I recommend it," notes Cappy McGarr of McGarr Capital Management.

In 1995, a leveraged buyout firm led by current Playtex chairman, Robert Haas, bought some 40 percent of the company's outstanding stock at $9 per share. "Back then, the company was overleveraged, poorly managed and losing market share," McGarr explains. Haas and his partners vowed to bring in new management, clean house, and increase the visibility of Playtex products. "They're doing exactly what they said they were going to do," McGarr insists. "The company has been a lousy investment for them so far, in terms of the stock price, but they brought on a new board and renegotiated the outstanding debt, and that should eventually pay off."

Haas's first order of business was hiring Michael Gallagher, a veteran of the consumer goods industry, as chief executive officer. "He gave Gallagher 800,000 options at $9.875 when he hired him," McGarr points out. "He also set in place a bonus structure whereby each time Playtex stock hits $15, $20, $25, and $30, he gets another $1 million bonus. So there's plenty of incentive for Gallagher to make the company succeed. Overall, company managers and directors own 48 percent of the outstanding stock."

Gallagher has made a series of noticeable changes, such as changing the package design for most Playtex goods, instituting a series of major product improvements, adding new items to the present lineup, giving out more trial samples, and investing in new plants and equipment to increase production capacity. The company is also doing more to reach the public. Playtex household gloves are now being advertised on TV for the first time in 20 years, and its Banana Boat products are attractively packaged in fun-store displays to grab the attention of young consumers, who use more sun care products than anyone else.

In addition, Gallagher reorganized the company's U.S. operations into two divisions with separate sales organizations and marketing teams. He also is putting more emphasis on growing business overseas. "International markets are a tremendous opportunity for the company, especially in South America," McGarr says. "The other positive is that Gallagher knows the international markets very well." The newly formed category development teams are staffed by highly skilled managers with data analysis and marketing expertise. Their job is to help the company build all of its categories to the maximum potential.

Reason for Recommendation

McGarr calls Playtex a classic turnaround play. "They've cleaned up the company and are increasing its market share in almost every single category," he observes. "Playtex has a 74 percent market share in spill-proof cups, 74 percent in disposable baby bottles, 41 percent in rubber gloves, and 21 percent in tampons. Plus, in 1997, it overtook Coppertone as the number one sun product in the United States with a 21 percent market share." The tampon business accounts for 45 percent of the company's total business, followed by infant care at 22 percent, sun care at 15 percent, household products at 12 percent, and hair care products at 6 percent.

But if business is improving, why is the stock still going nowhere? McGarr suggests it's because no one is paying attention. "A lot of times, Wall Street is behind," he contends. "Once Playtex has demonstrated it can turn around and generate higher earnings, the stock will go up." Smart investors, McGarr maintains, will buy shares in the company before then, to profit from Wall Street's delay in waking up to all of the positive things that are happening to it.

Procter & Gamble's buyout of Tambrands in 1997 sparked rumors that Playtex would be next. The most frequently mentioned suitor is the Kimberly-Clark Corporation, although neither company will confirm they're even talking. In terms of having to compete with P&G, McGarr is confident Playtex can handle it. "The company has proven it can play with the big names," he says. "You must also realize the tampon business is very profitable, and I can't imagine that Procter & Gamble would try to start a price war or anything similar." In terms of a possible buyout offer, McGarr says he wouldn't be surprised to see one. But either way, he's convinced this stock will do well this year. "I think earnings can grow by at least 17 percent annually," McGarr predicts. "I expect the stock to trade for $15 in 1998. If it is taken over by another company, I look for the offer price to be at least $18 per share."

Contact Information: Michael Gallagher
CEO
Playtex Products, Inc.
300 Nyala Farms Road
Westport, CT 06880
(203) 341-4000

Playtex Products Incorporated

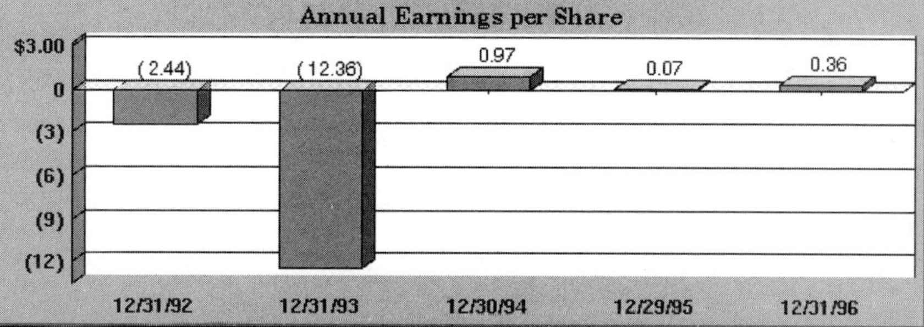

Playtex Products Incorporated

Symbol: PYX Exchange: NYSE

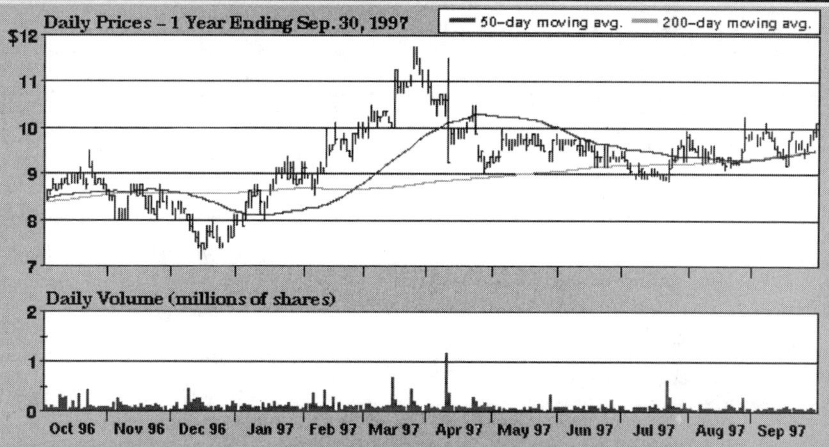

Latest Pricing Data (as of Sep. 30, 1997)		
Close (net change):	$10 1/8	(+3/16)
Day High & Low:	$10 1/8	$9 13/16
Volume & Avg. Volume:	54,400	121,627
52-Week High:	$11 3/4	Mar. 25, 1997
52-Week Low:	$7 1/8	Dec. 13, 1996
Latest Dividend:	$0.00	
Ind. Ann. Div. & Yield:	$0.00	N.A.
12 Month EPS:	$0.40	June 30, 1997
P/E Ratio & Beta Factor:	25.31	0.657
Shares Outstanding:	50.924 million	
Market Value:	$516 million	
Institutional Holdings:	34.64%	
Number of Institutions:	77	
Primary Market:	NYSE	

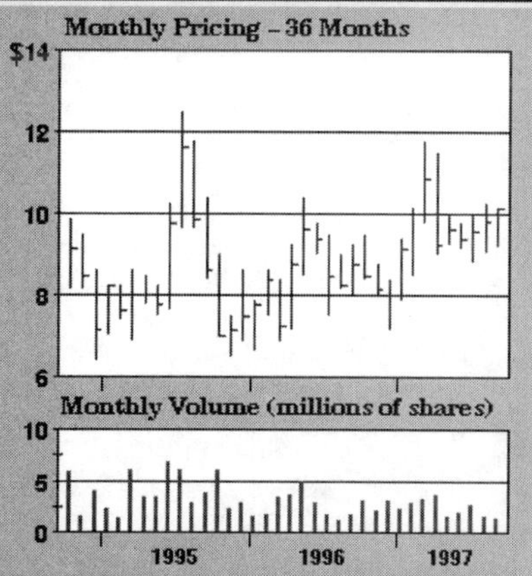

Currency: U.S. Dollars.

Source: IDD Information Services

Playtex Products Incorporated
Symbol: PYX

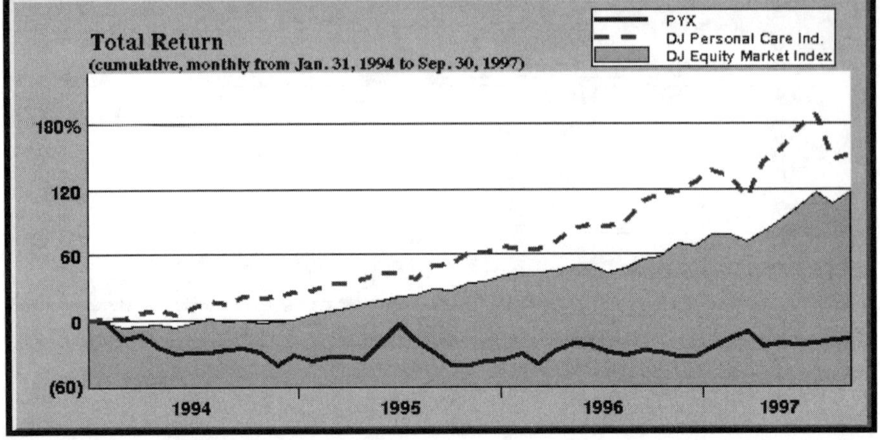

SELECTED INCOME STATEMENT AND BALANCE SHEET ITEMS

INCOME STATEMENT	12/31/92	12/31/93	12/30/94	12/29/95	12/31/96	LTM
Sales/Revenues	384.50	409.90	473.30	483.60	498.70	495.10
Cost of Goods Sold	118.30	90.900	154.20	177.40	181.50	182.10
Pre-tax Margin (%)	(2.70)	(30.00)	11.30	2.30	6.90	7.30
Operating Income	103.90	114.80	129.80	88.700	99.200	101.80
Net Income before Extras	(15.300)	(124.80)	29.500	2.800	18.200	20.000
Reported Net Income	(15.300)	(124.80)	29.500	2.800	18.200	20.000
Depreciation & Amortization	5.700	59.500	20.000	22.000	23.800	23.300
EPS from Net Income (Primary)	(2.440)	(12.360)	0.970	0.070	0.360	0.400
EPS from Net Income (Fully Diluted)	(2.440)	(12.360)	0.970	0.070	0.360	0.400
Dividend per Common Share	N.A.	N.A.	N.A.	N.A.	N.A.	N.A.
Dividend Yield (%)	N.A.	N.A.	N.A.	N.A.	N.A.	N.A.
Payout Ratio	N.A.	N.A.	N.A.	N.A.	N.A.	N.A.

BALANCE SHEET					
ASSETS					
Cash & Cash Equivalents	17.600	15.400	10.400	5.900	6.200
Inventories	25.700	33.000	41.600	49.200	37.600
Total Current Assets	97.200	124.30	113.90	130.80	122.50
Total Assets	716.10	588.50	599.40	682.90	660.30
LIABILITIES & EQUITY					
Short Term Debt	25.000	28.400	34.500	20.000	25.000
Long Term Debt	905.00	887.00	841.20	770.10	714.70
Total Liabilities	1,136.2	1,172.1	1,065.4	984.00	943.10
Shares Outstanding	50.158	50.158	30.880	50.880	50.887
Common Stockholder Equity	(544.90)	(723.40)	(466.00)	(301.00)	(282.70)
Total Stockholder Equity	(420.10)	(583.80)	(466.00)	(301.00)	(282.70)

Note: Figures in Millions of $ except: per share items, margins, yields, and ratios.

Source: IDD Information Services

PRE-PAID LEGAL SERVICES

Michael DiCarlo
DFS Advisors

Company Profile

It's a sign of the times. While people used to feel secure knowing they had a good health and dental plan in place, today they feel incomplete without legal insurance. That's right. Now you can be covered for an annual check up with both your doctor and lawyer thanks to Pre-Paid Legal Services, which makes the services of high-priced attorneys available at an affordable cost to the middle class. "It speaks volumes about the kind of society we live in today," says Michael DiCarlo, founding partner of DFS Advisors. "Unfortunately, we live in a very litigious society. People are always looking for reasons to sue one another. It's really pretty comical."

But it's profitable for Pre-Paid Legal. The company sells several different HMO-like insurance plans entitling policy holders to get unlimited access to one of 30 provider law firms and 6,000 referral attorneys in the 44 states in which it is currently licensed to do business. Although Pre-Paid Legal has been marketing and administering these policies for more than 25 years, they are more popular than ever. "The company has several different plans," DiCarlo explains. "There's a basic family plan, along with specialized plans for commercial drivers, law officers, school teachers, and small business owners." More than 90 percent of all customers take the basic plan, which costs as little as $14.95 per month if purchased through a qualifying affiliated group. In return, policyholders receive unlimited consultations with attorneys through a toll-free number, complimentary document reviews, preparation and annual revision of a simple will, and letter writing and phone calls by plan lawyers. For a little more money, you can add such features as defense coverage for moving traffic violations, assistance with personal injury or property damage claims, trial defense services for civil suits, and help in the event of an IRS audit. "At the top of the line part of the service, you can get a 25 percent discount from the provider's standard hourly rate," DiCarlo adds. "That's pretty significant when lawyers are charging $150 or more an hour these days."

Pre-Paid Legal sells its services through a commission-based multi-level marketing program. Nearly all of the 113,000 sales reps across the country are also clients, which means they comprise about a third of the company's total membership. The reps have to pay an enrollment fee to get started and are also responsible for the cost of all training and marketing material. It makes for a no-lose situation, because Pre-Paid takes on virtually no financial risk by bringing on additional associates.

The arrangement with its network of attorneys is equally as sweet. "The lawyer gets 35 percent of the total contract premium, and the marketing associates keep an estimated 25 cents on each dollar they bring in," DiCarlo notes. Beyond that, the company's liability for the policies is almost nonexistent. Unlike health insurers, which face the risk that patients will use up more in services than they pay out in premiums, Pre-Paid Legal has no further obligation beyond the set commission and fee share it has negotiated. "Its market is the middle 80 percent of the country," DiCarlo says. "The top 10 percent have their own attorney, and the bottom 10 percent can't afford one."

The company was started in 1972 after founder Harland Stonecipher was in an automobile accident and had trouble paying his legal bills. He realized a service like this was needed and initially ran it exclusively as a motor service club.

Reason for Recommendation

Perhaps we have the media to thank or blame, but increasingly, Americans are becoming more sensitive to the possibility of getting sued and therefore are growing more interested in the legal system. Otherwise the myriad of court-related TV shows wouldn't exist. Clearly, being covered just in case you get sued makes more sense than ever before. That's why Pre-Paid Legal stands to prosper as we enter the 21st century.

"This is a huge market, as you can imagine," DiCarlo exclaims. "The company has around 450,000 active contracts, and that's just the tip of the iceberg. It has easily been growing by 50 percent a year. It was doing $19 million in revenue in 1992. At the end of 1997, it will be around $95 million, up from $60 million in 1996. It has an absolutely pristine balance sheet, no debt, $15 million in cash, and a very stable business."

The company does have several competitors, but most market through direct mail and are much smaller in size. Pre-Paid Legal clearly has an edge with its enormous sales force, but there's no guarantee another firm won't emerge on the scene and steal a substantial amount of business. It's estimated that two-thirds of the American population is not covered by a legal services plan, which demonstrates the potential market for Pre-Paid Legal's products. "With the kind of high recurring revenue stream this company has, people will start to recognize it and place a much higher multiple on the stock than it has right now," DiCarlo predicts.

Contact Information: Harland Stonecipher
Chairman
Pre-Paid Legal Services, Inc.
321 E. Main
Ada, OK 74820
(405) 436-1234
http://www.pplsi.com

Pre Paid Legal Services Incorporated

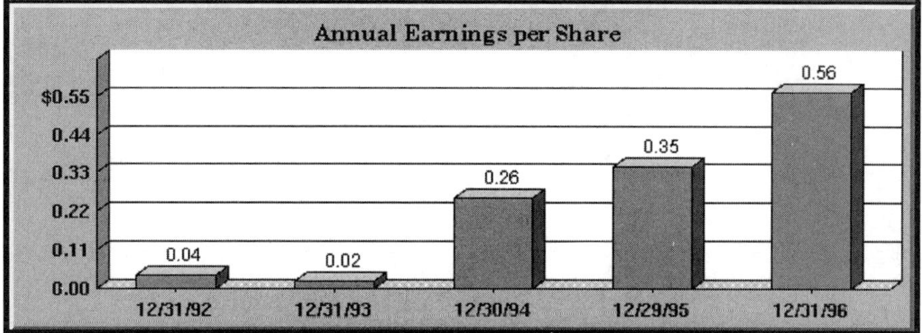

Pre Paid Legal Services Incorporated

Symbol: PPD Exchange: AMEX

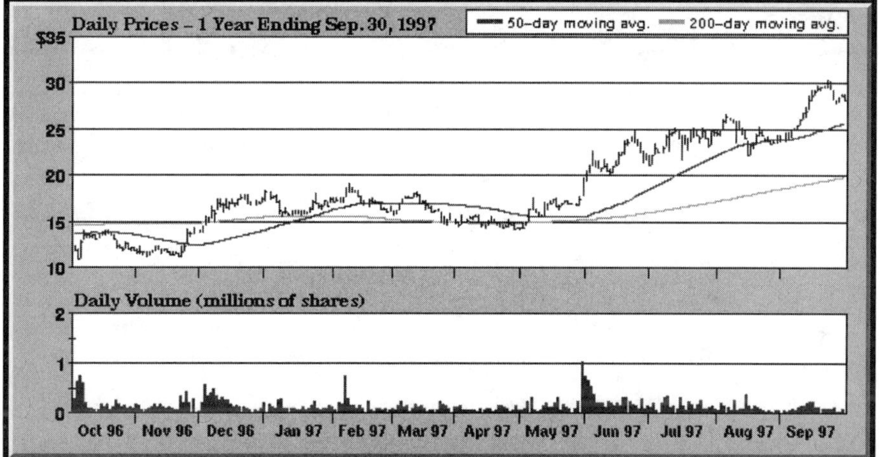

Latest Pricing Data (as of Sep. 30, 1997)		
Close (net change):	$28 1/4	(−3/8)
Day High & Low:	$28 7/8	$28
Volume & Avg. Volume:	94,000	198,320
52-Week High:	$30 5/16	Sep. 22, 1997
52-Week Low:	$10 7/8	Oct. 3, 1996
Latest Dividend:	$0.00	
Ind. Ann. Div. & Yield:	$0.00	N.A.
12 Month EPS:	$0.68	June 30, 1997
P/E Ratio & Beta Factor:	41.54	0.564
Shares Outstanding:	22.234 million	
Market Value:	$628 million	
Institutional Holdings:	37.68%	
Number of Institutions:	96	
Primary Market:	AMEX	

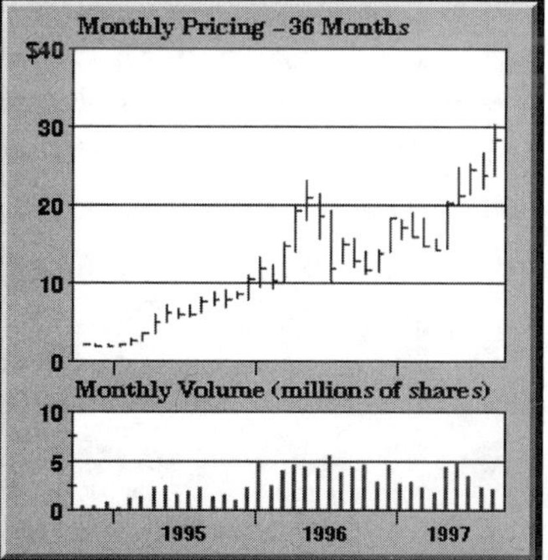

Currency: U.S. Dollars.

Source: IDD Information Services

Pre Paid Legal Services Incorporated
Symbol: PPD

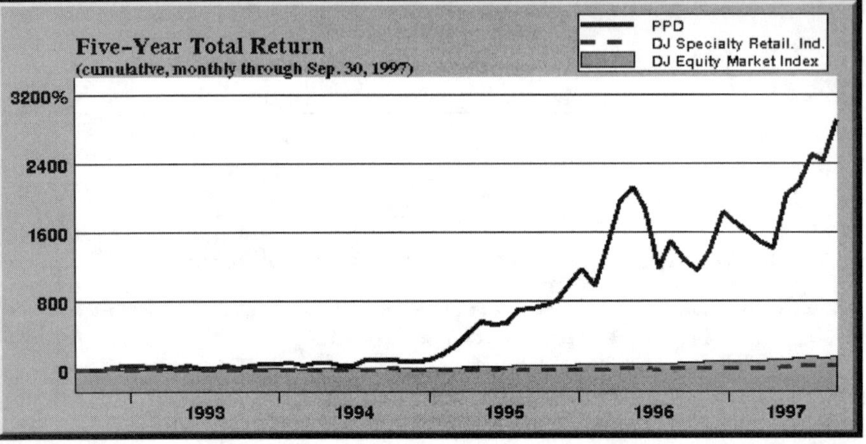

SELECTED INCOME STATEMENT AND BALANCE SHEET ITEMS

INCOME STATEMENT	12/31/92	12/31/93	12/30/94	12/29/95	12/31/96	LTM
Sales/Revenues	19.600	20.100	25.100	37.500	59.900	74.700
Cost of Goods Sold	N.A.	N.A.	N.A.	N.A.	N.A.	N.A.
Pre-tax Margin (%)	4.10	2.50	13.50	29.90	32.10	31.33
Operating Income	1.500	1.000	3.900	11.300	19.200	23.200
Net Income before Extras	0.500	0.300	3.700	7.300	12.500	15.200
Reported Net Income	0.500	0.300	3.700	7.300	12.500	15.200
Depreciation & Amortization	N.A.	N.A.	N.A.	N.A.	N.A.	N.A.
EPS from Net Income (Primary)	0.040	0.020	0.260	0.350	0.560	0.680
EPS from Net Income (Fully Diluted)	0.040	0.020	0.240	0.340	0.560	0.680
Dividend per Common Share	0.000	0.000	0.000	0.000	0.000	0.000
Dividend Yield (%)	N.A.	N.A.	N.A.	N.A.	N.A.	N.A.
Payout Ratio	N.A.	N.A.	N.A.	N.A.	N.A.	N.A.

BALANCE SHEET					
ASSETS					
Cash & Cash Equivalents	N.A.	N.A.	N.A.	N.A.	N.A.
Inventories	N.A.	N.A.	N.A.	N.A.	N.A.
Total Current Assets	N.A.	N.A.	N.A.	N.A.	N.A.
Total Assets	34.800	35.400	18.200	35.600	57.500
LIABILITIES & EQUITY					
Short Term Debt	0.000	2.600	0.000	0.000	0.000
Long Term Debt	5.400	1.200	0.000	0.000	0.000
Total Liabilities	11.400	11.700	2.300	5.800	12.100
Shares Outstanding	10.585	10.795	13.469	13.469	21.712
Common Stockholder Equity	23.300	23.500	15.400	29.700	45.500
Total Stockholder Equity	23.300	23.600	15.800	29.700	45.500

Note: Figures in Millions of $ except: per share items, margins, yields, and ratios.

Source: IDD Information Services

Q-ENTERTAINMENT

Andrew Addison
The Addison Report

Company Profile

At one time, kids and adults were amused by simply watching computer-generated characters battle each other on a video monitor. But no more. Such "safe" play is no longer cool. People want to do the actual fighting themselves. After all, why should a figment of some programmer's imagination have all the fun?

Enter the newest trend in amusement industry: laser tag. The game can be played by up to 40 people at a time and works something like this: Each player is equipped with a body pack and phaser. The battle is fought in a professionally designed arena that is full of unusual shapes and scenery, complete with realistic sound effects. If you tag your opponent with an accurate hit, you earn points. Opponents lose part of their laser activation each time they are struck and eventually are forced to get reenergized in order to stay alive (at least in the game).

Imagine, no more developing carpal tunnel by fighting your battles with a keyboard or joystick. Now you can wear the gear, hold the actual gun and pull the trigger with your own finger. Players know how many points they've racked up by listening to a voice synthesizer inside the laser device. At the end of the game, each warrior gets a printout of their team and individual performance, giving them a challenge and reason to come back to pay more money and play again. Even the Olympic athletes in Atlanta were seen zapping each other with laser tag equipment, and it was made by Q-Entertainment, formerly known as Q-Zar.

Like the laser tag industry in general, Q-Entertainment is a relatively young company. It was created in 1992 by company president and CEO Tom Butler, who had previously worked in the leisure business in Europe. The company's first laser tag center opened in North America that same year. Since then, Q-Entertainment has been aggressively expanding around the world, both through starting company-owned centers and by franchising the concept to independent operators, including Regal Cinemas, Six Flags, and the U.S. Navy. The company first went public in 1995 on the Toronto Stock Exchange, and has been trading on Nasdaq for less than two years. It also operates the Funtime Pizza chain.

"Q-Entertainment has created a niche for itself in a brand new industry," says Andrew Addison, editor of *The Addison Report*. "It's an entertainment company that operates arcades on a megascale. It just opened a 51,000-square-foot, three-story facility in Dallas that has the most incredible virtual reality games and areas where you can play things like laser tag. It's not just sitting in a seat racing a car. Either you or a group of people can have a race among yourselves and simulate the action physically as well as visually. It also has eating facilities and is very family-oriented."

The original Q-Entertainment concept seems to flourish in areas with immediate populations of 120,000 or more. The 12,000- to 14,000-square-foot centers do best when placed beside a mall or multiplex cinema and near tourist locations, colleges, and schools. The core market for these centers is teenagers, but all members of the family seem to enjoy playing the game.

The company's latest and most ambitious creation to date is Q-City, which it calls "the entertainment mall of tomorrow." Q-City is positioned to target the MTV generation, but will be marketed to a wider audience. It features trilevel futuristic buildings with laser tag, bowling, shops, eateries, and high-tech video games. Q-Kidz is another laser tag concept for smaller children between the ages of eight and ten.

"What's unique is you don't have to bring coins or bills to the center," Addison observes. "You use a plastic card. For $10 a year, you become a member and all games are charged to your account. The centers are also very well supervised. They don't allow any outlandish dress, smoking, or alcohol."

Reason for Recommendation

Addison first learned about Q-Entertainment from one of the money mangers he advises who visited the company's Dallas center and was impressed. "He literally had to be dragged away at closing time," Addison says. "I think it's a fascinating concept that plays on the family theme. It combines the entertainment and eating facilities so you can literally spend hours (and therefore a lot of money) there."

Q-Entertainment management expects most of its growth to come from wholly owned centers, because they are the most profitable, although it will continue to offer franchises to qualified buyers as well. While the market for laser tag appears to be large, be aware that Q-Entertainment is a small company fraught with risk. Company officers seem leery of releasing much material information about the operation, and its management team is relatively young and unproven. Still, revenues in the past year have doubled, and Addison is impressed with what he sees so far. "It's a company not too many people know about," he adds. "Q-Entertainment plans to open a number of units over the next 12 months. That will generate lots of excitement. My target for this stock is $10 a share."

Contact Information: Tom Butler
President and CEO
Q-Entertainment
1701 N. Market Street, Suite 200
Dallas, TX 75202
(214) 741-1376

Q-Entertainment Inc.

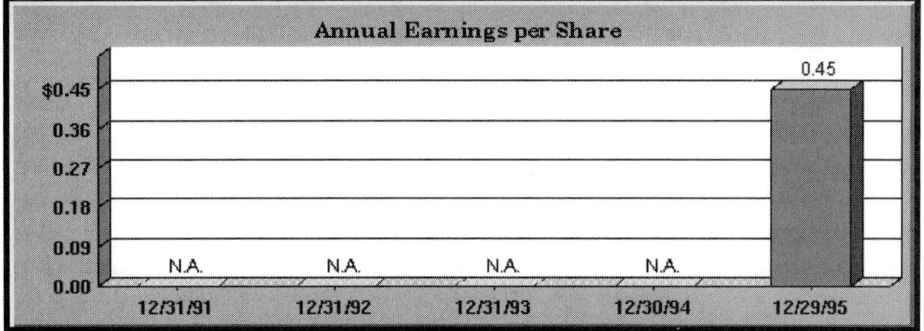

Q-Entertainment Incorporated

Symbol: QZARF Exchange: Nasdaq NMS

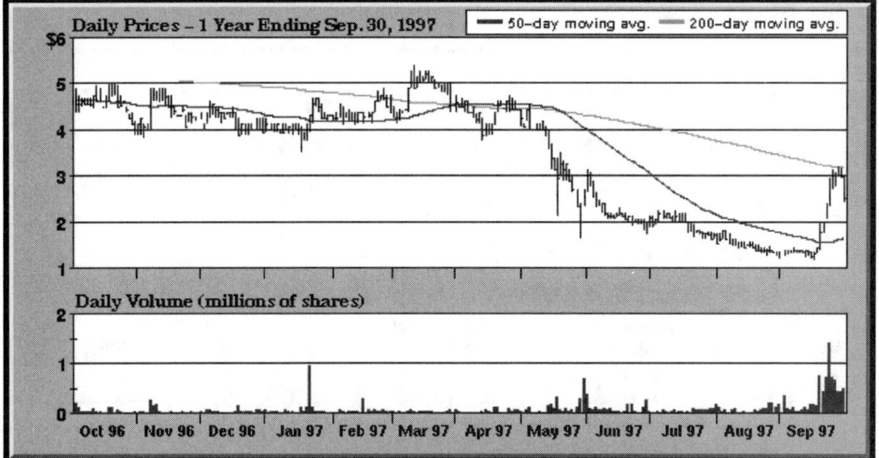

Latest Pricing Data (as of Sep. 30, 1997)		
Close (net change):	$2 1/2	(–15/32)
Day High & Low:	$3	$2 13/32
Volume & Avg. Volume:	483,400	53,201
52-Week High:	$5 3/8	Mar. 11, 1997
52-Week Low:	$1 5/32	Sep. 16, 1997
Latest Dividend:	$0.00	
Ind. Ann. Div. & Yield:	$0.00	N.A.
12 Month EPS:	$0.51	June 30, 1997
P/E Ratio & Beta Factor:	4.90	N.A.
Shares Outstanding:	21.479 million	
Market Value:	$53.7 million	
Institutional Holdings:	N.A.	
Number of Institutions:	N.A.	
Primary Market:	Nasdaq NMS	
Component of:	N.A.	

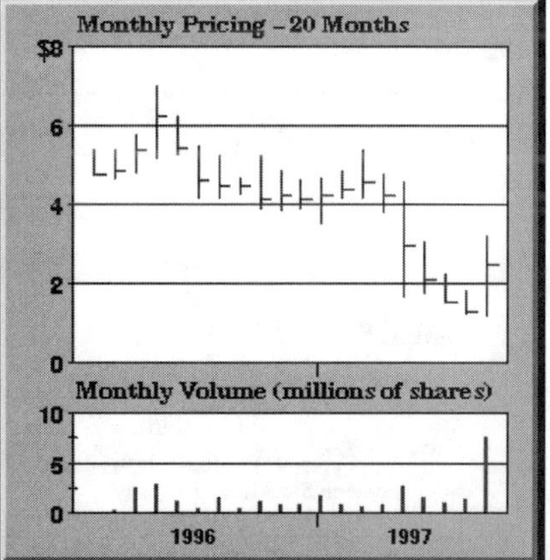

Currency: U.S. Dollars.

Source: IDD Information Services

Q-Entertainment Incorporated

Symbol: QZARF Exchange: Nasdaq NMS

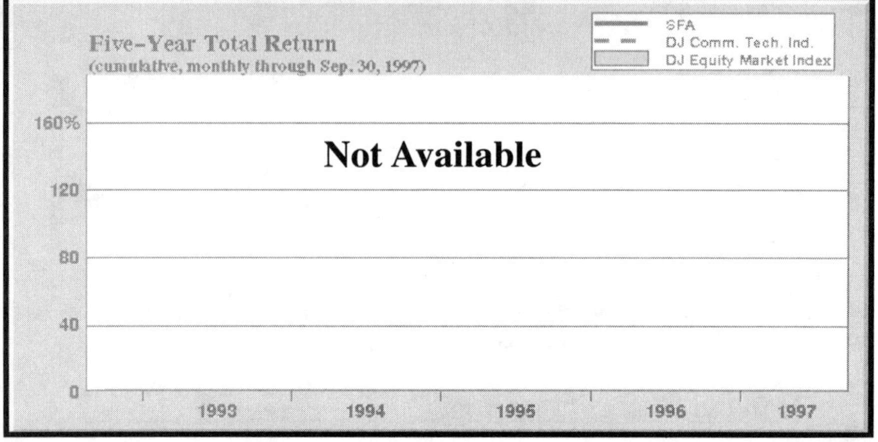

SELECTED INCOME STATEMENT AND BALANCE SHEET ITEMS

INCOME STATEMENT	12/31/91	12/31/92	12/31/93	12/30/94	12/29/95	LTM
Sales/Revenues	N.A.	N.A.	N.A.	N.A.	24.400	55.500
Cost of Goods Sold	N.A.	N.A.	N.A.	N.A.	7.000	N.A.
Pre-tax Margin (%)	N.A.	N.A.	N.A.	N.A.	37.70	N.A.
Operating Income	N.A.	N.A.	N.A.	N.A.	8.600	13.000
Net Income before Extras	N.A.	N.A.	N.A.	N.A.	8.600	N.A.
Reported Net Income	N.A.	N.A.	N.A.	N.A.	8.600	13.000
Depreciation & Amortization	N.A.	N.A.	N.A.	N.A.	2.300	N.A.
EPS from Net Income (Primary)	N.A.	N.A.	N.A.	N.A.	0.450	0.530
EPS from Net Income (Fully Diluted)	N.A.	N.A.	N.A.	N.A.	0.430	0.530
Dividend per Common Share	N.A.	N.A.	N.A.	N.A.	N.A.	N.A.
Dividend Yield (%)	N.A.	N.A.	N.A.	N.A.	N.A.	N.A.
Payout Ratio	N.A.	N.A.	N.A.	N.A.	N.A.	N.A.
BALANCE SHEET						
ASSETS						
Cash & Cash Equivalents	N.A.	N.A.	N.A.	N.A.	0.400	
Inventories	N.A.	N.A.	N.A.	N.A.	0.700	
Total Current Assets	N.A.	N.A.	N.A.	N.A.	15.000	
Total Assets	N.A.	N.A.	N.A.	N.A.	43.500	
LIABILITIES & EQUITY						
Short Term Debt	N.A.	N.A.	N.A.	N.A.	5.900	
Long Term Debt	N.A.	N.A.	N.A.	N.A.	0.000	
Total Liabilities	N.A.	N.A.	N.A.	N.A.	11.100	
Shares Outstanding	N.A.	N.A.	N.A.	N.A.	21.479	
Common Stockholder Equity	N.A.	N.A.	N.A.	N.A.	32.400	
Total Stockholder Equity	N.A.	N.A.	N.A.	N.A.	32.400	

Note: Figures in Millions of $ except: per share items, margins, yields, and ratios.

Source: IDD Information Services

RATIONAL SOFTWARE

Garrett Van Wagoner
Van Wagoner Capital Management

Company Profile

Today's fast-paced world is driven by computer software. It does everything from placing phone calls to trading stocks and funds. It is what makes certain planes depart and arrive safely, and at the same time allows you to enjoy the enormous array of information on the Internet. In its purest sense, you have probably purchased a computer software program at the store that you used to either play games with or balance your checkbook. But what many people don't realize is that it takes software to make software. And that's the business Rational Software knows best.

"This company is involved in enterprise-level software, particularly in the design, analysis, and writing of software code," explains Garrett Van Wagoner of Van Wagoner Capital Management. "The people who buy its products are professional code writers or software engineers. Rational's products allow them to write very complex software programs. It's very sophisticated stuff, unlike what you or I would use at home."

Rational's roots go back to the 1980s, when it was known as Verdix Corporation. Back then it mainly did work for the U.S. government. "This is one of those government-to-commercial conversions," Van Wagoner notes. "It worked in an arcane language called Ada, which is mainly used by the defense department. It's a very high-end system. The company had some great products that were used by Ada developers. Then, when it found out Ada was going the way of the dinosaur, it ported over its products to UNIX, Windows, and Windows NT. The commercial shipments have really started to kick in and to a grow very rapidly over the past couple of years. I first got interested in the company when it started to convert its product line in 1994." That was the year Verdix merged with a privately held California corporation called Rational and changed its name.

Software development projects are notorious for suffering from a high failure rate. This can be very costly, because it leads to project cancellations and significant product delays. That's why corporations are constantly looking for effective approaches to software development. Rational is extremely strong in two major areas: design and software testing. "On the design side, it uses something called object-oriented programming," Van Wagoner points out. "This is a way of programming software at a much faster rate than by just writing out the traditional code. In terms of the testing, when Microsoft writes a new release of Windows, for example, it will have a bunch of teams working on the project.

Various people will write different parts, and they need to keep track of the many versions done during the day to record any changes. It's something known as configuration management and Rational has a software program that's one of the best in this area."

Rational's current clients include such major organizations as Xerox, Smith Barney, TRW, and Ericsson. The company operates under what it calls "The Rational Approach," which is a comprehensive state-of-the-art solution for the construction of software systems. The Rational Approach consists of three integrated elements: processes for developing software, tools for automating the construction of software systems, and technical consulting services. To date, the company has sold more than 40,000 licenses for its software products to more than 2,500 customers worldwide. International sales account for roughly 36 percent of total revenues.

Reason for Recommendation

"The reason I think 1998 will be a big year for Rational is because it made a number of recent acquisitions that are now being integrated and will give it a full product suite to sell," Van Wagoner says. Most recently it merged with SQA, a provider of software quality-testing tools, and Requisite, a Colorado-based provider of software management tools and training. "These mergers have helped to eliminate most of Rational's competition," Van Wagoner contends. "Its major competition now is companies that decide to build this code writing software on their own."

So if it has little competition and such a strong product line, what's the major risk with this company? The possibility that one or more of its marriages will fail, according to Van Wagoner. "It could screw up these mergers," he says. "Either the personalities don't work out or the sales force can't get going. But, in my mind, this is highly unlikely and I think it will do great once these mergers are integrated. It gives the company a full product line and makes it the one to call when you're looking for these kinds of software tools."

Van Wagoner looks for Rational to earn around 80 cents for the year ending March 1998 and $1.15 to $1.20 in 1999. "By the end of 1998, I think the stock should sell for around $40," he adds.

Contact Information: Paul D. Levy
President and CEO
Rational Software Corporation
2800 San Tomas Expressway
Santa Clara, CA 95051-0951
(408) 496-3600
http://www.rational.com

Rational Software Corporation

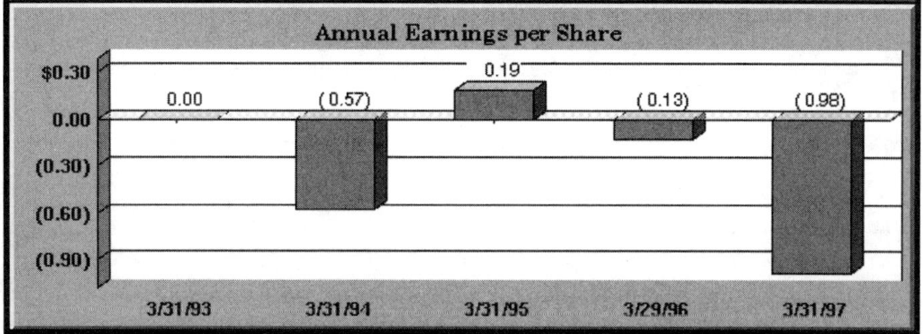

Rational Software Corporation

Symbol: RATL   Exchange: Nasdaq NMS

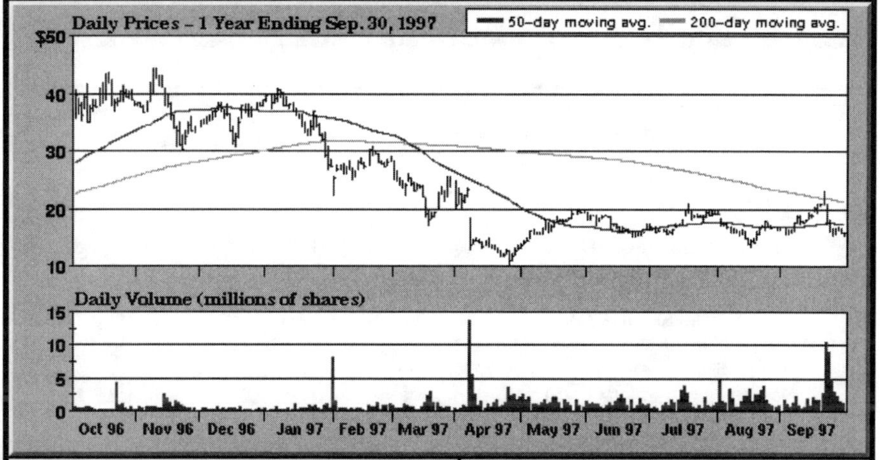

Latest Pricing Data (as of Sep. 30, 1997)		
Close (net change):	$16	(+1/8)
Day High & Low:	$16	$15 1/4
Volume & Avg. Volume:	1,362,800	565,224
52-Week High:	$44 1/4	Nov. 8, 1996
52-Week Low:	$10	Apr. 24, 1997
Latest Dividend:	$0.00	
Ind. Ann. Div. & Yield:	$0.00	N.A.
12 Month EPS:	($0.91)	June 30, 1997
P/E Ratio & Beta Factor:	N.A.	2.346
Shares Outstanding:	87.099 million	
Market Value:	$1.394 billion	
Institutional Holdings:	44.21%	
Number of Institutions:	283	
Primary Market:	Nasdaq NMS	

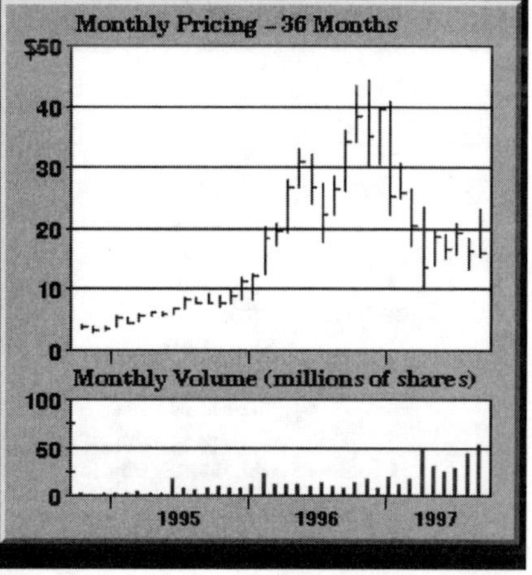

Currency: U.S. Dollars.

Source: IDD Information Services

Rational Software Corporation
Symbol: RATL

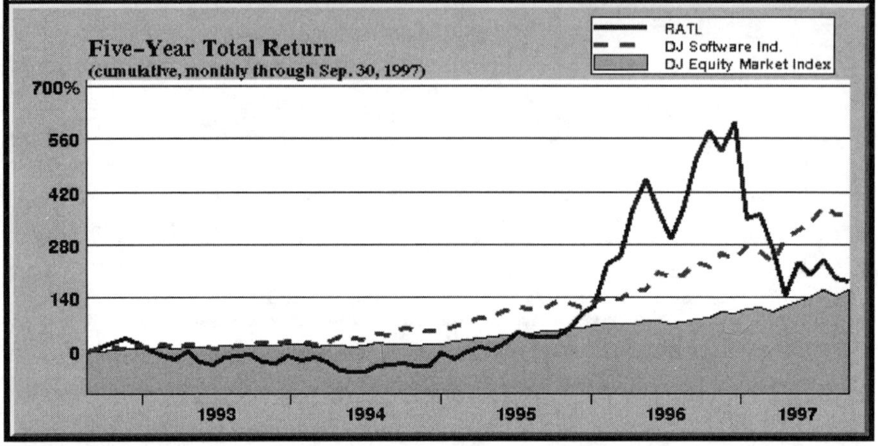

SELECTED INCOME STATEMENT AND BALANCE SHEET ITEMS

INCOME STATEMENT	3/31/93	3/31/94	3/31/95	3/29/96	3/31/97	LTM
Sales/Revenues	23.300	70.300	72.900	91.100	145.40	160.90
Cost of Goods Sold	3.000	15.300	20.100	21.900	30.000	32.200
Pre-tax Margin (%)	13.70	(19.30)	7.00	(3.30)	(26.50)	(14.65)
Operating Income	2.900	(13.700)	4.600	(4.500)	(39.100)	(36.400)
Net Income before Extras	2.000	(14.000)	4.700	(4.000)	(43.000)	(39.400)
Reported Net Income	0.200	(14.000)	4.700	(4.000)	(43.000)	(39.400)
Depreciation & Amortization	3.800	10.100	5.000	4.600	5.700	6.800
EPS from Net Income (Primary)	0.000	(0.570)	0.190	(0.130)	(0.980)	(0.910)
EPS from Net Income (Fully Diluted)	0.000	(0.570)	0.190	(0.130)	(0.980)	(0.910)
Dividend per Common Share	0.000	0.000	0.000	0.000	0.000	0.000
Dividend Yield (%)	N.A.	N.A.	N.A.	N.A.	N.A.	N.A.
Payout Ratio	N.A.	N.A.	N.A.	N.A.	N.A.	N.A.

BALANCE SHEET	3/31/93	3/31/94	3/31/95	3/29/96	3/31/97
ASSETS					
Cash & Cash Equivalents	2.000	7.400	9.400	43.900	227.50
Inventories	0.200	0.200	0.000	0.000	0.000
Total Current Assets	20.600	30.000	30.000	78.100	267.00
Total Assets	27.200	39.300	38.000	85.700	302.80
LIABILITIES & EQUITY					
Short Term Debt	0.800	2.600	2.600	0.700	2.000
Long Term Debt	0.600	3.000	0.600	1.300	1.700
Total Liabilities	9.800	32.900	26.000	34.900	62.900
Shares Outstanding	10.336	24.804	25.050	33.622	47.684
Common Stockholder Equity	17.400	6.500	12.100	50.900	239.90
Total Stockholder Equity	17.400	6.500	12.100	50.900	239.90

Note: Figures in Millions of $ except: per share items, margins, yields, and ratios.

Source: IDD Information Services

SCIENTIFIC-ATLANTA

Susan Byrne
Westwood Management

Company Profile

If you have cable TV, and who doesn't these days, you no doubt have a box on top of your set that your cable operator uses to scramble channels you haven't paid for. Chances are this box was made by Scientific-Atlanta. The company's core business is manufacturing these advanced analog set-tops for such customers as Continental Cablevision, Time Warner, and MediaOne. "Even if you don't have one of the company's boxes, some of its products are likely being used to bring that cable into your home, be it the cable connection itself or the uplinks and satellite dishes used to carry the various signals," says Susan Byrne of Westwood Management.

Scientific-Atlanta's business revolves around helping people connect with entertainment, information, and each other. It's an industry leader in pioneering satellite technology to deliver programming for entertainment giants like Disney, The Family Channel, HBO, Viacom, and ESPN. Its PowerVu digital video compression system allows users to save money by leasing less transponder space. Retailer JC Penney recently upgraded to this product, connecting 1,150 of its stores together, while providing for the transmission of in-store music and high-speed data downloads for catalog updates.

But what Byrne is most excited about is the company's new product called the Explorer 2000. "You can now get a cable modem with direct access to the Internet through either your PC or TV," she says. "The Internet is very cool, but it is so slow to download that it's frustrating. The cable modem has a direct fiber optic connection, and its speed is constrained only by the speed of the Internet itself. I recently saw an amazing demonstration put on by Scientific-Atlanta. On the left-hand side, it had a computer hooked up to a 56K modem, and on the right was a TV with this direct connection. It's amazing how much faster the TV on the right was, and it used the connection and software found only in these Scientific-Atlanta boxes. This is unlike anything being manufactured by the competition."

The Explorer 2000 boxes will sell for around $400 each, but that's a relatively small investment considering that cable operators can charge subscribers upwards of $20 a month to rent them. "The Explorer 2000 is the first set-top that makes both broadcast and future interactive digital cable services economically attractive compared to other digital alternatives," asserts Michael Harney, Scientific-Atlanta's vice president and general manager of digital video systems. "The Explorer 2000 will enable operators to deliver digital broadcast services immediately, support high-speed data and Internet access, and introduce new digital services as demand grows."

Reason for Recommendation

Because shipment of the Explorer 2000 has just begun, the orders should start to really roll in during 1998. The company has already received initial commitments from both Time Warner and Continental Cablevision. In fact, Scientific-Atlanta has been reporting one record after another in recent quarters, both in terms of bookings and sales. "I compare this company right now to where Boeing was four years ago when it had all of these backlogged orders for the 777 and you could see the business building up before the earnings surprises started to unfold," Byrne points out. "Even though current earnings are impressive, they don't reflect the business Scientific-Atlanta is booking today. But I have made the judgment that cable operators, who haven't spent any money on upgrades for two or three years, are going to start doing so, and Scientific-Atlanta will be a direct beneficiary."

Byrne also emphasizes that the company has no debt, yet remains relatively ignored by analysts. "They lump Scientific-Atlanta with other telecommunications companies, and this whole area has been a horrible performer in recent years," she points out. "I have a high degree of confidence this company's earnings are going to be surprisingly better over the next year-and-a-half than anyone thinks."

Furthermore, the company is taking steps to aggressively expand overseas. "The market for more traditional services in developing countries is enormous and growing," says Scientific-Atlanta president and chief executive officer Jim McDonald. "Consider that hundreds of millions of people do not yet have access to telephones, and for those areas of the world where television service is available, most providers still offer very few channels."

Consensus earnings estimates for fiscal year 1998, which ends in June, are $1 per share. However, Byrne thinks the company can earn at least $1.20. "I expect this Scientific-Atlanta to continue to grow by at least 20 percent a year and look for the stock to hit around $30," Byrne adds.

Contact Information: Jim McDonald
President and CEO
Scientific-Atlanta, Inc.
One Technology Parkway, South
Norcross, GA 30092-2967
(770) 903-5000
http://www.sciatl.com

Scientific Atlanta Incorporated

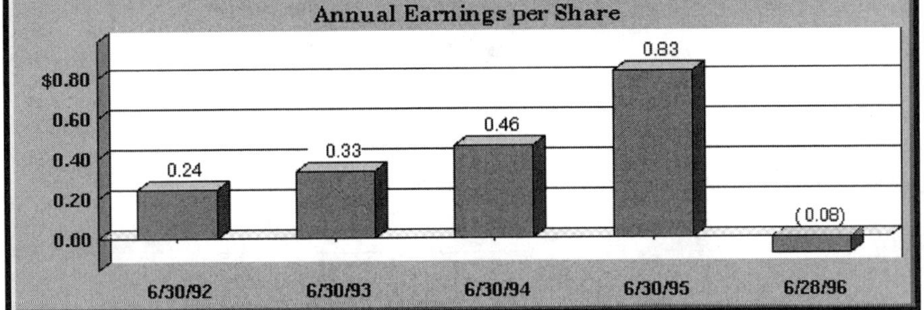

Scientific Atlanta Incorporated

Symbol: SFA Exchange: NYSE

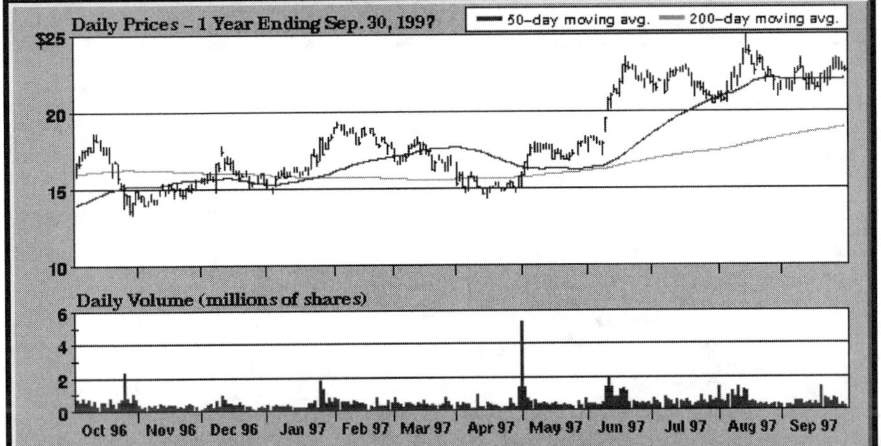

Latest Pricing Data (as of Sep. 30, 1997)		
Close (net change):	$22 5/8	(−1/16)
Day High & Low:	$22 3/4	$22 7/16
Volume & Avg. Volume:	197,700	387,141
52-Week High:	$24 15/16	Aug. 13, 1997
52-Week Low:	$13 1/4	Oct. 29, 1996
Latest Dividend:	$0.01	Sep. 5, 1997
Ind. Ann. Div. & Yield:	$0.06	0.27%
12 Month EPS:	$0.82	June 30, 1997
P/E Ratio & Beta Factor:	27.59	1.444
Shares Outstanding:	77.538 million	
Market Value:	$1.754 billion	
Institutional Holdings:	71.87%	
Number of Institutions:	366	
Primary Market:	NYSE	
Component of:	S&P 500	

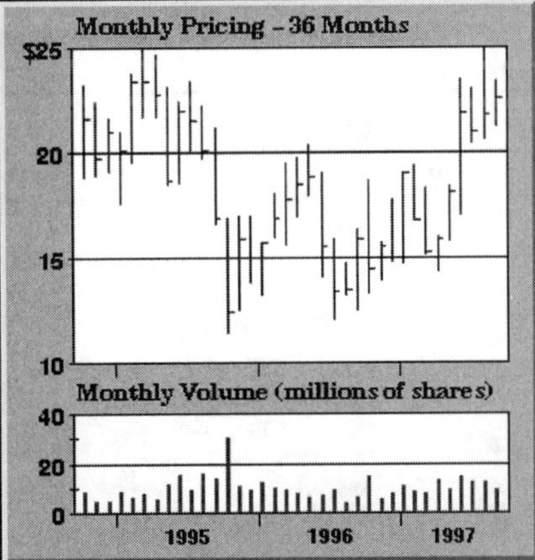

Currency: U.S. Dollars.

Source: IDD Information Services

Scientific Atlanta Incorporated
Symbol: SFA

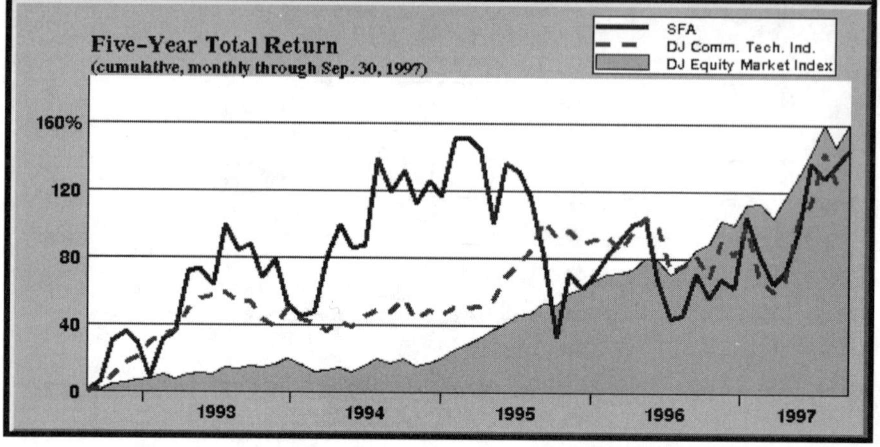

SELECTED INCOME STATEMENT AND BALANCE SHEET ITEMS

INCOME STATEMENT	6/30/92	6/30/93	6/30/94	6/30/95	6/28/96	LTM
Sales/Revenues	580.80	730.60	811.60	1,146.5	1,047.9	1,168.3
Cost of Goods Sold	392.70	507.20	545.80	795.50	725.30	N.A.
Pre-tax Margin (%)	3.70	4.50	6.30	8.10	1.00	N.A.
Operating Income	17.600	30.100	66.900	89.800	37.700	N.A.
Net Income before Extras	16.300	24.700	35.000	63.500	7.200	60.700
Reported Net Income	16.300	24.700	35.000	63.500	(6.000)	64.100
Depreciation & Amortization	16.100	19.100	20.900	29.800	36.600	N.A.
EPS from Net Income (Primary)	0.240	0.330	0.460	0.830	(0.080)	0.820
EPS from Net Income (Fully Diluted)	0.240	0.330	0.460	0.830	(0.080)	0.820
Dividend per Common Share	0.053	0.058	0.060	0.060	0.060	0.060
Dividend Yield (%)	0.67	0.36	0.35	0.27	0.39	0.27
Payout Ratio	0.22	0.18	0.13	0.07	N.A.	0.07

BALANCE SHEET					
ASSETS					
Cash & Cash Equivalents	90.900	103.50	123.40	80.300	20.900
Inventories	104.10	127.40	136.80	257.40	215.80
Total Current Assets	342.70	405.70	505.00	615.40	563.00
Total Assets	440.90	524.20	640.20	785.30	763.30
LIABILITIES & EQUITY					
Short Term Debt	4.100	6.000	6.500	1.400	1.600
Long Term Debt	1.700	1.400	1.100	0.800	0.400
Total Liabilities	141.30	171.40	244.60	311.10	299.60
Shares Outstanding	69.257	74.392	75.495	77.030	76.990
Common Stockholder Equity	299.70	352.90	395.60	474.20	463.70
Total Stockholder Equity	299.70	352.90	395.60	474.20	463.70

Note: Figures in Millions of $ except: per share items, margins, yields, and ratios.

Source: IDD Information Services

TOKIO MARINE & FIRE INSURANCE

Martin Whitman
Third Avenue Funds

Company Profile

Tokio Marine & Fire Insurance is by far the largest of 27 Japanese companies involved in writing nonlife policies, which is equivalent to what we refer to as property and casualty (P&C) insurance in the United States. This blue chip company has been around since 1879 and enjoys both a strong corporate and personal insurance business. It controls the largest share of the fire, marine, personal accident and auto markets of any insurer in Japan, based on the amount of premiums written. The firm boasts 50 subsidiaries, including overseas firms in 13 countries.

In its latest fiscal year, Tokio wrote more than $12 billion in premiums, 96 percent of which were in Japan. "This seemingly large premium volume, though, was dwarfed by the amount of assets Tokio employed in its business," observes Martin Whitman, manager of the Third Avenue Value Fund. "Stockholders equity was $22.8 billion, after deducting a reserve for deferred income taxes on unrealized appreciation. Of the $73.2 billion of total assets on the Tokio balance sheet as of March 31, 1996, $63.2 billion was in cash and securities, of which $31.4 billion was in equity securities, mostly Japanese common stocks valued at market."

Therefore, in addition to any underwriting profits, Tokio creates wealth for shareholders by managing a portfolio of investments. "The Tokio portfolio, valued at market, consists of almost 50 percent equity securities, mostly Japanese common stocks," Whitman says. "This common stock portfolio has been managed largely on a buy-and-hold basis. Realized capital gains on the common stock portfolio have been insignificant, as has net investment income in the form of dividends received."

Yet, while Tokio has enjoyed outstanding profitability, because its loss ratios are so low, net investment income results have been increasingly bad. In U.S. dollars, they have gone from $821 million in 1993 to $233 million in 1996. The company has no reported earnings, and the outlook for the nonlife insurance industry in Japan is terribly uncertain. "My speculation is there may be five principal reasons for Tokio's very poor returns," Whitman surmises. "First, about half of the portfolio is in common stocks where it is, in effect, managed for total return instead of dividend income. The net investment income return on the equity portfolio seems to have been under one-half of 1 percent for fiscal 1996. Second, interest rates in Japan are ultralow, averaging under 2 percent for risk-free credit instruments. This minimizes interest income for Tokio. Third, a small portion of the portfolio is in foreign securities, especially U.S. Treasuries, and net income here deteriorates as the yen gets weaker. Fourth, there was an increased write-off of nonperforming loans in 1996. Fifth, Tokio may have had to subsidize interest accruals and payments on approximately $21 billion of liabilities for 'deposit-type insurance products' where policies with a 3- to 30-year maturity are sold."

Given all of this, you'd probably conclude this is a stock to stay away from. But Whitman looks at it differently. "It's a very high quality business and the stock is cheap, selling at about 67 percent of its realistic market value," he insists. "I went to Tokyo and visited the company in person and found out it was even cheaper and better than I thought." After all, they don't call Whitman the premier vulture investor for nothing.

Reason for Recommendation

The low price, Whitman continues, takes out much of the risk "Given the huge size of Tokio's securities portfolio, it might best be viewed as an unregistered investment company masquerading as an insurance company," he suggests. "Assuming the accounting to be used to determine a net asset value (NAV) for Tokio ADRs was identical to that used for closed-end investment companies and mutual funds, the NAV assignable to Tokio on March 31, 1996 would have been $105.47." Realistically, Martin insists each ADR is worth $65 to $80. "This is a situation that couldn't exist in the United States in 1998," he adds. "You couldn't have a company whose stock is so cheap where the management doesn't own any stock and it not be the subject of some kind of activity, be it a takeover or another industry player making a substantial investment in it."

Nevertheless, Whitman admits the stock is fraught with risk. Thc Japanese nonlife insurance industry is currently in a state of turmoil, the Tokyo Stock Exchange has been in a free-fall, and it's unclear how the Japanese regulatory environment will impact Tokio going forward. What's more, it's not easy to get updated and reliable information about the company. "Tokio only publishes annual reports," Whitman says. "Its monthly and semiannual financial statements are filed with the Ministry of Finance and are nonpublic."

What will it take for this stock to move higher and recognize the value Whitman places on it? "Beats me," the honest portfolio manager says. "But I buy a lot of things that are cheap without a clear catalyst to make the share price grow in value."

Contact Information: Koukei Higuchi
President
Tokio Marine & Fire Insurance
2-1 Marunouchi 1-chome
Chiyoda-ku Tokyo 100, Japan
011-81-3-3212-6211

Tokio Marine and Fire Insurance Limited

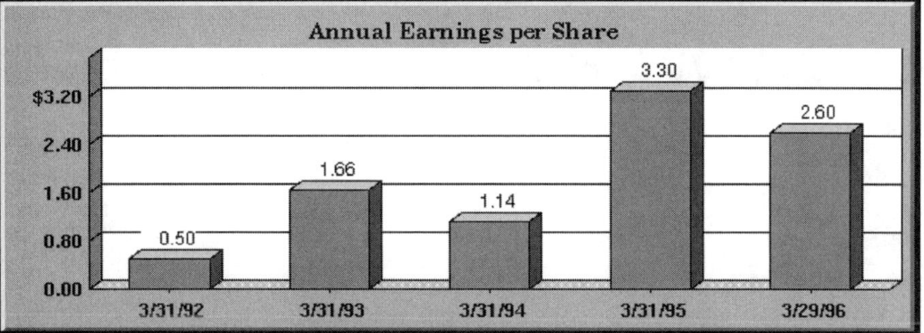

Tokio Marine and Fire Insurance Limited

Symbol: TKIOY Exchange: Nasdaq NMS

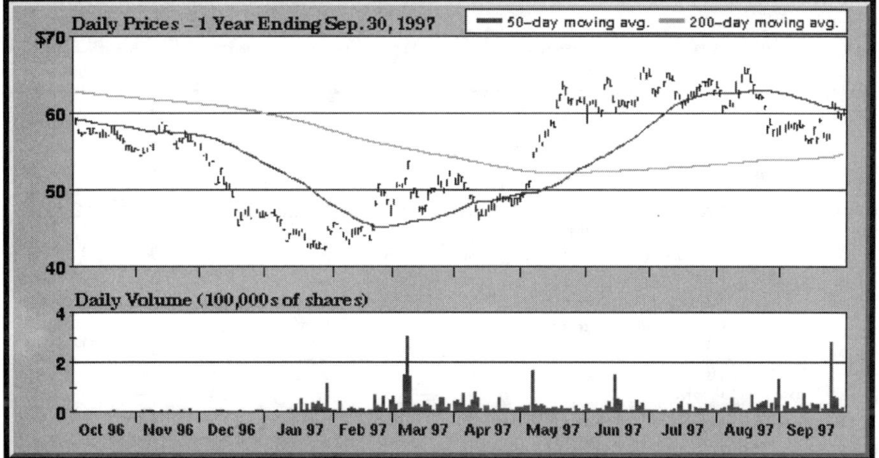

Latest Pricing Data (as of Sep. 30, 1997)

Close (net change):	$60 1/2	(+1/2)
Day High & Low:	$60 1/2	$59 5/8
Volume & Avg. Volume:	18,800	2,963
52-Week High:	$66	Aug. 13, 1997
52-Week Low:	$42	Jan. 28, 1997
Latest Dividend:	$0.32	Mar. 25, 1997
Ind. Ann. Div. & Yield:	$0.31	0.52%
12 Month EPS:	$2.60	Mar. 29, 1996
P/E Ratio & Beta Factor:	23.27	0.638
Shares Outstanding:	309.938 million	
Market Value:	$18.751 billion	
Institutional Holdings:	2.17%	
Number of Institutions:	59	
Primary Market:	Nasdaq NMS	

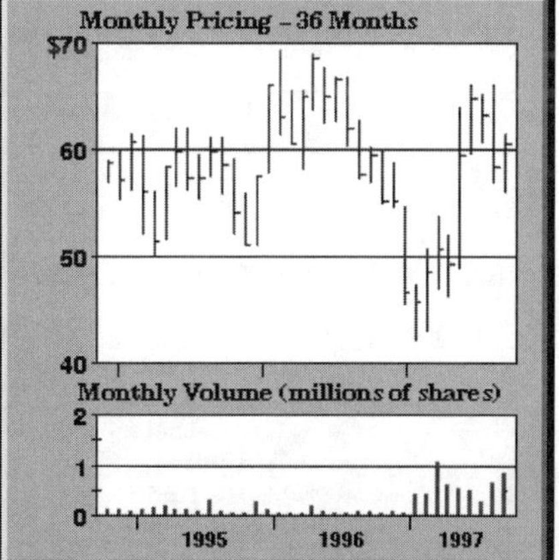

Currency: U.S. Dollars.

Source: IDD Information Services

Tokio Marine and Fire Insurance Limited
Symbol: TKIOY

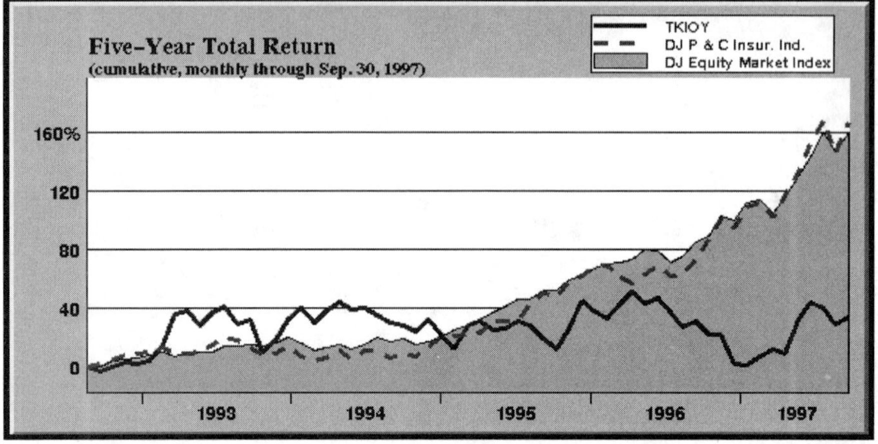

SELECTED INCOME STATEMENT AND BALANCE SHEET ITEMS

INCOME STATEMENT	3/31/92	3/31/93	3/31/94	3/31/95	3/29/96	LTM
Sales/Revenues	8,532.8	10,498	11,847	14,590	12,089	12,089
Cost of Goods Sold	N.A.	N.A.	N.A.	N.A.	N.A.	N.A.
Pre-tax Margin (%)	3.60	8.60	5.90	9.70	11.60	N.A.
Operating Income	307.70	899.10	697.10	1,410.8	1,398.5	N.A.
Net Income before Extras	154.70	518.80	353.60	1,021.0	806.40	806.40
Reported Net Income	154.70	518.80	353.60	1,021.0	806.40	806.40
Depreciation & Amortization	N.A.	N.A.	N.A.	N.A.	N.A.	N.A.
EPS from Net Income (Primary)	0.500	1.660	1.140	3.300	2.600	2.600
EPS from Net Income (Fully Diluted)	0.500	1.660	1.140	3.300	2.600	2.600
Dividend per Common Share	0.268	0.315	0.344	0.398	0.309	0.309
Dividend Yield (%)	0.70	0.59	0.58	0.68	0.48	0.48
Payout Ratio	0.54	0.19	0.30	0.12	0.12	0.12
BALANCE SHEET						
ASSETS						
Cash & Cash Equivalents	N.A.	N.A.	N.A.	N.A.	N.A.	
Inventories	N.A.	N.A.	N.A.	N.A.	N.A.	
Total Current Assets	N.A.	N.A.	N.A.	N.A.	N.A.	
Total Assets	50,283	59,496	70,904	79,361	73,235	
LIABILITIES & EQUITY						
Short Term Debt	0.000	0.000	0.000	0.000	0.000	
Long Term Debt	870.50	1,015.3	520.50	47.500	0.000	
Total Liabilities	36,450	43,269	49,729	56,546	50,414	
Shares Outstanding	309.031	309.105	309.346	309.414	309.938	
Common Stockholder Equity	13,833	16,227	21,175	22,815	22,820	
Total Stockholder Equity	13,833	16,227	21,175	22,815	22,820	

Note: Figures in Millions of $ except: per share items, margins, yields, and ratios.

Source: IDD Information Services

WELLS FARGO

Shelby Davis
Davis Selected Advisers

Company Profile

Wells Fargo is experiencing some growing pains. After acquiring First Interstate Bancorp for stock two years ago, the company became an entirely new entity. As chairman Paul Hazen puts it, "By the end of 1996, we were a very different looking company than we had been at the beginning of the year. Our assets had more than doubled, from $50.3 billion in January to $108.9 billion in December; we operated our retail business in ten states instead of one; staff numbered 36,900 at year end, up from 19,250 twelve months earlier; we had 1,950 retail locations throughout the west, instead of 975 only in California; plus we converted 6 million retail and wholesale accounts, over 1,500 ATMs, and nearly 900 retail outlets from First Interstate to the Wells Fargo system."

"This was the biggest merger in Wells Fargo's history, and it clearly caused some trouble for them," admits Shelby Davis of Davis Selected Advisers. "However, I think the company has worked through most of these problems, and management can now turn its attention toward growing the top-line revenue, which has been flat or down for several years."

In addition to restructuring its entire network, Wells Fargo is closing underperforming branches, adding supermarket locations, expanding its presence on the Internet and reducing its workforce to cut costs. "It is not afraid to test new things and tweak its delivery system," Davis observes. "It is constantly innovating and changing."

But the acquisition has clearly cost the bank more than just money. It also created ill feelings among some key clients. "Many random but significant telecommunications and systems problems occurred in the initial months after the merger, creating major service issues and inconveniences for our retail and wholesale customers," Hazen admits. "Systems slowdowns, clogged telephone service centers, errors in customer accounts, and long branch lines plagued our customers. Overall, it was a sorry experience for far too many."

But Wells Fargo is clearly still a leader in its field. It operates one of the largest and busiest consumer banking businesses in the United States, serving more than 10 million households through a network of some 1,900 branches and 4,300 ATMs. The company also provides a full range of banking services to small business, commercial, agribusiness, and real estate clients. In addition, it manages and administers some $300 billion in mutual fund and trust assets.

Reason for Recommendation

"What all of this means is that investors in 1998 get a shot at Wells Fargo at a reasonable price, because it was a year behind schedule in smoothly integrating the First Interstate merger," Davis insists. "That marriage was essentially completed in 1997, and the benefits should start to flow over the next three years and increasingly show up in the bottom line."

Davis believes Wells Fargo's strong management team will be able to reach its ambitious goals going forward. "Its model is to grow revenues at 5 percent a year, which is doable, but you must have a leap of faith it can actually accomplish that," he says. "It hasn't done it yet, but it should be able to, given its strong franchise. Plus, California is in a strong position now as a gateway to the Far East."

Furthermore, Davis notes that the company has a relatively small number of outstanding shares (around 85 million) and is repurchasing 6 million shares on the open market each year. It also has a more than adequate loss reserve built up.

"The bank generates lots of free cash flow, manages its capital well, and is buying back stock," Davis maintains. "It's known as one of the strongest banks in terms of expense control, and has a business formula that generates a high return on equity, because it has one of the widest spreads between lending rates and the cost of funds."

When you put it all together, Davis is convinced Wells Fargo can grow by at least 10 to 15 percent a year for the indefinite future, and you can buy the stock for around ten times estimated earnings. But what if interest rates go up this year? Won't that hurt the stock? "Not necessarily," says Davis. "If they go up gradually, it will sort of help the bank," he insists. "The reason: Its loan rates go up faster than its deposit rates. The risk from higher interest rates comes from higher credit losses. If the Fed causes a recession, that would be reason for concern. But California is one of the leading states for growth, so I think Wells Fargo will do just fine. My target price for the stock is $400 over the next two years."

Contact Information: Paul Hazan
Chairman
Wells Fargo & Company
420 Montgomery Street
San Francisco, CA 94163
(800) 411-4932
http://www.wellsfargo.com

Wells Fargo and Company

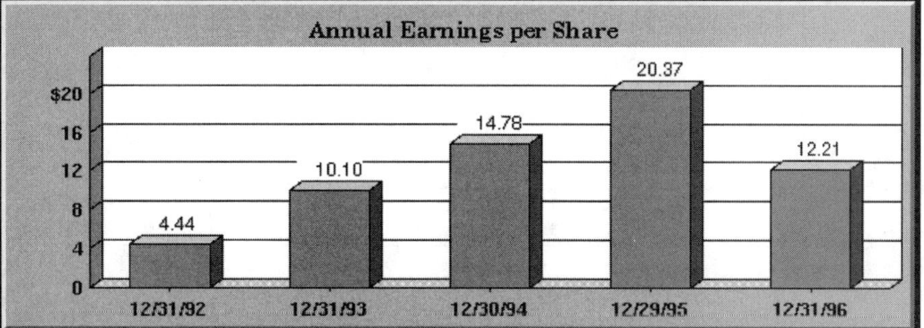

Wells Fargo and Company

Symbol: WFC Exchange: NYSE

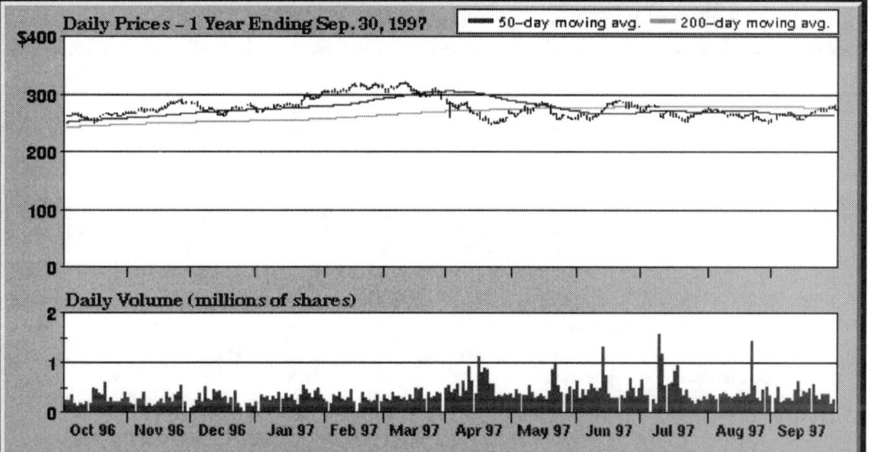

Latest Pricing Data (as of Sep. 30, 1997)		
Close (net change):	$275	(−4 7/8)
Day High & Low:	$280 1/2	$275
Volume & Avg. Volume:	254,800	279,150
52-Week High:	$320 1/2	Mar. 11, 1997
52-Week Low:	$245	Apr. 21, 1997
Latest Dividend:	$1.30	July 29, 1997
Ind. Ann. Div. & Yield:	$5.20	1.89%
12 Month EPS:	$10.13	June 30, 1997
P/E Ratio & Beta Factor:	27.15	1.074
Shares Outstanding:	87.913 million	
Market Value:	$24.176 billion	
Institutional Holdings:	62.15%	
Number of Institutions:	889	
Primary Market:	NYSE	
Component of:	S&P 500	

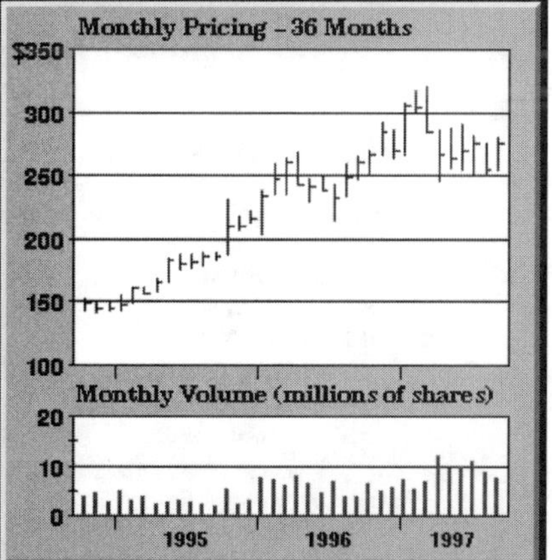

Currency: U.S. Dollars.

Source: IDD Information Services

Wells Fargo and Company
Symbol: WFC

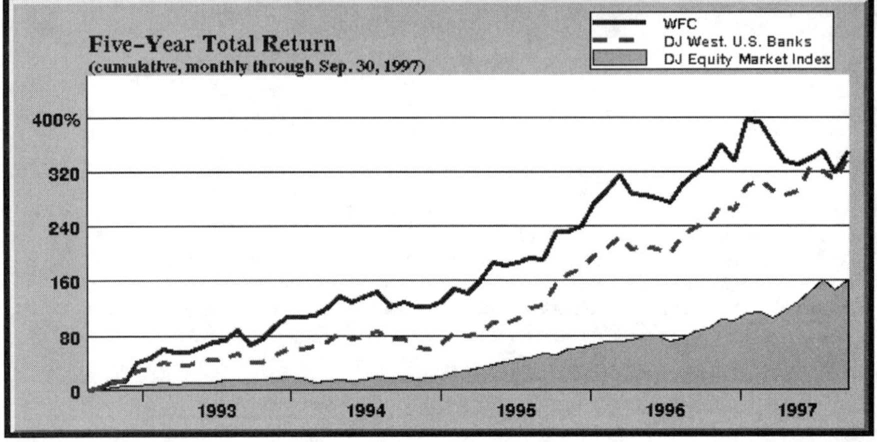

SELECTED INCOME STATEMENT AND BALANCE SHEET ITEMS

INCOME STATEMENT	12/31/92	12/31/93	12/30/94	12/29/95	12/31/96	LTM
Sales/Revenues	5,204.0	4,854.0	4,965.0	5,409.0	8,723.0	9,674.0
Cost of Goods Sold	N.A.	N.A.	N.A.	N.A.	N.A.	N.A.
Pre-tax Margin (%)	9.60	21.40	29.30	32.90	22.70	19.83
Operating Income	1,954.0	2,142.0	2,609.0	3,208.0	3,981.0	4,168.0
Net Income before Extras	283.00	612.00	841.00	1,032.0	1,071.0	1,011.0
Reported Net Income	283.00	612.00	841.00	1,032.0	1,071.0	1,011.0
Depreciation & Amortization	N.A.	N.A.	N.A.	N.A.	N.A.	N.A.
EPS from Net Income (Primary)	4.440	10.100	14.780	20.370	12.210	10.130
EPS from Net Income (Fully Diluted)	4.440	10.100	14.780	20.370	12.210	10.130
Dividend per Common Share	1.500	2.250	4.000	4.600	5.200	5.200
Dividend Yield (%)	1.96	1.74	2.76	2.13	1.93	1.93
Payout Ratio	0.34	0.22	0.27	0.23	0.43	0.51
BALANCE SHEET						
ASSETS						
Cash & Cash Equivalents	N.A.	N.A.	N.A.	N.A.	N.A.	
Inventories	N.A.	N.A.	N.A.	N.A.	N.A.	
Total Current Assets	N.A.	N.A.	N.A.	N.A.	N.A.	
Total Assets	52,537	52,513	53,374	50,316	108,888	
LIABILITIES & EQUITY						
Short Term Debt	202.00	188.00	189.00	195.00	401.00	
Long Term Debt	4,040.0	4,221.0	2,853.0	3,049.0	6,210.0	
Total Liabilities	48,728	48,198	49,463	46,261	94,776	
Shares Outstanding	55.191	55.813	51.252	46.973	91.474	
Common Stockholder Equity	3,170.0	3,676.0	3,422.0	3,566.0	13,512	
Total Stockholder Equity	3,809.0	4,315.0	3,911.0	4,055.0	14,112	

Note: Figures in Millions of $ except: per share items, margins, yields, and ratios.

Source: IDD Information Services

ZOOM TELEPHONICS

Al Frank

The Prudent Speculator

Company Profile

There's nothing more frustrating than trying to surf the Net with a slow modem. Downloading data can take forever, and it's easy to spend hours looking through just one Web site. Zoom Telephonics is trying to change all this by turning the information superhighway into just that, a fast and efficient network. The company has introduced a new 56K fax/modem, which is capable of transmitting data at up to 56,000 bps, or more than twice as fast as what you're probably used to. "It will make things much easier for anyone who uses a modem," says Al Frank, editor of *The Prudent Speculator*. "So much is being done over the Internet, and slow speeds can really create a bottleneck. You can now convert a relatively slow computer into a much faster machine by using Zoom's new modem. It costs around $200, and I expect it to sell millions of these things."

Growth in PC communications has exploded in recent years, driven by the popularity of both the Internet and such online services as America Online and the Microsoft Network. People are also accessing their computers at work, home, and on the road by phone. Zoom's fax/modems not only let one computer communicate with another, but also enable you to send and receive faxes instantly.

Boston-based Zoom has been a leading supplier of modems and other telecommunications products since 1977, when modems were expensive and extremely rare. Prices have now fallen, and the devices are a standard feature of almost every PC. To show you how fast this technology has advanced, the fastest modem transmission speed was 2400 bps in 1987. Today the current standard is 33,600 bps. Zoom's 56K modem is like nothing ever before available. The company also recently began shipping its first ISDN (Integrated Services Digital Network) product, which can transmit and receive data at up to 128,000 bps. In addition, most of Zoom's modems have voice mail, a full-duplex speakerphone, caller ID and distinctive ring features. Its more advanced modems can transmit voice and data simultaneously, which makes two-way conversations possible between computer users working on the same project at separate locations.

"Although the rollout of 56K modems will be slow, because Zoom and its competitor U.S. Robotics have yet to agree on an industry standard that will allow their products to communicate with each other, modem shipments should reach 40 million by 1998 compared to less than 20 million in 1995," Frank forecasts. "Research predicts that by the year 2000, more than 66 million U.S. households will be online, four times the number connected today." Zoom management also estimates that a substantial number of PC users will upgrade their present modems with the new 56K models.

Zoom outsources its fax/modem chipsets to Rockwell, rather than developing them internally. Its products are sold at most of the major computer retailers across the country, including CompUSA, Circuit City, MicroAge, and Best Buy. The company is currently trying to beef up sales overseas and has made strong inroads in both Western Europe and Japan.

Reason for Recommendation

Frank is convinced demand for the 56K modems will be huge. Yet he's even more enamored of Zoom's cheap stock price. "It trades for 67 percent of revenues, which is a great indication that it is undervalued," he maintains. "A high-tech company trading for 67 cents on $1 of sales is a super bargain."

The company's balance sheet is equally as impressive. "When we look at Zoom's financials, we see its book value is $6.33 and it has no long-term debt," he points out. "We think the company will earn about $1.15 per share over the next 12 months and feel it should trade for 18 times earnings. That would make it about a $20 stock." That's what it used to be, before the company came out with a disappointing earnings report in July 1996. The stock got slammed from $27 to about $7 a share in a matter of weeks.

As mentioned, Zoom competes with industry giant U.S. Robotics for the business of Internet surfers everywhere. U.S. Robotics is arguably more recognized in the industry and has more marketing muscle. However, Frank isn't worried. "Zoom's product is much better," he argues. "Even though U.S. Robotics is the major modem manufacturer in the industry, Zoom has built a nice niche for itself."

There are some concerns though. Because the 56K fax/modem is so new, there is no current standard for the technology. One is likely to emerge in 1998, but until then, performance may be impeded, thus preventing any strong initial demand for Zoom's product. "The other downside is the company might go out of business," Frank admits. "But I don't expect that to happen. I think this is a stock that will prosper."

Contact Information: Frank Manning
Zoom Telephonics, Inc.
207 South Street
Boston, MA 02111
(617) 423-1072
http://www.zoomtel.com

Zoom Telephonics Incorporated

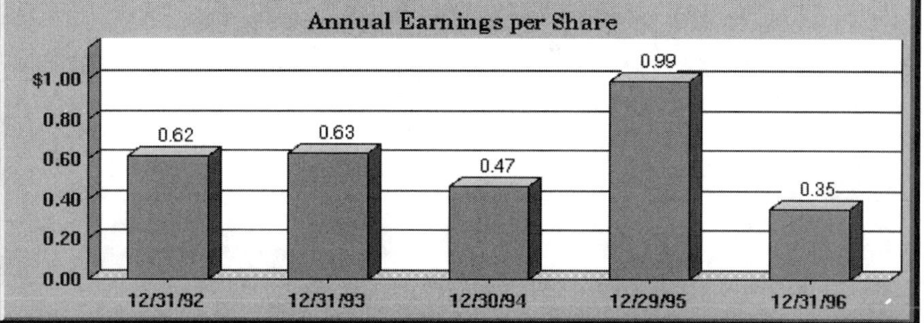

Zoom Telephonics Incorporated

Symbol: ZOOM Exchange: Nasdaq NMS

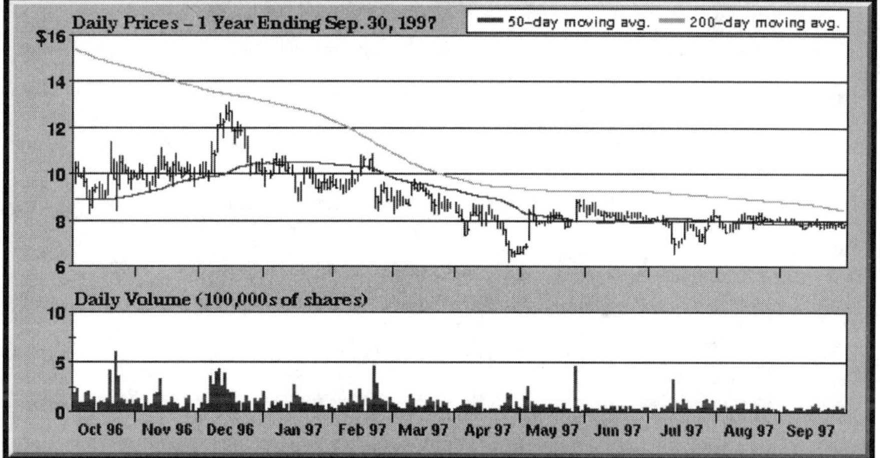

Latest Pricing Data (as of Sep. 30, 1997)		
Close (net change):	$7 7/8	(+1/8)
Day High & Low:	$7 7/8	$7 11/16
Volume & Avg. Volume:	48,400	203,799
52-Week High:	$13 1/8	Dec. 13, 1996
52-Week Low:	$6 1/8	Apr. 24, 1997
Latest Dividend:	$0.00	
Ind. Ann. Div. & Yield:	$0.00	N.A.
12 Month EPS:	($0.71)	June 30, 1997
P/E Ratio & Beta Factor:	N.A.	0.799
Shares Outstanding:	7.482 million	
Market Value:	$58.9 million	
Institutional Holdings:	2.87%	
Number of Institutions:	8	
Primary Market:	Nasdaq NMS	

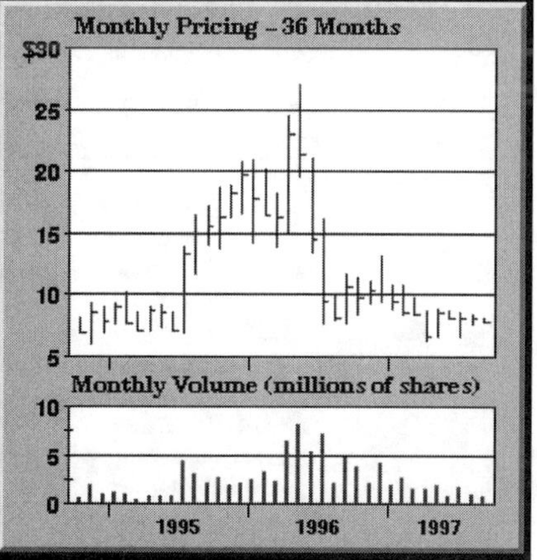

Currency: U.S. Dollars.

Source: IDD Information Services

Zoom Telephonics Incorporated
Symbol: ZOOM

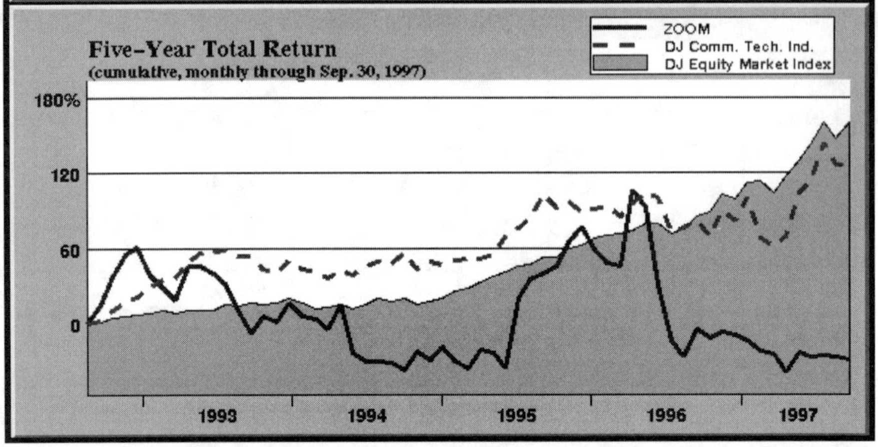

SELECTED INCOME STATEMENT AND BALANCE SHEET ITEMS

INCOME STATEMENT	12/31/92	12/31/93	12/30/94	12/29/95	12/31/96	LTM
Sales/Revenues	41.900	55.200	68.200	97.000	100.20	75.800
Cost of Goods Sold	30.200	41.900	53.100	73.100	79.100	65.200
Pre-tax Margin (%)	14.10	11.10	6.70	10.20	3.90	(16.35)
Operating Income	5.900	6.000	4.700	9.900	3.600	(9.100)
Net Income before Extras	3.600	3.800	2.800	6.100	2.500	(5.200)
Reported Net Income	3.600	3.800	2.800	6.100	2.500	(5.200)
Depreciation & Amortization	0.100	0.000	0.200	0.300	0.700	0.900
EPS from Net Income (Primary)	0.620	0.630	0.470	0.990	0.350	(0.710)
EPS from Net Income (Fully Diluted)	0.620	0.630	0.470	0.980	0.350	(0.710)
Dividend per Common Share	N.A.	N.A.	N.A.	N.A.	N.A.	N.A.
Dividend Yield (%)	N.A.	N.A.	N.A.	N.A.	N.A.	N.A.
Payout Ratio	N.A.	N.A.	N.A.	N.A.	N.A.	N.A.

BALANCE SHEET						
ASSETS						
Cash & Cash Equivalents	2.900	1.400	1.000	0.200	9.200	
Inventories	5.900	11.300	9.500	24.200	19.100	
Total Current Assets	14.100	22.500	25.000	46.500	51.000	
Total Assets	14.300	24.100	27.100	49.600	56.800	
LIABILITIES & EQUITY						
Short Term Debt	0.000	0.000	0.000	2.500	0.000	
Long Term Debt	0.000	0.000	0.000	0.000	0.000	
Total Liabilities	2.900	7.900	7.800	22.300	9.500	
Shares Outstanding	5.916	5.989	6.014	6.201	7.447	
Common Stockholder Equity	11.500	16.200	19.300	27.300	47.400	
Total Stockholder Equity	11.500	16.200	19.300	27.300	47.400	

Note: Figures in Millions of $ except: per share items, margins, yields, and ratios.

Source: IDD Information Services

part 2

THE TOP MUTUAL FUNDS FOR 1998

A FEW WORDS ABOUT MUTUAL FUNDS

Although mutual funds have been around for more than seven decades, they have experienced a plethora of popularity in the 1990s. There are now close to 8,000 funds on the market, which is roughly twice the number of issues on the New York and American Stock Exchanges combined.

You can literally find funds of every flavor, from conservative money market instruments to more aggressive small caps. It's easy to put money to work in a specific sector (like health care and technology), or diversify among a wide range of industries. It's even possible to take advantage of growth in exotic international markets, from Argentina to Zimbabwe, through funds.

The explosion of this industry is nothing short of phenomenal. Total fund assets stood at $500 million in 1940, skyrocketed to $500 billion in 1985, and stand in excess of $3.8 trillion today. Assets continue to flow in at a record pace. Furthermore, you can buy funds practically everywhere, from the local bank to your nearby discount broker. There's even a multilevel marketing company offering folks a chance to peddle these investment pools door to door.

The Appeal of Mutual Funds

What led to this sudden popularity? To begin with, people are more concerned than ever about savings. Baby boomers realize that without a carefully crafted investment plan they could fall short when it comes time to retire.

In addition, many businesses, both large and small, use mutual funds to manage employee benefit and profit sharing plans. This is a major growth area for the fund families that will continue to flourish for years to come.

Perhaps the number one reason for the public's insatiable appetite for funds rests with the overwhelming amount of publicity they have received in recent years. There are more than a dozen personal finance magazines currently available, all of which devote a lot of space to mutual fund investing. Moreover, virtually every major newspaper carries a regular column on funds, and financial commentators on radio and television continue to sing their praises.

Aside from all this free editorial space, the mutual fund companies themselves have spent millions educating and enticing the public to send in their hard-earned cash. The message is obviously getting through. New money now comes into funds at the astonishing rate of $1.6 billion a day.

Using Funds

There's no question mutual funds make a great deal of sense, especially for those unwilling to do the research and follow-up necessary to buy individual securities. Funds are most useful for equities. After all, the first rule of successful investing is *diversification.* You certainly don't want to put all your eggs in one basket when dealing with stocks. It is often argued that a rational person never keeps more than 5 percent of his or her money in any single security. Otherwise the risk is overwhelming.

When you buy a stock mutual fund, you automatically achieve instant diversification. Smaller funds, in terms of asset size, spread their money over dozens of companies, while larger ones may take positions in hundreds. Either way, your overall exposure is significantly reduced, though not entirely eliminated.

Funds make the process of investing a breeze. You simply send in a check and, for a small fee, hire a professional manager to make all the decisions for you. What could be easier? It's even possible and advisable to accumulate wealth in funds over time through dollar cost averaging, a method in which you invest on a regular basis regardless of market conditions, enabling you to buy more shares when prices are down, and less when they're up.

Just remember that not every fund is created equal. Roughly 75 percent of all stock funds actually *underperform* the unmanaged market indexes. These are funds supposedly spearheaded by top-notch investment professionals. Plus, with so many choices, picking a fund is about as complicated as sorting through individual stocks. Therefore, the key to success rests with proper selection, which is the focus of Part 2.

The Downside of Funds

There are disadvantages to owning funds. To begin with, they give you little control over exactly how your money is invested. Sure, you can buy a fund full of stocks, but you're not allowed to choose the companies. The fund manager can purchase anything he or she wants, within the guidelines of the prospectus, without regard to your preferences.

Additionally, fund companies can be extremely impersonal. Many are huge organizations that hire scantily trained representatives to answer shareholder questions. That's no problem if you just want to know your account balance or the fund's total return for a given year. However, should you have specific questions about what investments the fund is making or which stocks it recently purchased, you'll probably be out of luck. And you can forget about talking directly with the fund manager. This kind of access is almost unheard of.

Another problem is that good funds tend to grow quite large, which can hamper returns. A fund with $1 billion or more in assets is usually forced to diversify over dozens, if not hundreds, of companies. That makes it difficult to outperform the market, because each stock probably only comprises around 1 percent of total assets. Therefore, when one or two issues double or triple in value, they have little impact on overall results. It's a case of being overdiversified. Furthermore, funds are required to pay out any realized capital gains to shareholders each year, meaning you could have a tax liability even if you sit tight with your shares. When you buy stocks, you don't experience a gain until you liquidate your holdings.

Finally, funds can take some of the fun out of investing. Many people find the process of hunting down stocks and then watching them (hopefully) rise to be quite exciting. It's thrilling to match wits with the market in pursuit of profits. Because funds do everything for you, that pleasure is gone.

More on Asset Allocation

Still, mutual funds have a place in most portfolios, particularly for those more eager to spend time on the golf course or at the beach than reading through stock reports and monitoring price movements. If that describes you, simply choose from the following recommendations and relax.

I've divided the funds into four different categories: aggressive growth, growth, growth and income, and international. Aggressive growth funds typically invest in the stocks of smaller companies, making them susceptible to dramatic short-term price swings, but also potentially more rewarding. Growth funds these days generally hold a combination of small, midsize, and large companies, though the selections in this book tend to stick with the bigger names that are global powerhouses. Growth and income funds often use a combination of bonds and dividend paying stocks to create a portfolio that throws off a respectable yield, while reducing overall risk. International funds, as you might guess, invest primarily (and sometimes exclusively) in foreign-based securities of all sizes. While foreign funds are inherently volatile, due to factors such as currency fluctuations and political turmoil, they can actually help to reduce your portfolio's overall volatility, because overseas markets don't necessarily move in tandem with the United States.

Which types of funds should you buy? As a general rule, younger investors and those not requiring immediate income would be wise to focus on the more aggressive selections, while older and more conservative readers may want to pay close attention to the growth and income offerings.

I decided not to include pure bond funds for a couple of reasons. First of all, you can often do better by purchasing bonds, like Treasury bills, directly from the government or through a discount broker. Furthermore, when you look at the evidence, one thing is clear: Over time, stocks provide the highest returns. Since 1926, the S&P 500 has compounded at an average annual rate of 10.5 percent, compared with 4.3 percent for government bonds and 3.6 percent for money market funds. That means it's impossible for your capital to significantly increase without putting a large portion into equities.

Unfortunately, the stock market doesn't always go up, and losses in any given period can be dramatic. Luckily, so can the rewards, as we've seen in recent years. That's why it makes sense for younger investors to be more heavily and aggressively invested in equities than older ones, although almost everyone should have a respectable exposure to stocks.

There's a rule of thumb that states a person should subtract his or her age from 100 and put that percentage in equities, the rest in bonds. So, under this theory, if you're 40, you would have 60 percent of your assets in the stock market. Nevertheless, 101-year-old Philip Carret, who launched what is now called the Pioneer Fund in 1928, calls that philosophy, "Nonsense." As he puts it, "What difference does age make? That has nothing to do with it. Why, just because I'm 101, should I sell all my stocks and sit on bonds? I still have 75 to 80 percent of my money in stocks."

Even if you need a monthly check to live on, stock funds remain a good choice. You can always redeem a set number of shares each month to produce the required amount of income (it's called a systematic withdrawal plan), while your principal continues to grow.

Though there are no magic formulas, here are some general stock and bond asset allocation guidelines for each age group that might even be considered somewhat conservative. In fact, several of our panelists argue that you should avoid bonds entirely.

Age	Suggested Weighting
Under 40	80 to 100% Stocks, 0 to 20% Bonds
40–50	75% Stocks, 25% Bonds
50–60	65% Stocks, 35% Bonds
60–70	60% Stocks, 40% Bonds
70+	50% Stocks, 50% Bonds

Selecting Your Funds

The next question is how many funds do you need? The consensus varies widely, though if you have less than $10,000 to invest, one or two is probably enough. When you get up to $50,000, it makes sense to buy around five. If your investment capital exceeds $100,000, it's possible to own eight or ten different funds. However, each fund should have a slightly different focus or investment objective. Otherwise, you could end up owning a bunch of funds holding the exact same companies.

A well-rounded collection of stock funds might include one with each of the following objectives: large company growth, large company value, mid-cap growth, small-cap growth, small-cap value, and diversified international. The market tends to favor various groups at different times. By investing in numerous areas, your chances of always making money greatly increase. Our experts will offer more advice on this subject in Part 3.

Load versus No-Load

Fortunately, all but one of the funds listed in this book is offered on a "no-load," basis, meaning you won't pay any sales charges to get in or out, so every cent of your investment goes to work for you. You might ask, "How do the fund companies make any money then?" The answer is by charging an annual management fee, which is reflected in the fund's expense ratio. This is usually under 1 percent for bond funds, 2 percent for those invested in equities. You are never actually billed for this fee. Instead, it is taken directly out of the fund's daily net asset value, which is listed in the business section of most major newspapers.

It's important to note that both load and no-load funds carry management fees. The only difference is that funds with a load cost you up to 8 percent more. The load is simply a commission that comes off the top and goes directly into the pocket of the person who sells it to you, usually a broker or so-called financial planner. The fund companies generally don't get a penny. Therefore, if you do your homework and read books like this one, there's no reason to ever pay a load to buy a fund. In fact, several studies have shown that, as a group, no-loads actually perform better than their loaded counterparts. This means they not only save you money, but are also more profitable in the long run.

Buying Your Funds

After you figure out how many and which types of funds you want, it's time to decide where you should buy them. One option is to simply call the fund company directly to request a prospectus and application. You then merely fill in the blanks, send in a check for the required opening investment, and you're in business. Each confirmation slip comes with a coupon, enabling you to easily mail off additional contributions as often as you like, which is helpful for dollar cost averaging.

The latest and perhaps most convenient way to purchase funds is through the various national discount brokers, especially the big three: Charles Schwab, Fidelity Investments, and Jack White & Company. All offer no transaction fee programs, enabling you to buy hundreds of no-load funds from many different families without ever paying a commission. The brokers make their money through a service charge paid by the mutual fund companies. It doesn't cost you a penny more than if you were to buy the funds direct.

These no transaction fee programs are definitely worth investigating. They have two major advantages. The first is that all of your funds are consolidated on one easy-to-read monthly statement, which is very convenient. What's more, you can purchase shares and make trades on a specific day through your broker with a simple phone call. This saves you the hassle of writing out a check and mailing it in, and enables you to direct exactly when you want the trade to take place. With the postal service, it could take up to three weeks for your check to arrive.

At the end of each profile, if a fund can be purchased through any or all of these programs, this will be listed in italics. For more information on opening an account, just call the discount broker of your choice. They are all accessible through the following toll-free numbers and Internet addresses:

Charles Schwab & Co.	(800) 845-1714	http://www.schwab.com
Fidelity Investments	(800) 544-9697	http://www.fidelity.com
Jack White & Co.	(800) 233-3411	http://pawws.com/jwc

I have also included the Internet address for each fund that has one. By the way, I wrote an entire book on how to take advantage of these fantastic no-load fund supermarkets called *Buying Mutual Funds for Free* (Dearborn Financial Publishing). It shows you how to construct a winning portfolio using funds offered through these programs, compares each of the participating brokers, gives past performance statistics for every available fund and includes several model portfolios featuring the very best of more than 1,000 available choices. You should be able to find this book at your local bookstore.

About the Recommendations

What follows are some specific picks for 1998 from the world's leading mutual fund authorities. There are three aggressive growth, three growth, three growth and income, and two international selections. Each description lists the fund's primary objective and investment focus (to help you construct a diversified portfolio) along with its past performance record, expense ratio, top holdings, management profile, and contact information. As you read through this, remember that "past performance is no guarantee of future results." Keep in mind there are a lot of dogs in the mutual fund world, so stick with these gems, my friends, and savor the rewards.

AGGRESSIVE GROWTH FUND

BARON ASSET

Robert Bingham
Bingham, Osborn & Scarborough

Manager: Ronald Baron
Style: Small-Cap/Value-Oriented

Fund Profile

Unlike most aggressive fund managers, Ron Baron always keeps a close eye on value. The manager of Baron Asset searches for companies with unrecognized assets or favorable growth prospects selling at attractive prices. This not only helps him to find some hidden gems, but also reduces the risk in this inherently volatile segment of the market.

"He almost takes a value approach to picking growth stocks," notes Robert Bingham, a portfolio manager with Bingham, Osborn & Scarborough. "Baron looks for stocks that may be good buys because of timing or other considerations."

Baron likes to invest in businesses managed by hard-working, ethical, entrepreneurial executives. "These companies are usually small and midsized," Baron says. "They are almost always growing their businesses' values, in terms of earnings, cash flow, or asset value, by at least 15 to 20 percent a year. These companies are in emerging, job-creating industries in which our children are likely to work, not industries in which our parents and grandparents were employed." As a result, the fund currently has significant investments in health care, education, financial services, media, temporary help, and the casino gaming business. "These industries are favorably impacted by strong 'megatrends,' demographics ,and legislative initiatives and programs," Baron insists. "These areas of investment focus represent several of our investment themes."

"You'll notice the fund has very little participation in the highly volatile technology area," Bingham points out. "Instead, Baron tends to focus on companies that benefit from technology, instead of investing in the technology companies themselves."

Baron believes in doing strong fundamental analysis on every stock he owns, which includes company visits and frequent conversations with customers, employees, and management. "Twenty-two years of experience as a portfolio manager have taught me there are many ways to be a successful investor," Baron says. "We are long-term investors in publicly held businesses. We are not short-term traders of common stocks. The fund has often remained a shareholder of companies for years, regardless of stock market fluctuations." Baron is not afraid to take large positions in stocks he has a lot of faith in.

"He, like me, is a very long-term oriented investor who buys and holds," Bingham says. "He buys with at least a five-year perspective. I like his steady hand and strong philosophy, because this is an area of the market where you can find a lot of really mediocre managers and funds."

This strategy has clearly paid off. Baron Asset has consistently been at the top of its peer group since inception in 1987. Predictably, this stellar performance has not gone unnoticed. Ron Baron has been profiled in numerous personal finance magazines over the past few years, and the money has been flowing into his fund. Assets have gone from $290 million in 1995 to more than $2.5 billion today. Huge asset growth can sometimes cripple small-cap funds. But Bingham notes that Baron seems to be handling the new cash reasonably well.

"All of this money is a little bit of a red flag, but he may be able to handle it well," Bingham offers. "One thing I know is that he's not going to go out and start chasing after high multiple PE ratio stocks all of a sudden just to fill the portfolio."

Reason for Recommendation

"I'm trumpeting this fund as a reasonable man's choice for the growth portion of a portfolio, reflecting the fact that we have a very 'toppy' market where you might want to exhibit a little more caution in this part of your asset allocation," Bingham says. "This recommendation is not to say I think small-cap growth stocks are going to do real well in 1998. It's really to say I think every portfolio should have a component in the small-cap area, and this fund is a good way to fill that component."

Bingham also likes the fact that Baron has almost three decades of investment experience, which is rare today. "There are a lot of young guys and gals managing funds like this today, which is a little worrisome," he adds.

As for Baron, he has some very ambitious plans for the fund going forward. "We remain focused on our goal of doubling the per share asset value, including reinvested dividends, of Baron Asset by the end of the year 2000," he says. "Of course, there can obviously be no assurance that we will be able to achieve our objective."

Minimum Initial Investment: $2,000
(Available without a transaction fee from Schwab, Fidelity, and Jack White.)

Contact Information: Baron Asset
767 Fifth Avenue
New York, NY 10153
(800) 992-2766
http://www.baronfunds.com

Baron Asset Fund Sh Ben Int
Symbol: BARAX

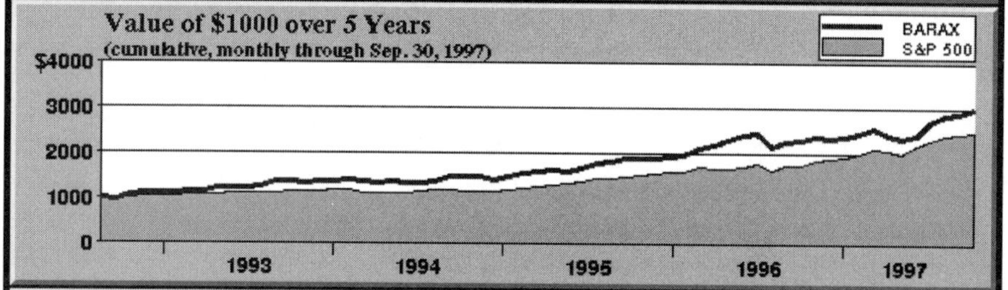

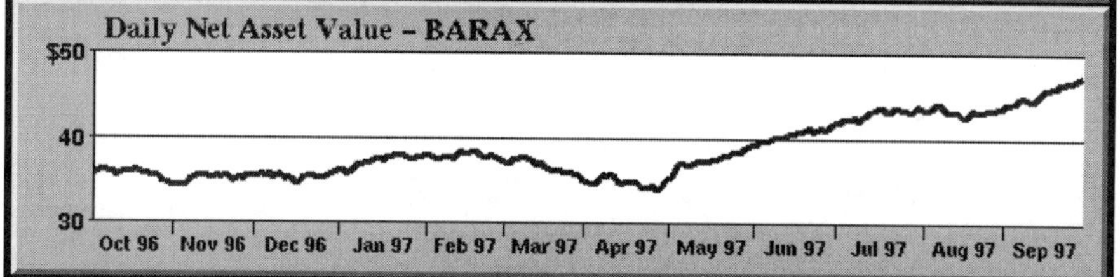

	Investment Period				
Value of $1000	**YTD**	**3 Months**	**1 Year**	**3 Years**	**5 Years**
BARAX	$1309.14	$1136.32	$1337.53	$2145.84	$3164.24
S&P 500	$1284.82	$1070.20	$1391.67	$2170.31	$2542.88
Total Return	**YTD**	**3 Months**	**1 Year**	**3 Years***	**5 Years***
BARAX	30.91%	13.63%	33.75%	28.98%	25.91%
S&P 500	28.48%	7.02%	39.17%	29.47%	20.52%

* - Total Return percentages for periods greater than 1 year are annualized.

Latest Pricing Data (as of Sep. 30, 1997)

52 Week High & Date:	$47.430	9/30/97	**52 Week Low & Date:**	$33.940	4/25/97
Last Distribution & Date:**	$0.04	12/27/96	**Ind. Ann. Div. & Yield:**	$0.00	N.A.
Offer Price:		$47.430	**Net Asset Value:**		$47.430

Source: IDD Information Services

Top 10 Holdings	Key Statistics	
Manor Care	Sales Load (max)	0.00%
Charles Schwab	Redemption Charge (max)	0.00%
Choice Hotels	Expense Ratio	1.40%
Vail Resorts	Management Fee	1.00%
Associates N/A	12b-1 Marketing Fees	0.25%
Heftel Broadcasting	PE Ratio	32.92
Robert Half Intl.	Dividend Yield	0.00%
Bristol Hotels	Turnover Ratio	19%
Dollar Tree Stores	Beta Factor	0.89
Stewart Enterprises	Total Assets	$2572 mil.

AGGRESSIVE GROWTH FUND

HARBOR CAPITAL APPRECIATION

Harold Evensky
Evensky, Brown & Katz

Manager: Spiros Segalas
Style: Large-Cap/Momentum-Based

Fund Profile

While funds that invest primarily in large-cap, blue chip stocks are normally considered to be conservative, Harbor Capital Appreciation is a notable exception. It's true that manager Spiro Segalas buys big names like Citicorp, PepsiCo, Hewlett-Packard, Microsoft, Merck, McDonald's, and Gillette, but he trades his positions with dizzying frequency and is willing to concentrate money in specific sectors, if he thinks that's the best way to pump up his performance. He can also put up to 20 percent of the portfolio in foreign stocks.

"Segalas has a very strong, detailed buy discipline," notes financial planner, Harold Evensky, of Evensky, Brown & Katz. "He's a bottom-up manager who looks for companies with strong sales growth, high returns on equity and quality balance sheets. He prefers firms with a unique competitive advantage in the areas of marketing and research." In order to be considered for purchase, companies must exhibit superior absolute and relative earnings growth. They must also be reasonably priced.

Segalas is an admitted momentum player. If a company fails to achieve or, preferably, exceed its expected earnings number, it is thrown out. "Segalas knows that he's playing in a volatile market and is buying the future," Evensky says. "That's why he and his analysts are constantly reevaluating their earnings expectations. Their philosophy is that they can make money from buying companies with strong earnings, especially if they get in before the rest of the world catches on. They monitor a pretty large universe of qualified candidates, and they stay fully invested."

Harbor Capital Appreciation was launched in 1987. Harbor Fund, the sponsor, contracted management of the portfolio out to Segalas's company, Jennison Associates Capital Corporation, in 1990. Jennison is a New York investment firm with $31 billion in assets. Founded in 1969, it is now a wholly owned subsidiary of Prudential Insurance.

Segalas, who is the founding director and chief investment officer of Jennison, graduated from Princeton University in 1955 and has been managing growth stock accounts for more than two decades. "Segalas has been running the fund for quite a while, but he's been making money using his style even longer," Evensky observes. "He also has a team of analysts, and their compensation structure is based largely on long-term performance. Clearly, this fund is managed by people who designed its philosophy and process, and who have been implementing it with passion for some time."

As previously mentioned, Segalas doesn't mind putting the majority of his cash in any one industry, if he's convinced that's the best place for it. Evensky doesn't mind this strategy. "At one point he had upwards of 60 percent of the portfolio in technology," Evensky says. "That comes from being a bottom-up manager. However, he historically hasn't outright fallen in love with a sector. If technology loses its luster, he has no trouble moving into another area. It's not that he's concentrating because he loves the concept of technology, or whatever area it might be. Rather, it's an indication of an area where he and his analysts feel they can enjoy the most growth."

Concentration can, however, have its drawbacks. While the fund's performance has far out paced the S&P 500 over the past five years, Segalas trailed the index slightly in 1996, due to his heavy technology weighting. The portfolio is slightly more diversified now, with 13.2 percent in drugs and health care, 10.4 percent in electronics, 8.9 percent in business services, 8.8 percent in computers, 4.9 percent in retailing, and 4.7 percent in insurance.

The fund's sell discipline is very straightforward. "If a company doesn't meet its earnings expectations, it gets replaced," Evensky says. "Segalas and his analysts are constantly scanning their universe of companies to find new ideas."

Reason for Recommendation

Evensky looks for three "Ps" when picking funds: philosophy, process, and people. Harbor Capital Appreciation passes on all three counts. Segalas's philosophy makes sense to Evensky and his process is clearly defined. "We want people who are passionate about what they do," he adds. "Segalas is almost a classic case. He has set out a specific process and sticks with it. And his performance, barring 1996, has been great. That temporary blip doesn't bother me. I'm real patient with short-term poor performance, if it's a result of a manager doing what he told me he was going to do, which it was. I'll stay with a manager as long as he's sticking to his guns." Evensky also points out that the fund has a relatively low expense ratio of just 0.75 percent. Plus, despite its moderately high turnover, Harbor Capital Appreciation is fairly tax efficient as well.

Minimum Initial Investment: $2,000 ($500 for IRAs)

Contact Information: Harbor Capital Appreciation Fund
One SeaGate
Toledo, OH 43666
(800) 422-1050

Harbor Fund Cap Apprec Fd
Symbol: HACAX

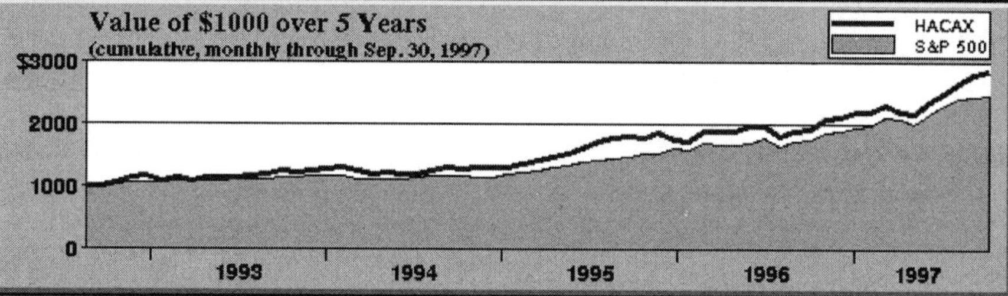

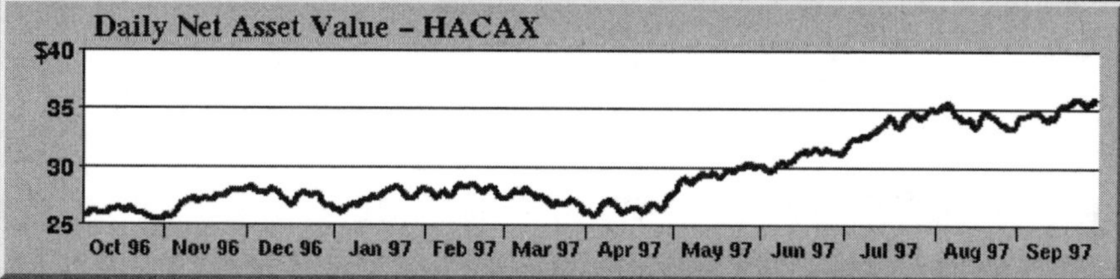

	Investment Period				
Value of $1000	**YTD**	**3 Months**	**1 Year**	**3 Years**	**5 Years**
HACAX	$1353.59	$1146.35	$1439.20	$2281.28	$2950.56
S&P 500	$1284.82	$1070.20	$1391.67	$2170.31	$2542.88
Total Return	**YTD**	**3 Months**	**1 Year**	**3 Years***	**5 Years***
HACAX	35.36%	14.63%	43.92%	31.64%	24.16%
S&P 500	28.48%	7.02%	39.17%	29.47%	20.52%

* – Total Return percentages for periods greater than 1 year are annualized.

Latest Pricing Data (as of Sep. 30, 1997)					
52 Week High & Date:	$35.930	9/22/97	**52 Week Low & Date:**	$25.420	10/29/96
Last Distribution & Date:**	$0.88	12/26/96	**Ind. Ann. Div. & Yield:**	$0.02	0.06%
Offer Price:		$35.640	**Net Asset Value:**		$35.640

Source: IDD Information Services

Top 10 Holdings
Pfizer
Cisco Systems
Boeing
SmithKline Beecham
Hewlett-Packard
Eli Lilly
Schlumberger
Walt Disney
Compaq Computer
Intel

Key Statistics	
Sales Load (max)	0.00%
Redemption Charge (max)	0.00%
Expense Ratio	0.75%
Management Fee	0.60%
12b-1 Marketing Fees	0.00%
PE Ratio	34.21
Dividend Yield	0.06%
Turnover Ratio	74%
Beta Factor	1.25
Total Assets	$2384 mil.

AGGRESSIVE GROWTH FUND

TEMPLETON GLOBAL SMALLER COMPANIES

Eric Roseman

Global Mutual Fund Investor

Manager: Team Managed
Style: Small-Cap/International and U.S.

Fund Profile

Although my general rule is that you should stay away from mutual funds with sales loads, especially when you're making your own investment decisions, Eric Roseman has asked for an exception this year. That's because he believes he's uncovered a fund perfectly poised to prosper from 1998's economic backdrop.

The fund is Templeton Global Smaller Companies. It comes in two different classes. Class one levies a 5.75 percent upfront load, but has a relatively low annual expense ratio of 1.27 percent. Class two charges a 1 percent upfront load, a 1 percent deferred load, and sports an expense ratio of 2.07 percent. Since Roseman's assumption is that investors are buying this fund for the long haul, he prefers the class one shares.

As its name implies, the fund invests primarily in smaller companies traded on both the American and foreign exchanges. It normally sticks with stocks boasting market capitalizations above $250 million and below $5 billion. It can also buy rights, warrants, and preferred stock. During its most recent reporting period, the fund had 41 percent of its money in Europe, followed by 20 percent in the United States, 14 percent in Asia, and 5 percent in Latin America.

"Templeton Global Smaller Companies is the best long-term performer in the global small-cap sector," observes Roseman, editor of the *Global Mutual Fund Investor.* "The firm employs a value approach to equity selection, looking for companies trading at low price-to-book and price-earnings multiples, along with good dividend yields. It seeks out firms with above average earnings growth around the world."

The fund has been managed by Peter Nori since June 1997, following the resignation of Marc Joseph, who had been in charge since 1992. This means that the fund's stellar record is somewhat useless as a barometer for the future, since Nori wasn't responsible for producing these numbers. Nori has been an equity analyst with Templeton since 1990, and he's assisted by three other managers.

But what's important to remember, according to Roseman, is that he has the help of Templeton's two other high profile international experts: chief investment officer Mark Holowesko and emerging markets guru (and former *Wall Street's Picks* panelist) Mark Mobius. "Templeton pioneered global investing back in 1947," Roseman adds. "It's really a first-class organization and the grand old dean of foreign investors."

Reason for Recommendation

The reason Roseman views this fund as such a timely pick is that global smaller companies, as a group, have badly trailed the performance of the larger blue chips since 1995, during one of the greatest bull markets in history. "There's a value discrepancy between the two asset classes of roughly 10 percent," he notes. "That means there's 10 percent better value right now in the global smaller company arena. Smaller companies are also behind the curve when it comes to reporting earnings. They typically do extremely well right at the peak of an economic cycle, which is what we're probably at or near right now. The dollar is also strong, and that usually helps small-cap earnings. This makes it a great time to invest in global small companies."

What's more, Roseman is pleased with the fund's heavy exposure to Europe. "Relative valuations are better in Europe, because the economic cycle there lags the United States by about two years," he maintains. He further notes that the fund's managers have been raising cash lately, which suggests they are turning somewhat cautious.

Of course, investing in small-cap stocks in general can be risky business. When you add in the elements of foreign politics and currency fluctuations, the volatility gets even greater. Still, Roseman insists that if you stick with this fund, you won't lose a lot of sleep. "Risk depends in large part on who is managing your fund," he says. "This fund employs a value approach that has been methodically proven to be successful over the past 50 years. I think that reduces your risk substantially, especially in contrast to other global funds that have only been around for a few years and are run by young, inexperienced portfolio managers."

That's why Roseman maintains it's worth forking over the steep 5.75 commission to get into this Templeton offering. "Personally, I think loads are really immaterial," he insists. "If an investor's going to dollar-cost average every month, I agree it can hurt. But if you're making a one-time lump sum investment, or perhaps putting money in once a year, I don't think it's going to have much of a bearing on your long-term results. I believe buying a fund with a high management fee will hurt you more."

Minimum Initial Investment: $100 (Sales Load: 5.75 percent for class-two shares)

Contact Information: Franklin Templeton Group
700 Central Avenue
St. Petersburg, FL 33704-3628
(800) 342-5236
http://www.franklin-templeton.com

Templeton Globl Smallr Company Fund Cl I
Symbol: TEMGX

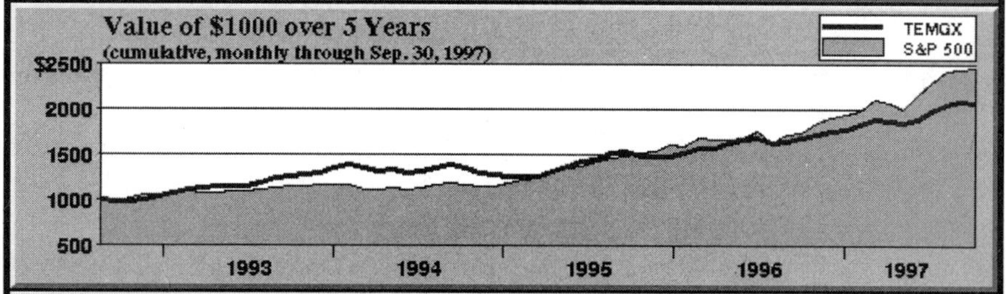

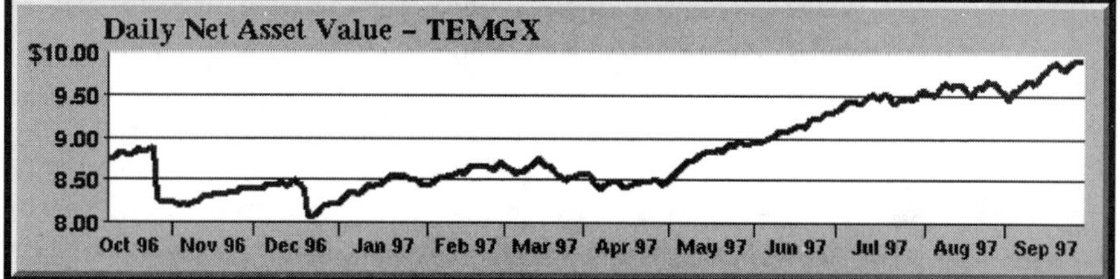

	Investment Period				
Value of $1000	**YTD**	**3 Months**	**1 Year**	**3 Years**	**5 Years**
TEMGX	$1186.88	$1065.66	$1268.29	$1579.39	$2175.40
S&P 500	$1284.82	$1070.20	$1391.67	$2170.31	$2542.88
Total Return	**YTD**	**3 Months**	**1 Year**	**3 Years***	**5 Years***
TEMGX	18.69%	6.57%	26.83%	16.46%	16.82%
S&P 500	28.48%	7.02%	39.17%	29.47%	20.52%

* - Total Return percentages for periods greater than 1 year are annualized.

Latest Pricing Data (as of Sep. 30, 1997)

52 Week High & Date:	$9.920	9/30/97	**52 Week Low & Date:**	$8.070	12/17/96
Last Distribution & Date:**	$0.29	12/16/96	**Ind. Ann. Div. & Yield:**	$0.06	0.60%
Offer Price:		$10.530	**Net Asset Value:**		$9.920

Source: IDD Information Services

Top 10 Holdings	Key Statistics	
News Corporation	Sales Load (max)	5.75%
Conseco	Redemption Charge (max)	0.00%
Internatio-Mueller	Expense Ratio	1.27%
Gesa-Gas y Electridad	Management Fee	0.75%
Hollandsche Beton Groep	12b-1 Marketing Fees	0.25%
Medeva	PE Ratio	20.76
Koninklijke Ahrend	Dividend Yield	1.21%
SIG Schweizerische	Turnover Ratio	32.71%
Wing Hang Bank	Beta Factor	0.46
Fairfax Financial	Total Assets	$1845 mil.

CLIPPER FUND

Catherine Voss Sanders
Morningstar Investor

Manager: James Gipson
Style: Large-Cap/Long-Term Growth

Fund Profile

"This fund doesn't have wrong with it several things that tend to be wrong with a lot of funds," surmises Catherine Voss Sanders of *Morningstar Investor* as she begins to describe her favorite pick for 1998, the Clipper Fund. "Here's what I mean: If you look at the fund industry today, a lot of funds are making several mistakes. They cost too much, they trade too much, and they hold too much. Clipper's not really guilty of any of those things."

In terms of cost, Clipper's annual expense ratio is 1.11 percent, which is slightly below average, but Voss Sanders admits it could still be lower. You certainly can't accuse fund president James Gipson of trading too much, either. "We see fund managers who want shareholders to give them several years to perform, but they don't extend that courtesy to the stocks they own," Voss Sanders points out. "Clipper is one fund that really tries to invest in companies, instead of trading around. It has a turnover ratio of 25 percent, which means it holds on for an average of four or five years." And Gipson clearly doesn't own too much. At last check, he had just 20 names in his portfolio. "Many funds are too diversified," Voss Sanders concludes. "If you're going to pay for active management, you don't want something that looks like an index. Clipper holds 20 to 25 securities. It's not uncommon for a top holding to take up 10 percent of the portfolio."

Now for some background on the fund and its investment process. Clipper is a value-oriented growth vehicle that tries to generate long-term growth of capital. It is managed by Pacific Financial Research, a firm founded in 1980 that manages portfolios for institutions, wealthy individuals, and endowments. The fund's value philosophy calls for finding companies whose current share prices don't reflect their long-term intrinsic worth. This measure is calculated by looking at a combination of dividend and cash flow discounting models, price-earnings ratios, and how much comparable companies have been selling for in the marketplace. "They kind of play the contrarian game," Voss Sanders says. "It is willing to go in and scoop up huge positions in battered growth stocks if the value is there. They are definitely applying a value strategy, but they're flexible in the way they do it."

Balance sheet strength and the ability to generate earnings are important considerations for Gipson and his crew, but he doesn't care much about dividends. If he can't find anything to buy, he's not afraid to build up cash, which is exactly what he's been doing lately. "In addition to cash, we employ two strategies to preserve and increase capital," Gipson says. "Our first step is to avoid overvalued areas of the market where investor sentiment is most enthusiastic, such as Internet technology stocks. On the positive side, we continue to concentrate the portfolio on good, understandable companies selling at reasonable prices. Executing those strategies in a disciplined fashion is the best way we know to add value to the portfolio in the years ahead."

As you might have guessed, Clipper was established as a "nondiversified" fund, meaning it can invest up to 25 percent of its assets in any one issuer. At present, it is not nearly that concentrated. It is also able to stock up on fixed-income and even foreign securities if the value is there. "Gipson is very flexible," Voss Sanders observes. "He'll even buy bonds as a total return play. He did that in the eighties and made a killing."

Reason for Recommendation

Need I tell you why Voss Sanders likes this fund? You should know by now that it does everything she expects, and avoids those practices that usually cause funds to wind up in the mediocre performers category. Clipper has a good track record, although it has only managed to beat the S&P 500 by the slimmest of margins since inception in 1984. On the other hand, it tends to be relatively stable and has kept pace with the all-stock S&P while holding a considerable amount of cash at times. The fund also tends to be relatively tax efficient given its low turnover. "Gipson finds companies he likes, that he thinks are undervalued, and commits to them for several years," Voss Sanders adds. "This approach has paid off for investors."

One final thing to consider: Pacific Financial Research, which is owned by Gipson, was sold to publicly traded United Asset Management in 1997. This has caused some to wonder whether Gipson will still give the fund his full attention because he no longer has as much at stake. Voss Sanders bets he will. "UAM provides support, but in a very hands-off fashion," she maintains. "Besides, Gipson has a huge chunk of his personal wealth tied up in the fund."

Minimum Initial Investment: $5,000 ($2,000 for IRAs)

Contact Information: Clipper Fund
9601 Wilshire Boulevard
Beverly Hills, CA 90210
(800) 776-5033

Clipper Fund Incorporated
Symbol: CFIMX

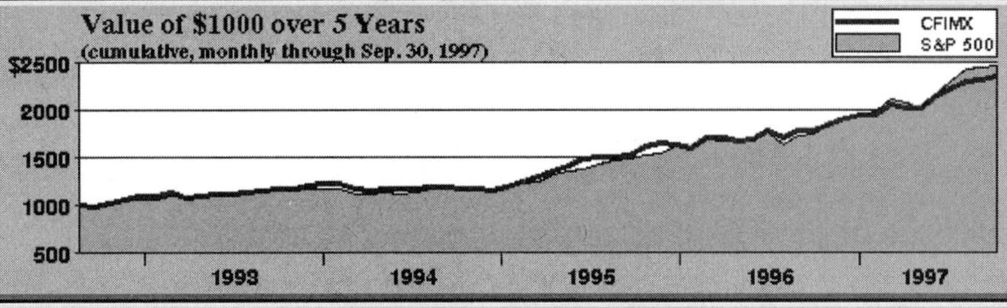

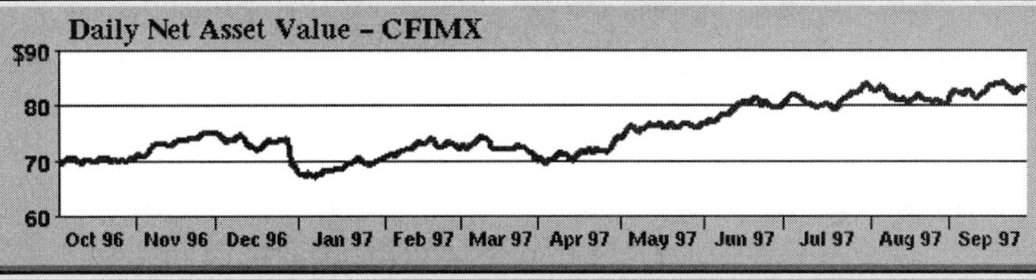

Value of $1000	YTD	3 Months	1 Year	3 Years	5 Years
			Investment Period		
CFIMX	$1231.61	$1044.43	$1300.26	$2014.51	$2353.77
S&P 500	$1284.82	$1070.20	$1391.67	$2170.31	$2542.88

Total Return	YTD	3 Months	1 Year	3 Years*	5 Years*
CFIMX	23.16%	4.44%	30.03%	26.30%	18.67%
S&P 500	28.48%	7.02%	39.17%	29.47%	20.52%

* – Total Return percentages for periods greater than 1 year are annualized.

Latest Pricing Data (as of Sep. 30, 1997)

52 Week High & Date:	$84.510	9/22/97	52 Week Low & Date:	$67.030	1/06/97
Last Distribution** & Date:	$5.11	12/27/96	Ind. Ann. Div. & Yield:	$0.84	1.01%
Offer Price:		$83.220	Net Asset Value:		$83.220

Source: IDD Information Services

Top 10 Holdings	Key Statistics	
FHLMC	Sales Load (max)	0.00%
Fannie Mae	Redemption Charge (max)	0.00%
Wal-Mart Stores	Expense Ratio	1.08%
US Treasury Note	Management Fee	1.00%
US Treasury Strip	12b-1 Marketing Fees	0.00%
McDonald's	PE Ratio	24.23
Mattel	Dividend Yield	0.95%
US Treasury Strip	Turnover Ratio	24%
Philip Morris	Beta Factor	0.89
Johnson & Johnson	Total Assets	$702 mil.

GROWTH FUND

DREYFUS AGGRESSIVE VALUE

Thurman Smith
Equity Fund Research

Manager: Timothy Ghriskey
Style: Large-Cap/Long-Term Growth

Fund Profile

Dreyfus Aggressive Value is part of a new series of funds Dreyfus has introduced in recent years in an effort to pump up its lagging equity offerings. But despite its name, Thurman Smith of Equity Fund Research contends this fund holds a lot of large blue chip names and is far less aggressive than some of its peers. "Aggressive just means the manager has a lot of flexibility," he reasons. "He's allowed to short stocks if he wants to and has the freedom to overweight sectors." That's why Smith believes this fund fits better in the growth, as opposed to aggressive growth, category. "It's amazingly resistant to downward movements, yet it moves up smartly when the market is rising," he observes. "There is 70 percent more reward on the upside but sports an average market risk on the downside. This means it really moves when the market goes up, but won't kill you when it goes down."

Dreyfus Aggressive Value tries to achieve capital appreciation by investing in companies selected on a "value" basis. Among the factors portfolio manager Timothy Ghriskey looks at for determining value are low price-to-book ratios, low PE ratios, and higher-than-average dividend yields. "Ghriskey has a very effective way of comparing what he calls the earnings yield to the five-year Treasury note yield," Smith points out. "The earnings yield is simply the expected earnings in the next 12 months divided by the current price. He compares that with the T-bill yield for five years. If it's higher, and he owns the stock, he'll sell it. If it's lower, it becomes a candidate for consideration, which is when you bring in the fundamental analysts and see what's going on and apply a lot of different tests. It's just a first screen to determine whether or not a stock is well priced."

Ghriskey buys companies of all sizes, as long as they meet his criteria, and is an active trader. He is also able to purchase options and futures, and can even sell stocks short. All of these are aggressive strategies, as the fund's name suggests, although they have been used sparingly thus far. Ghriskey contends that he and his cohorts are passionate practitioners of fundamental analysis. "This method of determining the value of a security starts with our analysts and often our portfolio managers communicating directly with the management of companies that are being considered for investment," Ghriskey says. "Not only do we interview management by telephone on a regular basis, but we also periodically visit corporate headquarters, divisional headquarters, factories, and distribution outlets."

The fund maintains a rather concentrated portfolio, although it is highly diversified among companies and industries. "Ghriskey owns about 56 issues right now, which is about where he wants it," Smith notes. "His sector weightings tend to be neutral, meaning he doesn't overweight unless he's really keen on an area for a specific reason."

Reason for Recommendation

"I like this fund because the manager's style works and makes sense," Smith adds. "He's saying, 'I'll pay you more for something if it's worth it.' So it combines a concern for value and a consideration for how much a stock is likely to grow. I also think the integration with T-bill rates is a real world overlay. He's got a very systematic research process that finds things that move but doesn't pay too much for them. That's just what you want. This is my top-rated market risk fund. I have it in every one of my model portfolios and private accounts." Furthermore, Smith is somewhat cautious on the outlook for 1998 and believes this fund will help to cushion investors in the event of a downfall.

Smith also notes that this fund is relatively undiscovered, which is another reason he likes it. "It only has about $50 million in assets, despite its great performance, so the word isn't out yet," he exclaims. "Dreyfus appears to have quite a good battery of funds right now. It has got a great bunch on board and it's not fully recognized yet." Until recently, Dreyfus's stock funds had an extremely poor reputation. But when the company was taken over by Mellon Bank several years ago, it made a concerted effort to change that.

One possible negative is that Ghriskey is responsible for managing seven other funds at Dreyfus, which brings into question how much time he really has to concentrate on this portfolio. But Smith says this doesn't appear to be a problem. "He has 37 analysts at Dreyfus he can draw on for help," Smith contends. "Ghriskey says he uses the same research database for all of his funds and just allocates the ideas according to the requirements of each fund. He's also got a lot of support from his assistant portfolio managers."

Minimum Initial Investment: $2,500 ($750 for IRAs)
(Available without a transaction fee through Schwab, Fidelity, and Jack White.)

Contact Information: Dreyfus Aggressive Value Fund
200 Park Avenue
New York, NY 10166
(800) 645-6561
http://www.dreyfus.com

Dreyfus Grth and Value Funds Incorporated Aggressive Val
Symbol: DAGVX

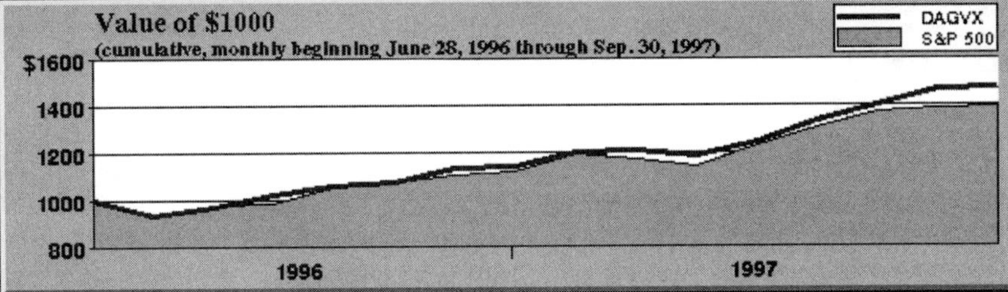

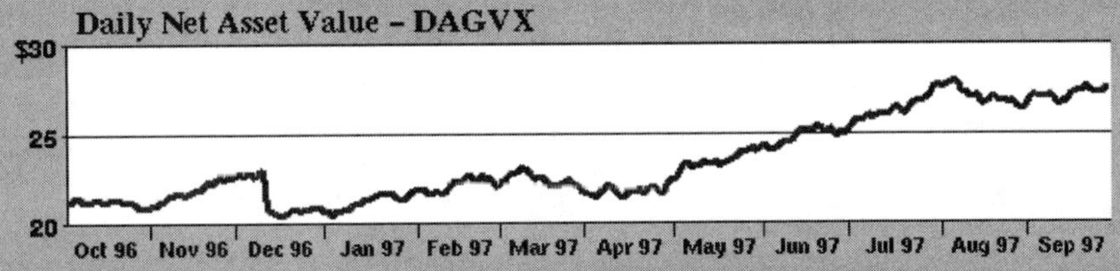

			Investment Period		
Value of $1000	**YTD**	**3 Months**	**1 Year**	**3 Years**	**5 Years**
DAGVX	$1325.93	$1101.48	$1416.32	N.A.	N.A.
S&P 500	$1284.82	$1070.20	$1391.67	$2170.31	$2542.88
Total Return	**YTD**	**3 Months**	**1 Year**	**3 Years***	**5 Years***
DAGVX	32.59%	10.15%	41.63%	N.A.	N.A.
S&P 500	28.48%	7.02%	39.17%	29.47%	20.52%

* - Total Return percentages for periods greater than 1 year are annualized.

Latest Pricing Data (as of Sep. 30, 1997)

52 Week High & Date:	$27.910	8/06/97	**52 Week Low & Date:**	$20.400	12/16/96
Last Distribution & Date:**	$1.91	12/11/96	**Ind. Ann. Div. & Yield:**	$0.05	0.18%
Offer Price:		$27.460	**Net Asset Value:**		$27.460

Source: IDD Information Services

Top 10 Holdings	Key Statistics	
Lone Star Industries	Sales Load (max)	0.00%
Yellow	Redemption Charge (max)	0.00%
Ciba Specialty	Expense Ratio	N/A
Airborne Freight	Management Fee	0.75%
Millennium Chemicals	12b-1 Marketing Fees	0.00%
Coastal	PE Ratio	N/A
Phillips Petroleum	Dividend Yield	0.17%
Forest Laboratories	Turnover Ratio	N/A
Tosco	Beta Factor	N/A
Tenaga National	Total Assets	$160 mil.

YACKTMAN FOCUSED

Michael Stolper
Stolper & Company

Manager: Donald Yacktman
Style: Mid-Cap/Concentrated Growth

Fund Profile

One of the inherent problems with most mutual funds is they are often forced to buy a lot of stocks they only *like* not *love* as more money flows in. In addition, a majority of funds are legally prevented from having any one company make up a significant portion of the overall portfolio. Yacktman Focused is different. Not only is it run by Don Yacktman, one of the top fund managers in the country, but it also contains just 10 to 15 of his favorite stocks. No fillers. Just the best ideas he and his analysts come across. "Yacktman says back-testing has led him to believe that concentrating on one's best ideas should improve performance by about three percentage points annually," notes Michael Stolper of Stolper & Company. "The Focused Fund will have all of the same names as those in his current Yacktman Fund, but in higher percentages. Five names will have a 10 percent weighting each, while the remaining ten stocks will have about a 5 percent weighting."

Yacktman, who is featured on this year's *Wall Street's Picks* panel, looks for growth companies, but will only buy them when they are attractively priced. "Yacktman likes to say his investment style 'squeezes out' risk," Stolper observes. "Business risk is alleviated by owning only very good businesses. Management risk is dealt with by the fund's emphasis on identifying capable capital allocators. And price risk is minimized by buying stocks at substantial discounts to private market values. Choosing this fund, with its value-oriented approach to large-cap growth stocks, is like turning over one's money to a knowing, responsible, and proven caretaker."

In addition to the highly concentrated portfolio, the new Yacktman Focused fund contains two additional wrinkles. "We'll have the ability to buy or sell put options and borrow money," Yacktman tells me. "We're using these tools to enhance what we already think we do well, which is get the highest returns consistent with a minimum level of risk. If you borrow money and buy things that are selling above private market value, you're asking to have your head handed to you. But if you're buying businesses selling at a big discount to what they're worth with borrowed money, it enhances your returns."

Stolper doesn't mind giving Yacktman these extra options, although he hopes they are implemented sparingly. "I don't like short selling, because I view it largely as a distraction," Stolper says. "Having the ability to do it and then doing it with any frequency are two entirely different matters. I hope Yacktman chooses not to pull the trigger, even though it's available to him." Yacktman Focused will primarily own quality large-cap growth stocks. However, Yacktman isn't dogmatic and will buy smaller stocks if he determines they are more attractively priced.

Reason for Recommendation

According to Stolper, the best way to choose a mutual fund is by finding a manager who picks stocks the same way you would if you had the time to do it yourself. He believes Don Yacktman is such a person. "He knows his business," Stolper insists. "He has very clear ideas as to what an appropriate investment is and the fidelity to stick with his valuation techniques. His point of entry is typically when there has been an event or corporate problem that whacks the stock. He has to make a judgment as to whether the event is terminal or transient. It isn't bottom fishing in the traditional sense. It's just being careful and being convinced that the problem will reconcile and there's been a gross market overreaction. It's a nice way to own classic mid- to large-cap growth stocks in a more favorable way than just climbing aboard Coca-Cola and hoping it all works out. He combines a dedication to the achievement of high returns with a healthy dislike of unnecessary risk."

You can read more about Yacktman's investment style in Part 3 of this book. In a nutshell, he looks for a good business with a high return on assets whose private market value is less than the price of its stock. "Yacktman starts with a universe of about 600 names that seem like they might meet their criteria, but not many more than 100 make the final cut," Stolper notes. "A private market value is established for each, company fundamentals are studied, and management is assessed before an investment decision is made."

Perhaps you're thinking that a portfolio with only 15 stocks is extremely risky. But Stolper has a different view. "From a practical standpoint, I think you get your best outcomes over time with short high-conviction lists," Stolper maintains. "There tends to be a greater depth of analyses as to the opportunity. To me, concentration is sort of an after burner. The consequence is you tend to diversify risk and return. If you think someone knows their craft, that amplification will work out well for you."

Minimum Initial Investment: $2,500 ($500 for IRAs)
(Available without a transaction fee through Schwab, Fidelity, and Jack White.)

Contact Information: Yacktman Focused
303 West Madison Street, Suite 1925
Chicago, IL 60606
(800) 525-8258
http://www.yacktman.com

Yacktman Fund Incorporated Focused Fd
Symbol: YAFFX

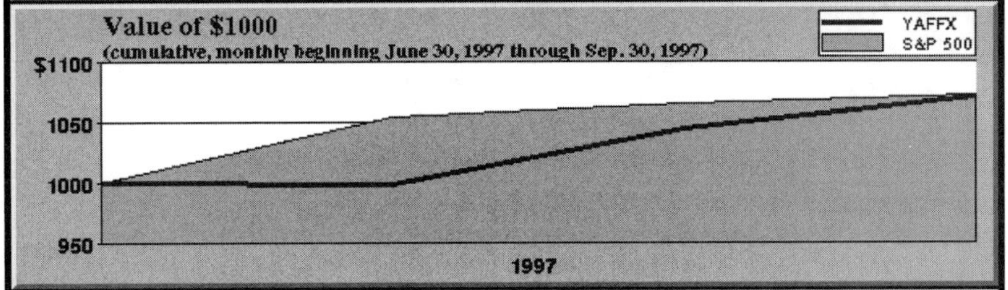

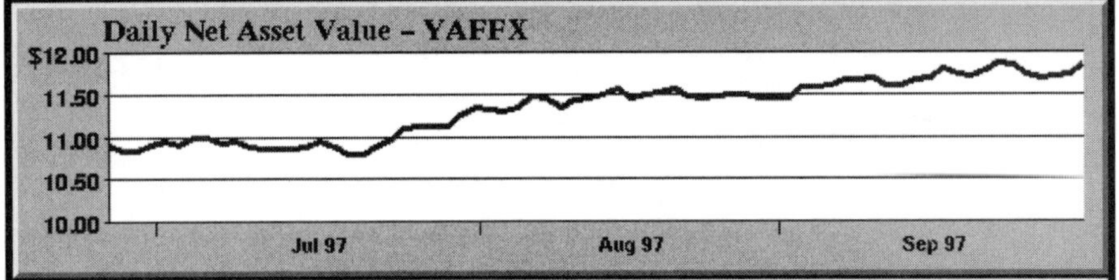

	Investment Period				
Value of $1000	**YTD**	**3 Months**	**1 Year**	**3 Years**	**5 Years**
YAFFX	N.A.	$1087.16	N.A.	N.A.	N.A.
S&P 500	$1284.82	$1070.20	$1391.67	$2170.31	$2542.88

Total Return	**YTD**	**3 Months**	**1 Year**	**3 Years***	**5 Years***
YAFFX	N.A.	8.72%	N.A.	N.A.	N.A.
S&P 500	28.48%	7.02%	39.17%	29.47%	20.52%

* - Total Return percentages for periods greater than 1 year are annualized.

Latest Pricing Data (as of Sep. 30, 1997)

52 Week High & Date:	$11.860	9/22/97	**52 Week Low & Date:**	$10.790	7/21/97
Last Distribution & Date:**	$0.02	6/30/97	**Ind. Ann. Div. & Yield:**	$0.00	N.A.
Offer Price:		$11.850	**Net Asset Value:**		$11.850

Source: IDD Information Services

Top 10 Holdings	Key Statistics	
Department 56	Sales Load (max)	0.00%
Philip Morris	Redemption Charge (max)	0.00%
Franklin Covey	Expense Ratio	N/A
Fruit of the Loom	Management Fee	1.00%
Whitman Corp.	12b-1 Marketing Fees	0.00%
Intimate Brands	PE Ratio	N/A
United Asset Management	Dividend Yield	N/A
Clorox	Turnover Ratio	N/A
Tootsie Roll	Beta Factor	N/A
Reebok	Total Assets	$27 mil.

MATTHEWS ASIAN CONVERTIBLE SECURITIES

Stephen Savage
Value Line Mutual Fund Survey

Manager: Paul Matthews
Style: Large-Cap/Foreign Convertible Securities

Fund Profile

Stephen Savage exudes optimism when talking about the Asian Tiger markets. "The potential there is great. They are very dynamic and growing rapidly," exclaims the director of the *Value Line Mutual Fund Survey*. "The problem, particularly for someone in the growth and income realm, is that the volatility there is extremely high." But Savage has found a solution. Through buying the Matthews Asian Convertible Securities fund, you can capitalize on the region's promising future while tempering risk.

The Tiger economies include Hong Kong, Singapore, South Korea, Taiwan, Indonesia, Malaysia, the Philippines, Thailand, and China. They encompass most of the major regions of Asia, excluding Japan. These economies are far less developed, yet have been attracting a great deal of investor interest. "There's a whole flood of capital going into the Asian markets right now," Savage says. "There's a shift by companies to do their manufacturing in the region because it is rich in resources and has a great labor force."

The problem is that securities traded in these countries tend to be highly volatile and illiquid. That's why investing directly in the stocks of Asian Tiger companies can feel like a real roller coaster ride. But Savage maintains that Matthews Asian Convertible is different because the securities it buys tend to tame some of the Tiger's risk. "This is a unique vehicle that takes advantage of the emergence of convertible securities in the Asian markets," he notes. "The advantage of convertibles is they afford a means of participating in the upside of the equity markets without as great a risk, because the downside is buffered by the debt aspect and the yield. It's a nice way to participate in the dynamic growth opportunities offered by the Asian markets without experiencing the full load of volatility."

In the United States, traditional convertible securities are instruments that can be exchanged under certain conditions for some other security from the issuer. Usually this means you can turn a preferred stock or bond into shares of the common stock at a certain price. Until then, you enjoy a much higher dividend yield than that offered by the common stock, which adds an extra element of stability. Savage says the convertibles issued in Asia are much more conventional than those now being peddled in America. "In this country, you can get into some synthetic convertibles," he points out. "They're not at that point in Asia. The issuers of convertibles tend to be stable, larger, more established blue chip-type companies."

Matthews Asian Convertible is managed by Paul Matthews, who has been investing in the Asian Tiger markets since 1982. He's based in San Francisco now, but lived in Hong Kong from 1982 to 1988. At last check, Matthews had 31.3 percent of this tiny $3.4 million fund invested in Hong Kong, with 15.5 percent in Taiwan, 9.1 percent in the Philippines, 8.3 percent in Thailand, 7.4 percent in Singapore, 7.3 percent is South Korea, 5.2 Percent in Malaysia, 2.3 percent in Indonesia, and 1.1 percent in India. He also runs a stock-only Pacific Tiger fund and another that invests exclusively in Korea.

Reason for Recommendation

Savage maintains that Matthews Asian Convertible allows you to participate in 70 percent of the upside potential of Asian common stocks while getting nice protection on the downside, which is just what a growth and income investor usually looks for. But there are some drawbacks. "The availability of convertible securities in Asia is not so great," he warns. "There are not as many companies that offer them there, and you can't participate in as many markets as you can with stocks."

Savage is quite fond of Paul Matthews. "I think he has a sensible approach," Savage says. "He's a very highly skilled money manger. He's got international expertise and his firm has a presence overseas. He personally goes and visits companies on-site and evaluates each country's political and economic stability."

Although Savage believes this is a perfect complement to a U.S.-based growth and income fund, he argues Matthews Asian Convertible isn't just for conservative investors. "This type of investment is, by nature, aggressive to begin with," he adds. "You might want to mix it with another Asian equity fund. It's a versatile vehicle. You can use it to get your initial Southeast Asian exposure or to soften the risk of an existing equity position you might already have there. So if you believe, as I do, that the Southeast Asian market is going to be a great investment, but you don't want to worry about a couple of bad stock or country picks and want to play the region without going full tilt, this is the way to do it."

Minimum Initial Investment: $1,000 ($250 for IRAs)

(Available without a transaction fee through Schwab, Fidelity, and Jack White.)

Contact Information: Matthews Asian Convertible Securities Fund
655 Montgomery Street, Suite 1438
San Francisco, CA 94111
(800) 789-2742

Matthews International Funds Asian Cv Secs
Symbol: MACSX

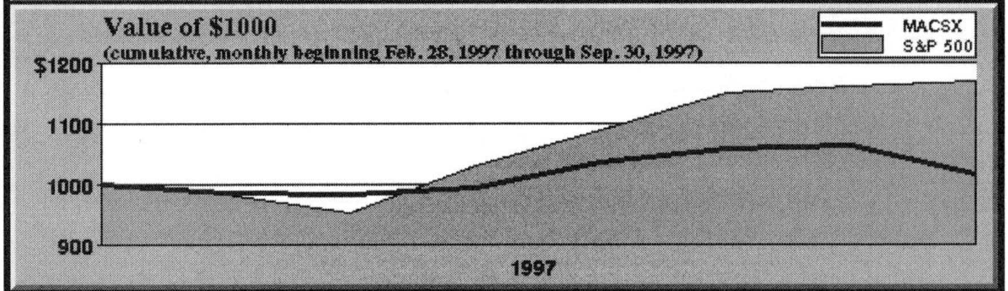

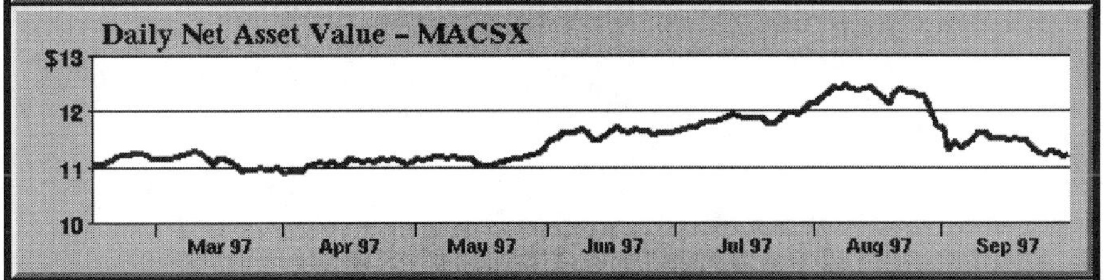

Value of $1000	YTD	3 Months	1 Year	3 Years	5 Years
	Investment Period				
MACSX	N.A.	$964.75	N.A.	N.A.	N.A.
S&P 500	$1284.82	$1070.20	$1391.67	$2170.31	$2542.88

Total Return	YTD	3 Months	1 Year	3 Years*	5 Years*
MACSX	N.A.	(3.53%)	N.A.	N.A.	N.A.
S&P 500	28.48%	7.02%	39.17%	29.47%	20.52%

* – Total Return percentages for periods greater than 1 year are annualized.

Latest Pricing Data (as of Sep. 30, 1997)

52 Week High & Date:	$12.480	8/08/97	52 Week Low & Date:	$10.880	4/01/97
Last Distribution** & Date:	$0.07	6/25/97	Ind. Ann. Div. & Yield:	$0.14	1.20%
Offer Price:		$11.220	Net Asset Value:		$11.220

Source: IDD Information Services

Top 10 Holdings
China Travel Intl. Cv 4.25%
Dairy Farm Intl. Cv 6.5%
Samsung Electronics Cv 0.25%
China Overseas Land Cv 5.25%
Bangkok Bank Cv 1.5%
Bank of East Asia Cv 2%
Hon Kwok Land Cv 5.3%
Commerce Asset Holdings Cv 1.75%
Hong Kong/Shanghai Hotels Cv 5%
Regal Hotels Intl. Cv 5.25%

Key Statistics	
Sales Load (max)	0.00%
Redemption Charge (max)	1.00%
Expense Ratio	1.85%
Management Fee	1.00%
12b-1 Marketing Fees	0.00%
PE Ratio	27.37
Dividend Yield	1.18%
Turnover Ratio	88%
Beta Factor	N/A
Total Assets	$6.3 mil.

T. ROWE PRICE DIVIDEND GROWTH

Walter Frank
Moneyletter

Manager: William Stromberg
Style: Large-Cap/Growth and Income

Fund Profile

Walter Frank is nervous about the United States stock market going into 1998. In fact, he's not expecting the averages to make much progress, if any. "But at any point in time, there are always good stock pickers who can outperform, and that's what I am looking for," he says. This search has led him to T. Rowe Price Dividend Growth.

"It's a value-oriented fund, and it has performed well," he explains. "It's got a very low beta, which is something I like at the moment. It goes after beaten-down companies that will offer some potentially high returns, and it has been outperforming the market of late."

T. Rowe Price Dividend Growth is structured to provide increasing dividend income and long-term capital appreciation by investing primarily in dividend-paying stocks. The fund is managed by an investment advisory committee headed by William Stromberg, who joined T. Rowe Price in 1987 and has been managing investments since 1989. (Brian Rogers, who manages T. Rowe Price Equity Income, the next fund you'll be reading about, is also on the committee.)

Stromberg and his team typically invest at least 65 percent of the portfolio in dividend-paying common stocks that are out of favor, but expected to increase their dividends over time. They view a track record of dividend increases as an excellent indicator of a company's financial health and growth prospects. They also point out that a stock yielding 3 percent today with a dividend yield growing at 8 percent annually would yield nearly 14 percent on the original investment 20 years from now. This means a $10,000 investment would generate $1,400 in annual income after two decades of growth.

What's more, dividends can generate a significant amount of overall capital appreciation in the form of compounding interest when regularly reinvested. (Dividends from the fund are declared and paid quarterly. You can receive them by check, or request that they be automatically reinvested. If you don't need the monthly income, the reinvestment route is the way to go.)

Reason for Recommendation

"Stromberg is a quite capable manager who does some very unique things," Frank says. "For example, he invested heavily in real estate investment trusts in 1996 and got some excellent performance out of them."

In addition to the dividend growth aspect, Stromberg and his colleagues seek out companies with sound balance sheets, solid cash flow, a sustainable competitive advantage, leading market position, and low valuation.

"This bias clearly makes it a large-cap fund, but it does contain some small-cap names as well," Frank says. "The important thing to remember is that I believe this fund can ride out a rocky market like the one I expect us to have this year. Its past performance has proven this." The dividend yield will also serve as a buffer if the difficult market environment Frank envisions becomes a reality.

By the same token, because the fund invests primarily in blue chip, established companies, its potential for significant capital appreciation could be less than that of more aggressive, small-cap funds, like those listed earlier. However, even with its conservative approach, T. Rowe Price Dividend Growth has been a standout performer in recent years.

The fund has a highly diversified portfolio, keeping exposure to any one stock at less than 2 percent. Some of the top holdings include familiar names like Mobil, Fannie Mae (one of *Wall Street's Picks for 1998*) and AlliedSignal, along with lesser-known Tomkins and Hubbel.

"Given my somewhat negative outlook on the U.S. market for 1998, this is a fund I can easily recommend for the domestic equity portion of a portfolio," Frank adds.

Minimum Initial Investment: $2,500 ($1,000 for IRAs)

Contact Information: T. Rowe Price Dividend Growth
100 East Pratt Street
Baltimore, MD 21202
(800) 638-5660
http://www.troweprice.com

Rowe T Price Dividend Growth Fund
Symbol: PRDGX

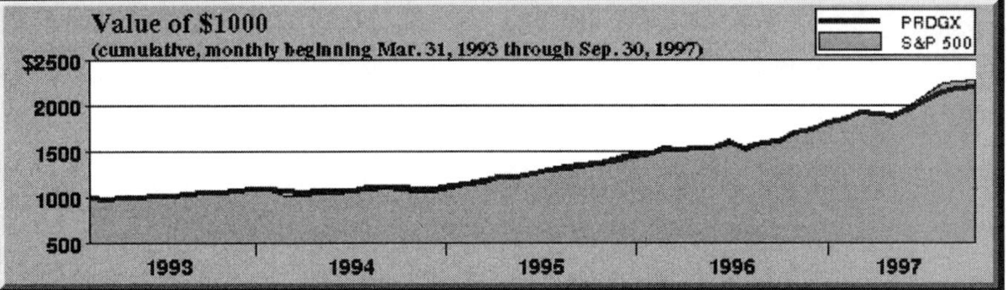

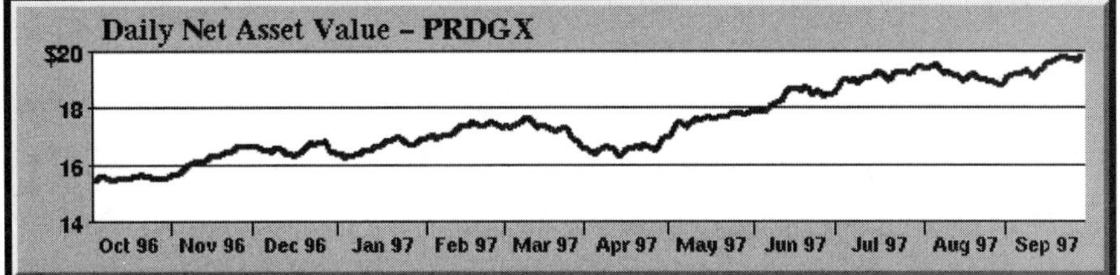

			Investment Period		
Value of $1000	**YTD**	**3 Months**	**1 Year**	**3 Years**	**5 Years**
PRDGX	$1242.05	$1077.90	$1365.48	$2062.54	N.A.
S&P 500	$1284.82	$1070.20	$1391.67	$2170.31	$2542.88
Total Return	**YTD**	**3 Months**	**1 Year**	**3 Years***	**5 Years***
PRDGX	24.20%	7.79%	36.55%	27.29%	N.A.
S&P 500	28.48%	7.02%	39.17%	29.47%	20.52%

* - Total Return percentages for periods greater than 1 year are annualized.

Latest Pricing Data (as of Sep. 30, 1997)					
52 Week High & Date:	$19.830	9/30/97	**52 Week Low & Date:**	$15.440	10/10/96
Last Distribution & Date:**	$0.11	9/26/97	**Ind. Ann. Div. & Yield:**	$0.36	1.82%
Offer Price:		$19.830	**Net Asset Value:**		$19.830

Source: IDD Information Services

Top 10 Holdings	Key Statistics	
Fannie Mae	Sales Load (max)	0.00%
Time Warner	Redemption Charge (max)	0.00%
Mobil	Expense Ratio	1.10%
Ace Limited	Management Fee	0.20%
Security Capital Industrial Trust	12b-1 Marketing Fees	0.00%
Mid Ocean Limited	PE Ratio	22.04
SBC Communications	Dividend Yield	1.95%
Mellon Bank	Turnover Ratio	43%
AlliedSignal	Beta Factor	0.63
Exel	Total Assets	$548 mil.

T. ROWE PRICE EQUITY INCOME

Michael Hirsch
Freedom Capital Management

Manager: Brian Rogers
Style: Large-Cap/Growth and Income

Fund Profile

Mutual fund pioneer Michael Hirsch calls T. Rowe Price Equity Income manager Brian Rogers "a real up-and-comer who will be among the next generation of mutual fund leading lights." The fund's primary goal is to provide substantial dividend income along with long-term capital appreciation. You're probably thinking this sounds a lot like the previous fund, T. Rowe Price Dividend Income. The fact is, Rogers is part of the investment committee for that fund as well. Conversely, Dividend Growth manager William Stromberg helps to run Equity Income. So what's the difference? The answer is, "not much." One major distinction is that Equity Income adheres to a value-driven investment style, while Dividend Growth takes a more blended approach. But both funds, while similar, could fit well within the conservative stock portion of your portfolio.

Now for more on Equity Income's value approach. Rogers seeks out stocks that are temporarily unloved and priced low relative to their potential. Like all value managers, he hopes to profit once other investors recognize the stock's true worth and drive its price higher. Rogers puts money primarily in the stocks of established U.S. companies that pay above-average dividends (higher than the S&P 500), although he can also buy bonds, foreign stocks, and convertible securities.

The dividend helps to increase the fund's overall total return, while cushioning the fall during market declines. "It's an excellent fund that fits my profile of providing good upside participation with downside protection," Hirsch says. As one example, during the fund's worst period since inception, the last quarter of 1987, the S&P 500 fell 22.5 percent, while Equity Income declined by 13.9 percent. Clearly, if all stocks fall, so will this fund. Just not as much.

Research is the cornerstone of Rogers' investment philosophy. He screens hundreds of companies and does a thorough bottom-up evaluation of each one. Some of the things he looks at are each stock's PE ratio, price-to-book value ratio, dividend yield, price-to-cash flow ratio, any undervalued assets the company has and the potential for restructuring opportunities. He also generally keeps part of the portfolio in bonds. "To run a good equity income fund, you must have good equity analysts, and T. Rowe Price certainly does," Hirsch maintains. "But you also have to be good on the fixed-income side, because these securities are so sensitive to interest rate movements. T. Rowe Price is excellent on that front as well."

Due to the fund's value orientation, its holdings are less vulnerable to market downturns, because Wall Street is already expecting the worst. Therefore, when a disappointment comes to fruition, it's not likely to be that noticeable. On the other hand, if a company comes out with a positive earnings surprise, this could cause its shares to rise significantly, especially when it catches investors off guard. "Most importantly, at the end of the day, Brian is an excellent portfolio manager," Hirsch insists. "You sit with him and you can just see a bright, young manager. He has the knack. When you speak to Brian, you feel like you're in the presence of genius. He knows exactly how to play the game and play it successfully."

Rogers earned his MBA at Harvard and was a loan officer at Banker's Trust before joining T. Rowe Price in 1982. He began managing money for them a year later and took over Equity Income at its inception in 1985. His performance at the fund has been outstanding. Over the past five years, Equity Income's returns have topped the S&P 500 with about 30 percent less risk. The fund has also consistently towered above all of its growth and income peers.

Reason for Recommendation

In addition to his high regard for portfolio manager Brian Rogers, Hirsch believes every investor should have an equity income fund in their portfolio, especially because he's somewhat cautious on the outlook for the market. "It's a great style diversifier," he explains. "It's going to bail you out in down times and give you the courage to stay around and wait for the market to go back up."

The fund's total expense ratio is a relatively low 0.83 percent. The one negative is the portfolio's large size. As usual, money follows performance, and some $10 billion has been handed to Rogers in recent years. Size can often impede performance. In fact, Hirsch says fast asset growth is one thing that will make him sell an otherwise good fund. But in this case, Hirsch maintains, size really isn't a problem. "In the growth and income category, you can get away with it," he reasons. "After all, his portfolio is full of names like GE, Atlantic Richfield, AT&T, Chase, Warner-Lambert, and Texaco. These stocks can absorb a lot of assets."

Minimum Initial Investment: $2,500 ($1,000 for IRAs)

Contact Information: T. Rowe Price Equity Income
100 East Pratt Street
Baltimore, MD 21202
(800) 638-5660
http://www.troweprice.com.

Rowe T Price Equity Incorporated Fund
Symbol: PRFDX

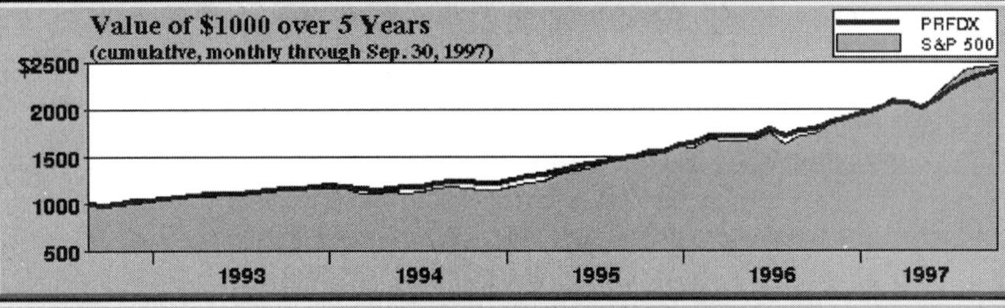

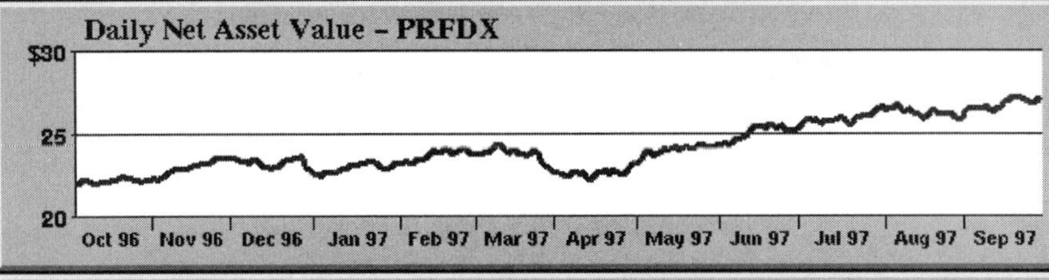

	Investment Period				
Value of $1000	YTD	3 Months	1 Year	3 Years	5 Years
PRFDX	$1237.05	$1078.91	$1330.37	$1985.09	$2465.41
S&P 500	$1284.82	$1070.20	$1391.67	$2170.31	$2542.88

Total Return	YTD	3 Months	1 Year	3 Years*	5 Years*
PRFDX	23.70%	7.89%	33.04%	25.68%	19.78%
S&P 500	28.48%	7.02%	39.17%	29.47%	20.52%

* – Total Return percentages for periods greater than 1 year are annualized.

Latest Pricing Data (as of Sep. 30, 1997)					
52 Week High & Date:	$27.150	9/18/97	52 Week Low & Date:	$21.970	10/03/96
Last Distribution** & Date:	$0.16	9/26/97	Ind. Ann. Div. & Yield:	$0.60	2.23%
Offer Price:		$26.930	Net Asset Value:		$26.930

Source: IDD Information Services

Top 10 Holdings	Key Statistics	
Mellon Bank	Sales Load (max)	0.00%
Dow Chemical	Redemption Charge (max)	0.00%
Arco	Expense Ratio	0.85%
Exxon	Management Fee	0.25%
General Electric	12b-1 Marketing Fees	0.00%
Chase Manhattan	PE Ratio	23.84
International Flavors & Frag.	Dividend Yield	2.31%
DuPont	Turnover Ratio	25%
Texaco	Beta Factor	0.65
Alltel	Total Assets	$10604 mil.

INTERNATIONAL FUND

ARTISAN INTERNATIONAL

Bob Markman
Markman Capital Management

Manager: Mark Yockey
Style: International/Broad-Based

Fund Profile

One of Bob Markman's greatest conquests is uncovering brand new funds spearheaded by experienced managers with proven track records. He compares it to finding old wine in a new bottle. Artisan International is just such a fund. Manager Mark Yockey built an impressive record with the United International Growth Fund from 1990 to 1995 before joining Artisan. "He was in the top 2 percent of his peer group," Markman observes. "We know he can successfully manage a portfolio. He's just been given a new set of clothes."

Yockey runs the fund from his office in San Francisco. He follows the exact same style as before, investing in foreign stocks mostly in developed countries with strong growth prospects. He builds his portfolio using both a "top-down" and "bottom-up" approach, meaning that country and individual stock selection are equally important parts of his investment process. "He doesn't invest on auto pilot like so many other international managers," Markman says. "Most international funds are closet index funds. Their portfolios are constructed close to the EAFE (an international stock index) weightings, which means they're going to have fairly high Japanese holdings and fairly low holdings in some areas that have great growth potential."

When examining individual countries, Yockey tries to identify those areas of the world that are experiencing improving or rapid economic growth and have what he deems to be undervalued markets. Next, he seeks to find those companies that are best positioned to capitalize on that growth. He emphasizes well-managed businesses with dominant or increasing market share in solid industries. "I like the fact that, while not a value fund, it has a reasonable price criteria for growth," Markman notes. "The PEs tend to be lower than the growth rates of the stocks. The average PE of the companies in the portfolio is 15, with an average growth rate of 20 percent a year."

Yockey buys stocks of all sizes, but has a natural bias toward small-caps. He predicts that up to half of his portfolio will be in stocks of companies with market capitalizations below $5 billion. The characteristics most important to him when evaluating a company include quality management, a strong balance sheet, a dominant market share, and an identifiable catalyst for continued growth. He also likes to find underfollowed stocks and frequently takes positions in turnaround situations as well.

Artisan International is broadly diversified, although its heaviest concentration is in Europe (at 60 percent), followed by Asia (30 percent), Latin America (6 percent), and the United States (1 percent). "We continue to be optimistic about the overseas markets in an environment of low global interest rates and attractive valuations," Yockey says. "We remain cautious on Japan. We like Europe, and are finding attractive valuations in the Philippines, Thailand, and Indonesia."

Reason for Recommendation

"I want my international funds managed by independent thinkers who will take advantage of the fact that there are some 30 odd countries in this world to choose from," Markman says. "With Artisan, you've got a fund with 25 percent of its money in Scandinavia and less than 5 percent in Japan. If you were constructing a portfolio based on the traditional market weightings, those numbers would be reversed. I think the way Yockey is doing it leads to better performance."

So far, it certainly has. Artisan was ranked as the number one international fund in the nation for 1996, its first full year in business, with a total return of 34.4 percent. That performance attracted a lot of attention and assets, causing the fund's total assets to swell past the $450 million mark. Its start in 1997 was less auspicious, which raises the question of whether this fund is just a one-year wonder or an excellent long-term achiever. Markman is betting on the latter. "In the grand scheme of mutual funds, this fund still has less money than most others," he says. "And Yockey has a terrific record. I have full faith that he will continue to post excellent numbers."

Markman's typical stock portfolio has a 25 to 30 percent overseas weighting right now, with special emphasis on Europe, just like Artisan. And while he singles this out as his favorite foreign fund, he's also fond of the next international pick you'll read about, Oakmark International. In fact, most of his accounts contain both funds. And he recommends that you consider buying both as well. "When a manager is searching for stocks among such a wide range of countries, they're going to have huge variations in short-term performance," he reasons. "On a year-to-year basis, they will look very different. By splitting your money among the two funds, you can lessen the short-term volatility in your portfolio."

Minimum Initial Investment: $1,000
(Available without a transaction fee from Schwab, Fidelity, and Jack White.)

Contact Information: Artisan International
P.O. Box 8412
Boston, MA 02266-8412
(800) 344-1770

Artisan Funds Incorporated Intl Fd

Symbol: ARTIX

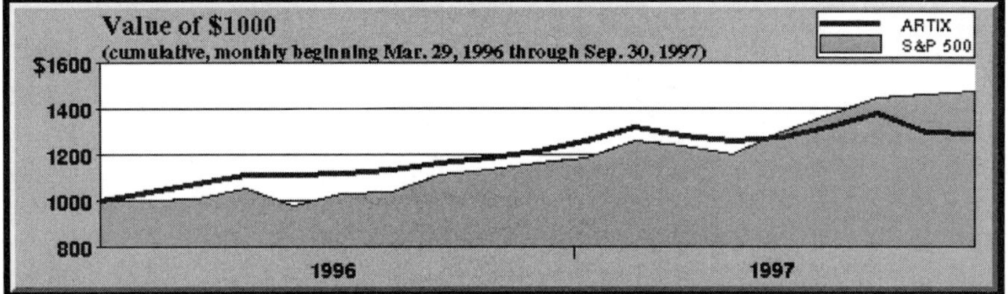

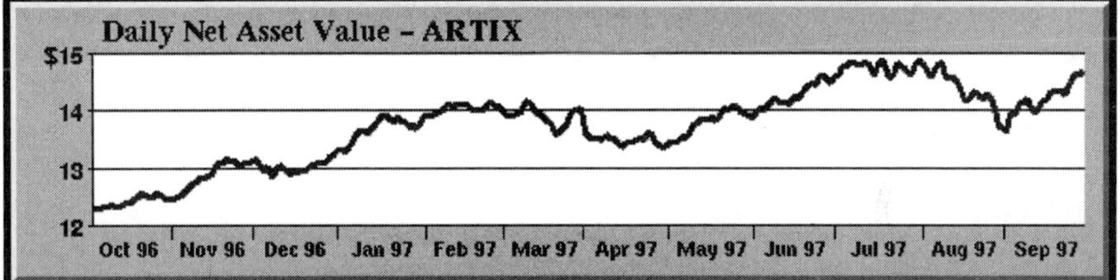

	Investment Period				
Value of $1000	**YTD**	**3 Months**	**1 Year**	**3 Years**	**5 Years**
ARTIX	$1104.35	$1015.88	$1203.76	N.A.	N.A.
S&P 500	$1284.82	$1070.20	$1391.67	$2170.31	$2542.88

Total Return	**YTD**	**3 Months**	**1 Year**	**3 Years***	**5 Years***
ARTIX	10.44%	1.59%	20.38%	N.A.	N.A.
S&P 500	28.48%	7.02%	39.17%	29.47%	20.52%

* - Total Return percentages for periods greater than 1 year are annualized.

Latest Pricing Data (as of Sep. 30, 1997)

52 Week High & Date:	$14.900	7/17/97	**52 Week Low & Date:**	$12.290	10/03/96
Last Distribution & Date:**	$0.00		**Ind. Ann. Div. & Yield:**	$0.00	N.A.
Offer Price:		$14.710	**Net Asset Value:**		$14.710

Source: IDD Information Services

Top 10 Holdings	Key Statistics	
Credit Suisse Group	Sales Load (max)	0.00%
Novartis	Redemption Charge (max)	0.00%
Sankyo	Expense Ratio	2.50%
UBS-Union Bank Switz.	Management Fee	1.00%
Tabacalera	12b-1 Marketing Fees	0.00%
CLF-Dexia France	PE Ratio	28.01
Credito Italiano	Dividend Yield	0.00%
Schibsted	Turnover Ratio	N/A
Whitbread	Beta Factor	N/A
Guangzhou Investment	Total Assets	$451 mil.

OAKMARK INTERNATIONAL

Louis Stanasolovich
Legend Financial Advisors

Manager: David Herro
Style: International/Value-Based

Fund Profile

"When the U.S. market tends not to perform that well, foreign markets tend to do much better," says Louis Stanasolovich of Legend Financial Advisors in Pittsburgh. That's exactly the type of scenario he's forecasting for 1998. Therefore, he believes investors should keep at least 35 percent of their money overseas this year. His favorite fund to do the job is Oakmark International. "It's a value-oriented fund," Stanasolovich explains. "Manager David Herro doesn't own a single Japanese stock. He's extremely dedicated to his investment process. He has a strict method of evaluating companies to determine whether they are too expensive. He makes his buy or sell decisions based on where the numbers come out."

Herro also manages the Oakmark International Small Cap fund, so it comes as no surprise that Oakmark International has roughly a quarter of the portfolio in stocks of companies headquartered in one of the emerging markets nations, such as Indonesia, Israel, Argentina, Brazil, and Mexico. "I'm the biggest believer in the world in emerging markets," Stanasolovich says. "I think if you were picking one investment that you expected to do well, and that could withstand all kinds of volatility, you'd do best in emerging markets equities."

Half of the $1.6 billion fund's assets are invested in Europe, with the largest weightings in Great Britain, Sweden, France, and the Netherlands. "When you think about it, Europe is inherently a turnaround situation," Stanasolovich observes. "Hence, the companies there tend to sell at much cheaper valuations. Herro likes Europe a lot. That makes perfect sense to me, particularly given his strong small-cap weighting there."

Herro joined Oakmark International at its inception in 1992. Before that, he was an international portfolio manager for the State of Wisconsin Investment Board and The Principal Financial Group. "He does a lot of traveling and tries to visit many of the companies in his portfolio," Stanasolovich points out. "When I see managers doing this kind of good qualitative work, I'm immediately attracted, especially if they have a good track record."

Herro certainly does. Oakmark International is currently among the country's top foreign funds, although its record in the past has been somewhat spotty. "In late 1994 and early 1995, he not only had trouble with some of his stocks but also started hedging currency a little too early," Stanasolovich admits. "While it hurt performance in the short run, it has worked out extremely well. What people don't know is that David Herro had an excellent private track record, prior to joining Oakmark. He actually had one of the best track records in the business."

Reason for Recommendation

"I really do believe that foreign markets will outperform the U.S. market in 1998," Stanasolovich asserts. But that's not the only reason he recommends Oakmark International. Even in years when the U.S. market is going through the roof, Stanasolovich believes overseas investing makes sense. "It offers an extra element of diversification," he says. "In 1996, when the U.S. market did well, Oakmark International still managed to beat a lot of domestic funds."

However, in recent years, some pundits have argued that all markets around the world move together. In other words, if the U.S. market falls today, foreign markets are bound to fall tomorrow, and vice versa. Stanasolovich takes issue with that conclusion. "In the short run, like two weeks or a month, all markets are highly correlated," he admits. "But when you spread out that time frame, the correlation is much less. There's no question that it pays to be internationally diversified."

He specifically singles out Oakmark International for its great record, strict value discipline, and proven management team. "They've really got their act together and do very hard-core value analysis," he says. "To me, that's particularly important when dealing with foreign markets."

Among other things, Herro considers the relative political and economic stability of each issuer's home country before making an investment, along with the ownership structure of the company and its accounting practices. There are no limits on the fund's geographic asset allocation, but it will ordinarily invest in at least five different countries outside of the United States at all times.

While international markets are inherently volatile, Stanasolovich doesn't think investors have much to worry about in 1998. "A big downside is limited and I think a big upside is probably more possible," he predicts. "I believe Herro will continue to show his good colors this year and going forward."

Minimum Initial Investment: $1,000
(Available without a transaction fee through Schwab and Jack White.)

Contact Information: Oakmark International Fund
2 North LaSalle Street
Chicago, IL 60602
(800) 625-6275
http://www.oakmark.com

Harris Associates Investment Trust Oakmark Intl Fd
Symbol: OAKIX

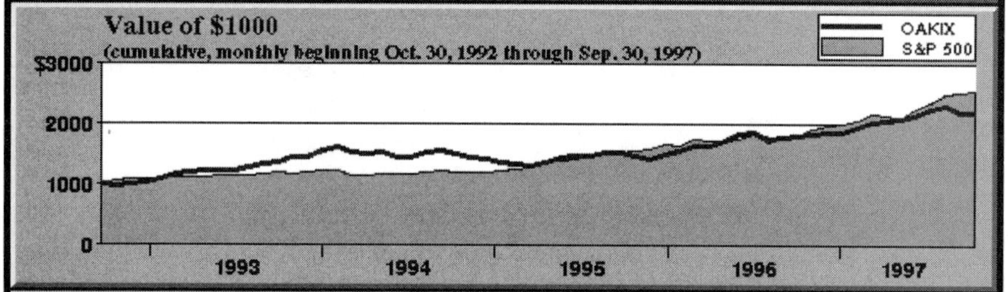

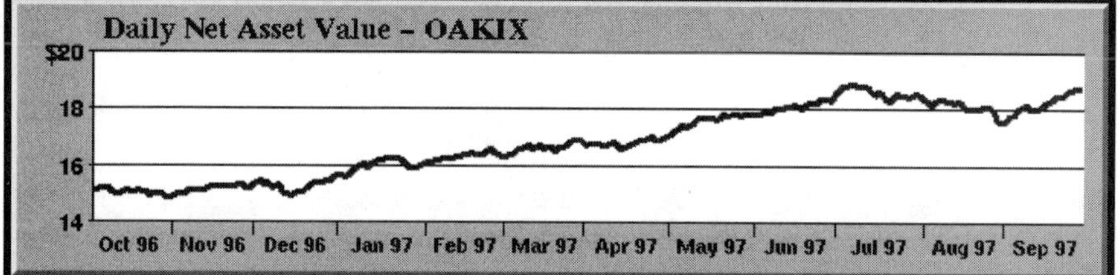

	Investment Period				
Value of $1000	**YTD**	**3 Months**	**1 Year**	**3 Years**	**5 Years**
OAKIX	$1197.07	$1025.68	$1272.34	$1527.74	N.A.
S&P 500	$1284.82	$1070.20	$1391.67	$2170.31	$2542.88
Total Return	**YTD**	**3 Months**	**1 Year**	**3 Years***	**5 Years***
OAKIX	19.71%	2.57%	27.23%	15.17%	N.A.
S&P 500	28.48%	7.02%	39.17%	29.47%	20.52%

* - Total Return percentages for periods greater than 1 year are annualized.

Latest Pricing Data (as of Sep. 30, 1997)

52 Week High & Date:	$18.870	7/07/97	**52 Week Low & Date:**	$14.860	10/30/96
Last Distribution & Date:**	$0.20	12/11/96	**Ind. Ann. Div. & Yield:**	$0.16	0.85%
Offer Price:		$18.770	**Net Asset Value:**		$18.770

Source: IDD Information Services

Top 10 Holdings	Key Statistics	
Cordiant	Sales Load (max)	0.00%
Volvo Class B	Redemption Charge (max)	0.00%
Telefonos de Mexico	Expense Ratio	1.32%
Guinness	Management Fee	1.00%
Nestle	12b-1 Marketing Fees	0.00%
Tomkins	PE Ratio	16.50
Lion Nathan	Dividend Yield	0.87%
Sedgwick Group	Turnover Ratio	42%
YPF	Beta Factor	0.39
Asia Pulp & Paper	Total Assets	$1685 mil.

part 3

UP CLOSE WITH THE EXPERTS

GETTING TO KNOW WALL STREET'S FINEST

This is always my favorite part of the book. Now that you've read about the many stocks and mutual funds my distinguished panelists are buying in 1998, it's time to learn a little bit more about what makes them so great. What follows are complete biographies of each expert, presented in alphabetical order. You'll find a picture (so you can see they're not only savvy, but also good-looking), followed by a brief overview of what they do and how they got where they are. Every profile ends with thoughts on the biggest mistakes investors make and strategies for success in the stock market. Also included is the panelist's occupation, birth date, educational background, market outlook, and the best and worst investments he or she ever made. (This last statistic is proof that no one is perfect, although everyone hits an occasional home run.)

Each luminary has a different way of choosing stocks and/or a unique field of expertise, so you will get truly a diversified list of disciplines and techniques to help you become a better buyer and seller of both stocks and mutual funds.

I'm often asked what characteristics the world's greatest investors have in common. After doing some careful analysis, I came up with five traits they all seem to share. First of all, they have adopted very specific strategies that they consistently follow, regardless of what's happening with the overall market. Clearly, there isn't just one technique that works all the time. Nevertheless, if you develop a system you understand and heed without fail, over time you will make a lot of money. Second, the pros are highly suspicious of "hot tips" and anything recommended by a stockbroker. Many go as far as to say people should avoid taking the advice of a broker altogether, because most are mere salespeople who don't know very much about the market to begin with. Next, the masters don't pay attention to what they see and hear on the news. Instead, they ignore the day-to-day direction of the Dow and focus on uncovering new ideas while closely following the holdings in their own portfolios. Along those same lines, the wealthiest investors avoid market timing. They are always fully invested, although the specific stocks and funds they hold might change depending on their outlook for such things as interest rates and the economy. Finally, and this should come as no surprise, the gurus all agree that diversification is the secret to achieving long-term investment success.

It's interesting to note that only a handful of these experts actually majored in business or planned to invest other people's money for a living. I guess that goes to show you don't need a Harvard MBA to become a first-class portfolio manager. It's also striking how open and easygoing most of these living investment legends are. Even though they work in a fast-paced, often frenetic industry, these folks have a great deal of confidence and faith in their decisions. They aren't constant traders, yet are willing to accept both success and failure, and aren't afraid to move on when they're wrong. Without question, they understand the true essence of what makes the stock market work.

In addition to giving you a lot of insight into who these people are, the profiles will teach you how to pick stocks and mutual funds, when to sell, and what to expect from your investments in the future. You are sure to uncover valuable advice you can profit from for decades to come.

One last observation I will leave you with is that last year most of my panelists were cautious and forecasting a correction of between 10 and 20 percent, which is exactly what we got. In 1996, they were accurately bullish. This time around, although they are overwhelmingly positive, most warn that stock market returns are likely to be more in line with their historic norms of between 8 and 10 percent a year starting in 1998. In other words, it's time to lower your expectations. If my panelists are on the money again, and I have every reason to believe they will be, careful stock and fund selection, as always, is of vital importance. Now let's hear from them about how to properly pick your investments now and into the future.

ANDREW ADDISON

The Addison Report

As a piano player, Andrew Addison knows the key to perfecting his craft is practice, practice, practice. The same principle applies to his investment career. He's been practicing with the bulls and bears for more than two decades now and has dramatically changed the way he picks stocks during that time. While he used to rely exclusively on technical analysis, he now pays much more attention to the fundamentals.

Addison has had an interest in stocks ever since he was a young boy growing up in New Jersey. "I was always fascinated with seeing pages in the newspaper that were nothing but numbers," he recalls. He began charting companies around age ten, and remembers investing birthday and lawn mowing money in the market. "I just kept adding to my positions and was able to use the proceeds to pay a good portion of my college education," he adds.

After earning his undergraduate degree, Addison surprisingly opted to go to law school, instead of working toward an MBA. However, he found the only course he liked was one on contracts, because it was business related. He dropped out after just one semester and transferred to Babson College, where he completed half of the MBA program. To distinguish himself from fellow classmates when it came time to find a job, he formed several hypothetical stock portfolios and tracked them for a number of months, as a way of demonstrating his stock-picking prowess to potential employers.

His first break came in 1974, when Shawmut County Bank offered him a job coordinating investment operations, primarily on the fixed-income side. Six years later, he left to start his own newsletter, *The Addison Report*. Today, in addition to this publication, he publishes another one for institutional investors, called *The Institutional View*, and serves as an outside consultant to several mutual funds, trust departments, and money managers.

Addison is always on the prowl for new investments. "Because I'm constantly taking the market's pulse to analyze developing trends, many of my ideas come from the work I do to determine which groups or sectors are performing best," he says. "But, at the same time, I also get ideas on a bottom-up basis by looking at individual companies. My interest could be sparked by a big surge in revenues or earnings during the quarter, a new product introduction, change in management, or an investor group acquiring a position that may stir up the pot."

That's a departure from how Addison used to find his investments. Before, he was strictly a technical analyst, going by the numbers and charts. Now he says his work breaks down to something like 60 percent technical and 40 percent fundamental. "Technical analysis works because it's very objective and can help you spot promising companies before the crowd," he explains. "It's especially good for determining when to buy stocks that have been out of favor and are undergoing a turnaround, because very often a stock will exhibit the characteristics of what we call 'bottoming,' and start to turn up ahead of any apparent improvement in fundamentals."

Specifically, the most important technical indicators Addison looks at are pricing action, volume flows, and relative strength. "I like to see a stock, if it's been out of favor, reverse its pattern of making lower highs and lows," he says. "Ideally I'm looking for stocks that have begun to trade in a well-defined range with strengthening volume flows and an improvement in relative strength compared to the market."

On the fundamental side, he wants to own companies that are industry leaders, have unique products or services, and enjoy great pricing flexibility. "I also look for changes in the rate of earnings and revenue gains," he says. "Additionally, I like to find companies where management owns a good position and is buying more." Sometimes he's attracted to a company after noticing a broad trend that is likely to help it. "As an example, when grape prices are advancing strongly, that creates opportunities for fertilizer or farm equipment concerns," he reasons. "In sum, every investment recommendation we make must have a good composite rating on both its technical and fundamental criteria." He says it's a strategy that can dramatically lower risk. "If you have a stock that measures up on the technical side and also has supporting fundamentals, you're less likely to get egg on your face."

Occupation: Editor, *The Addison Report*
Franklin, Massachusetts

Birth Date: March 6, 1951

Education: BA, Amherst College, 1973

Biggest Mistake Investors Make: "Not having a game plan and getting caught up in what you read or hear at a cocktail party. If you have a game plan, it will help to ensure your losses are not large."

Best Investment: Culbro (He bought it for $15 a share in March 1995, and it more than tripled in a few months.)

Worst Investment: Diapulse Corp. (Purchased the stock in 1968 and rode it all the way down to zero.)

Advice: "Have a game plan, set limits so you're willing to sell if a stock declines a certain percentage, and be ready to take money off the table if it does what you expect it to."

Market Outlook: Bullish. "I expect to see Dow 10,000 in the next few years, assuming we don't have a major recession."

ROBERT BINGHAM

Bingham, Osborn & Scarborough

Bob Bingham has finally found his calling. After spending most of his life going from job to job, he's now celebrating his fifteenth year as a money manager, specializing in no-load mutual funds. "It took me until I was 33 to find what I loved and the kind of work that was my passion," he says. "I was always a big believer that if you're not sure about what you want to do forever, you choose something that presently engages you and that's what I always did."

Not only has Bingham held dozens of jobs, he's also traveled extensively. After graduating from Amherst College in 1970, he spent two-and-a-half years working his way around the world. He drove a 12-year-old Volkswagen from Europe to Nepal, spending time as a ski instructor, English teacher, and discotheque promoter along the way. He later flew to Japan and Africa before returning to California, doing everything from selling chemicals to landscaping lawns.

He finally decided to settle down in 1981 when, at the age of 31, he was unemployed and contemplating what to do next. His wife suggested he'd be good at helping people with their investments, even though he had no formal training in the field. A short time later, he spotted an ad in *The Wall Street Journal* from a financial planning firm looking for commission-based account executives with "no experience necessary." He applied and got the job. Of course, he didn't stay there long. Four years later, he left with a fellow broker to form Bingham, Osborn & Scarborough, a San Francisco-based investment firm that manages more than $350 million, mostly through mutual funds.

Why has this profession worked out so well? "It combines several of the things I love," Bingham explains. "I love teaching, and this gives me an opportunity to teach both clients and junior partners-to-be. I also enjoy variety, and this business changes its composition daily."

Bingham is both a financial planner and investment manager. He uses funds, instead of individual stocks and bonds, because he's convinced they enable him to construct more sophisticated portfolios. "Mutual funds have become the medium of exchange in the securities markets," he maintains. "It used to be it was individual issues. But modern portfolio theory changed the ball game. It's been quite convincingly demonstrated that asset allocation is what makes the difference in long-term investment performance."

He cites one study that shows 94 percent of the performance in a portfolio comes from asset allocation, compared with 4 percent for stock selection and 2 percent for market timing. "If you believe that, you want to diversify among markets, not individual securities," he concludes. "To do that, unless you have millions of dollars, you must be able to purchase and sell portfolios of securities that represent those markets. Mutual funds enable you to do that."

Bingham chooses his funds based on the asset classes he wants represented, not on managers or past performance records. "We throw all of the funds in our database up on a computer screen and probably the single biggest factors we look at are expense ratios, turnover, and consistency of management," he shares. "We don't like a star fund, because once the star leaves, you have a major change of management. We'd rather see stability in the overall management company, not just the individual pulling the trigger."

Right now, his portfolio strategy calls for an increased weighting in real estate investment trusts, along with respectable representation overseas. "Typically we'll have 15 to 30 percent of the stock portion of a portfolio invested internationally," he says. While his average turnover is low, ranging from 10 to 20 percent a year, Bingham will sell a fund if it is no longer doing the job it was hired to do. "That doesn't happen very much, because we're not trying to find the numero uno fund in the business," he notes.

When you walk into Bingham's office or talk to him on the phone, you're bound to hear the sounds of classical music playing in the background. "My personality is somewhat eclectic, and I like the calming effect of the music," he admits. "It probably keeps me a little more even-keeled." Away from the office, Bingham is an avid squash player and loves to visit the ski slopes. "Athletics is a major outlet for me," he adds.

Occupation: Partner, Bingham, Osborn & Scarborough
San Francisco, California

Birth Date: October 7, 1948

Education: BA, Amherst College, 1970

Biggest Mistake Investors Make: "Following the herd and hot money. The worst thing you can do is read the headlines, see what's hot, and invest in it."

Best Investment: Vanguard S&P 500 Index Fund (He's owned it for the past eight years, and it has outperformed most of his other funds.)

Worst Investment: Investing in a real estate limited partnership in the 1980s. (It lost 80 percent of its value in six years.)

Advice: "Come to a philosophy of how you're going to make your money grow and make sure it is long-term oriented."

Market Outlook: Cautious. "I think we're in for several years of significantly lower returns in the stock and bond markets."

SCOTT BLACK

Delphi Management

What do fine art and value investing have in common? The answer: Scott Black is an expert in both. Although he makes his living from picking stocks, Black's true passion came to fruition in 1984 when a former girlfriend took him to an art auction. "Once I found out I could afford this stuff, I sort of caught the fever," he says. "I now have by far the largest collection of French impressionist art in New England."

Black grew up in Maine, and originally planned on a career as a doctor. He was accepted as a premed student at Johns Hopkins University at age 16, but once he got there, found out he wasn't as intrigued by science as he thought. "So I majored in math and economics instead," he reflects. "I then decided to apply to graduate school straight out of college."

Unfortunately, the Vietnam War came along and forced him to postpone those plans for a year. But he ultimately graduated from the Harvard Business School at the age of 24 and went on to work in the corporate finance departments at Xerox, Seagram's, and Merrill Lynch. "I started to invest in stocks on my own in 1966 at the bottom of the market just for fun," he recalls. "That was right after the market was blown out under Lyndon Johnson. Then a good friend of mine introduced me to value investing."

Investing remained a hobby for Black until William O'Neil, who has a stock data gathering operation and now also publishes *Investor's Business Daily*, hired him to restructure his California company back in 1978. O'Neil paid Black well, and once his assignment there was over, he decided to start his own investment management firm.

"I was able to meet the people from Sunkist while I was in California, and they became my first clients in November of 1979," he says. "I'm proud to say they're still with me today."

Black now manages $900 million dollars for about 20 institutions. He works with one analyst, although he makes most of the investment decisions himself. He even answers his own phone. Black's portfolios hold anywhere from 60 to 85 stocks at any given time and are often concentrated by industry.

"Right now we're overweighted in media stocks with more than 20 percent of the portfolio," he shares. "We also own a lot of financial services stocks, especially regional banks and small insurance companies."

Black finds his companies by doing an enormous amount of computer screening. "We basically break the world of Ben Graham into two subdivisions," he explains. "One I call earnings power plays. Those are companies that have good, sustainable earnings power with a minimum of 15 percent return on equity. We don't want to pay more than 10 to 10.5 times expected earnings for these companies."

The second type of stock he likes is what he refers to as an asset play. "These are companies with strong balance sheets and positive free cash flow," he says. "In good years, they earn a high return on equity, but they sell at big discounts to break up value." In other words, he's always looking for a bargain, like his original mentor, Warren Buffett. "We're opportunistic," he admits. "We're usually buying when the bad news is coming out and all of the analysts are issuing sell recommendations."

Black always visits or calls every company before making an investment and stays in regular contact with top management. He'll sell a stock for two primary reasons: The company starts trading for what he considers to be its full value or he realizes he's made a mistake.

When he's not searching for investment ideas, Black is active with the Democratic party and has set up his own charitable foundation. "I give 15 to 20 percent of my gross income to charity," he claims. "Most of the money goes for education and helping children around the globe." Black also loves to travel and, of course, attends a lot of art auctions. "I could quit now and be a curator of 19th and 20th century French paintings," he adds.

Occupation: Founder and President, Delphi Management, Inc.
Boston, Massachusetts

Birth Date: February 14, 1947

Education: BA, Johns Hopkins University, 1968
MBA, Harvard Business School, 1971

Biggest Mistake Investors Make: "Buying stories and overpaying for promises."

Best Investment: Fisher Scientific (The stock went up 500 percent in just nine months during the early 1980s.)

Worst Investment: Several discount retailers, including Caldor and Venture Stores, which he bought about three years ago. "I lost about 40 percent of my money on them," he says.

Advice: "Be disciplined and know that value will out. Don't get your head turned by easy money or what some guy on the golf course says."

Market Outlook: "I'm not smart enough to know what's going to happen with the market. People who are successful don't try to time the market, they just buy good businesses."

ELIZABETH BRAMWELL

Bramwell Capital Management

Between remodeling her New York office, managing her team of analysts, staying in touch with clients, attending meetings, monitoring what's been a very volatile market and managing some $500 million, Elizabeth Bramwell has little free time these days. But that's the price you pay for running your own successful investment firm. "This is the ultimate way to go," she says. "I don't think it's the first thing one should do in one's career, but having your own business is very interesting."

Bramwell went out on her own in February 1994, following a successful seven-year stint running the Gabelli Growth Fund. It grew to $700 million under her command, posting an average annual return of 16.6. Her performance often bested boss Mario Gabelli, who managed several funds of his own. Bramwell parted company with Gabelli following a series of highly publicized disputes and launched her own self-named fund six months later. "I left with the idea that if I were going to go out on my own, I was going to prove that I could start a fund and succeed," she reveals. The National Association of Securities Dealers, in binding arbitration, awarded her a settlement of almost $1 million in 1996 for unpaid compensation Bramwell claimed Gabelli owed her.

Growing up, Bramwell never had much of a financial vocabulary. Her father was a musician and she dreamed of becoming a doctor. That's why she was a chemistry major in college. However, economics was more interesting to her than science and, after graduation, she enrolled at the Columbia Business School to get an MBA in finance. That's where she first met Gabelli, who was one of her classmates.

Bramwell says her investment discipline has evolved after more than 27 years in the business. "I consider myself to be a growth investor," she explains. "When I started out, I worked on analyzing emerging public companies, so I own a lot of the smaller names. But what I don't want to do is ignore some of the larger firms that are big movers." In addition to managing the Bramwell Growth Fund, which holds many of those larger companies, she is a subadviser to the Selected Special Shares Fund, which concentrates on small-cap stocks.

She prides herself on being both a top-down and bottom-up analyst. "From a top-down standpoint, I really think about things like inflation, interest rates, tax rates, currencies, and political events," she shares. "Right now, I think inflation is minimal. You've got a very competitive world out there. You have worldwide manufacturing, a strong dollar, and technology driving costs and the whole pricing structure down. I think interest rates are quite high relative to inflation and the rest of the world and the quality of earnings is very good." Bramwell's conclusion is that we are in an expanding global economy where free trade is opening up opportunities in places one could only dream about before.

From a bottom-up, more sector-specific perspective, she concentrates on companies that are major users of technology. "I like financial services companies very much," she says. "They have huge databases and a real drive toward consolidation, which creates an opportunity to cross-market products to customers." She's also keen on outsourcing companies and the makers of technology themselves.

Once Bramwell has determined which areas she's interested in, she begins looking closely at specific companies. "I'm trying to figure out how they're going to grow going forward with new products and markets," she tells me. "Are the margins going to continue expanding, and what's happening with tax rates? Do they need to raise more money, or will they buy back shares?" She also gets a lot of insight from attending the many road shows that come through the Big Apple. "Companies do these 30- to 45-minute presentations that are followed by a question-and-answer period," she explains. "I think having several other analysts there asking questions provides for a very insightful and synergistic experience."

Unfortunately, although Bramwell continually whipped the S&P 500 in her Gabelli days, she's been running slightly behind it ever since. "This is a problem for all of us active managers," she admits, contending that her day in the sun will return, most likely sooner than later. "I think the pendulum will eventually swing in our favor. The problem is the S&P index is different from the way it used to be. It has become much more technology- and growth-oriented. But a lot of the stocks in it are expensive, and I believe the kinds of companies I buy are more attractive."

Occupation: President and CIO, Bramwell Capital Management
New York, New York

Birth Date: December 1, 1940

Education: BA, Bryn Mawr College, 1962
MBA, Columbia University, 1967

Biggest Mistake Investors Make: "Acting impulsively and not objectively. Also, not planning ahead and becoming educated."

Best Investment: Robert Half International (First bought in 1994 for $9.50 a share. It now trades for more than $60.)

Worst Investment: U.S. Satellite

Advice: "Equities are a long-term investment so don't try to trade in and out."

Market Outlook: Bullish.

SUSAN BYRNE

Westwood Management

Growing up in Pasadena, California, Susan Byrne didn't even know what Wall Street was. But following her short-lived first marriage, she headed for New York at the age of 24 with her 4-year-old son and a lot of ambition. "I thought New York would be a neat place to go and start my grownup life," she recalls. "I had my choice of three secretarial jobs, and the one that paid the most was with E.F. Hutton."

Byrne was assigned to be the appointment secretary for company president Robert Fomon. By always volunteering, overselling her abilities, and yearning to make more money, she was able to talk her way into a job as a research editor at another brokerage firm. "It wasn't a very glamorous job," she admits. "I took all of the material from the analysts and edited it into proper English."

From there, she worked her way up to becoming a member of the investment team, specializing in the area of political economics, where she used a lot of the knowledge gained from her time studying history at the University of California at Berkeley. "I loved this job and felt I had really found something that I not only enjoyed, but also could make a contribution in," she shares. "I was also really encouraged by my clients. They would say, 'Based on the way you look at things, Susan, you should really consider managing money.'" Amazingly, despite being surrounded by portfolio managers, Byrne never thought about striving for this position herself. But one thing led to another, and in 1977, she was hired as an apprentice portfolio manager by Banker's Trust. Two-and-a-half years later, she was offered a chance to work as an assistant treasurer and in-house pension fund manager at GAF Corporation. "This job gave me the opportunity to clearly demonstrate an ability to manage money, because in the bank you had committees and guidelines, but here I was on my own," she recalls. "I was with them for almost four years, and with their blessing, I started my own firm, Westwood Management, on April 1, 1983." GAF was her first client.

Byrne pauses at this point to note that her journey must sound awfully unconventional. But she maintains it's simply a function of the fact that she's over 50 and female. "There was a horrible bear market in the early 1970s, and the securities industry wasn't attracting a bunch of people," she explains. "My first five years in the business were from 1970 to 1975. These were terrible times, and there wasn't a lot of competition. Today the firms want to see a certain type of person from the best and brightest schools."

Still, Byrne admits she started her own company because she knew that was the only way she'd ever become a big player in the business. "I was waiting for these firms to come knock down my door and make me a partner, which was clearly not happening," she shares. "So I decided to start my own company and demonstrate clearly to myself and my peers that I had a talent for managing money." She started with $35 million and today has grown to more than $1 billion in private accounts and mutual funds.

You don't gather that much money unless you know how to make it multiply, and Byrne has clearly proven she does. Her first rule of investing is don't lose money. "That may sound silly, but it's one of those things people sometimes forget," she says. "I begin with a top-down viewpoint, by looking at what's happening with inflation. If the environment seems right for financial securities, I look at a combination of the expected 12- to 18-month economic cycle, along with the outlook for corporate profits, interest rates, inflation, and the dollar."

She then chooses stocks by searching for a catalyst that can drive a company's share price higher. Once she's found that, she looks at what other analysts are saying about the stock, and will only buy if she thinks they are underestimating its potential. "This sounds easier than it is, because we only own about 40 stocks out of a universe of 6,400, so you can see that we agree with other analysts 95 percent of the time," she notes. "We'll only invest in those companies that we have a high degree of confidence will come through with a positive earnings surprise."

Every stock in her portfolio has a price target based on her estimated forward-looking growth rate, and Byrne says her goal is to buy value stocks that will ultimately turn into high growers.

Nine years ago, Byrne left New York for Dallas after marrying her second husband. "It was a good move," she says. "Now I have three new stepsons and a great spouse."

Occupation: President and Chief Investment Officer,
Westwood Management
Dallas, Texas and New York, New York

Birth Date: August 5, 1948

Education: Attended but didn't graduate from the University of California at Berkeley.

Biggest Mistake Investors Make: "Trying to make money too fast."

Best Investment: Dell Computer (It's grown tenfold since she first bought it in 1994.)

Worst Investment: Trying to buy options almost 25 years ago.

Advice: "Be too busy to fool around with your portfolio. Have a program, decide what you're going to save, come up with a sensible asset mix, and stick with it."

Market Outlook: Cautious. (Expecting returns of around 8 to 10 percent, and feels bonds look more attractive than stocks.)

JAMES COLLINS

Insight Capital

Jim Collins is ecstatic about the market's prospects for 1998, especially when it comes to small-cap stocks. "I think we're looking at five times as much upside as downside potential," he predicts. "The downside is on the order of 4 to 8 percent, and the upside could be anywhere from 20 to 40 percent." One reason for this optimism is that his fund went through some tough times in 1997, falling more than 16 percent at one point during the year. "We know there will be down periods in the market and we'll underperform it at times," he reasons. "But we've found that when we do go down by close to 20 percent, that usually leads to a period of great outperformance." For instance, his managed accounts dropped 23 percent during the second quarter of 1990, only to roar back 121 percent from the second to third quarter of 1991. The only thing that could spoil Collins's positive picture, he says, is a rapid increase in interest rates by the Fed, which he considers to be highly unlikely.

Collins originally began following the stock market in high school, but for unorthodox reasons. He wanted to own a manufacturing plant and knew he would have to come up with capital to do it. He figured learning about stocks would give him the knowledge he needed to come up with this cash. But things didn't turn out like he planned. "After graduating from college with an engineering degree, I went into the Navy," he reflects. "For about ten years, I tried everything conceivable out there to get an edge on the marketplace."

After his tour of duty was over, he joined General Electric as an engineer and spent his off hours trading stocks. He managed to turn $1,500 into $487,000 in just four years. "I hadn't been at GE very long before I was making more money trading stocks than I was as an engineer," he confesses. "I was pretty much a speculator and trader in those days. I ran a concentrated portfolio of over-the-counter stocks. I typically held no more than six to eight names at a time, with most of the money invested in three issues." His portfolio eventually zoomed to $1.5 million, before plummeting back down to $30,000 after a series of bad gambles. "I took that money, married a lovely girl from Asheville, North Carolina, and as soon as I graduated from the Harvard Business School, we took off for Europe and spent the whole $30,000 traveling for three months," he says. "I never looked at is as money. I just looked at it as a score. My thinking is still pretty much the same. I want to rack up as big a score as I can."

So far, that's exactly what he's done. His firm, Insight Capital, is ranked among the top 1 percent of all money manager's in the nation, and his *OTC Insight* is the number one investment newsletter over the past eight years, according to the

Hulbert Financial Digest, producing a total return of 762 percent, or 31 percent a year.

Collins's first professional job in the industry was working for a friend picking stocks for his mutual fund company in 1967. He later became a stockbroker before starting his own firm in 1983. "I'm primarily a fundamentalist in what I do," he explains. "I have a three-step buying process of running quantitative screens, doing fundamental analysis and then what I call performance analysis. Performance analysis for me is really taking a look at the relative strength of a stock."

He maintains a database of 6,500 stocks, which he screens every morning. "First and foremost I like to find stocks with a track record of beating the market over a long period of time," he reveals. "The primary purpose of the screening is to see if a company has a track record of beating the market. Then I move on to fundamental analysis to verify that the industry looks good, and that the company is a notch ahead of the rest of the players in its business. I then like to dig deeper to see that earnings are indeed growing rapidly, preferably by 20 percent a year or better, and that they have solid cash flow."

Because he demands such strong growth, he most often gravitates toward smaller stocks that trade over the counter. The average company in his portfolio right now should grow its earnings by 31 percent in 1998 and has a PE ratio of between 24 and 26. "The number one reason I'll sell a stock is because it's not beating its benchmark index," he adds. This can lead to extremely high turnover.

When Collins wants to escape the hustle and bustle of the investment world, he and his wife jet over to the hills of merry England where they like to hike. Other times they'll take the weekend off to see a Broadway show in New York.

Occupation: President, Insight Capital Research & Management
Walnut Creek, California

Birth Date: August 26, 1934

Education: BEE, Georgia Tech, 1956
MBA, Harvard College, 1963

Biggest Mistake Investors Make: "Hitting the panic button when the market goes down."

Best Investment: Cisco Systems (First bought in 1991 and it has gone up almost tenfold since.)

Worst Investment: Gantos (Purchased shares of this clothing company in the 1980s for between $9 and $12 per share. Got out of it around $5, before it went down to $3.)

Advice: "Pick an investment manager or fund with a good three- to five-year track record. Don't try to do it on your own in today's volatile market environment."

Market Outlook: Bullish.

SHELBY DAVIS

Davis Selected Advisers

Call him coach Shelby. Sure, his title may have changed, but Shelby Davis insists he's still as active in the investment business as ever before. In February 1997, he turned portfolio manager duties for his New York Venture and no-load sibling Selected American Shares funds over to his 32-year-old son Chris. "I did it exactly on the 28th anniversary of my running the Venture Fund," he explains. "I was getting ready to turn 60, and Chris already had a fine record of running the Davis Financial Fund at our firm. Besides, he had been my comanager on Venture and Selected American for three years and I felt it was time for him to be promoted."

He also sought to prepare his family-owned firm, with $8 billion in assets, for the next generation. The fact is, investing runs deeply through the Davis bloodline. Shelby's late father founded the investment firm Shelby Cullom Davis, and his 90-year-old mother is still a member of the New York Stock Exchange. Meanwhile, his son Andrew is president of Davis Selected Advisers and manages the company's Real Estate Fund.

"I worked at my dad's firm in high school and college, which is where I first learned to appreciate the compounding of financial companies," Shelby recalls. "I also discovered that stocks were not pieces of paper, but fractional ownership positions in the earnings and dividend streams of companies. So even today, when I think of owning a stock, I ask myself if I were rich enough, would I be interested in buying the whole company at that price, not just this fractional position."

While Shelby is no longer the portfolio manager for his popular mutual funds, he's still the chief investment officer and CEO of Davis Selected Advisers and has one of the most enviable records in the mutual fund industry. "In essence, I'm the coach and Chris is the quarterback," he says. "The change means my life will hopefully be more simplified, giving me more time to do what I like best, which is working on picking stocks and coming up with a strategy for investing. I also hope to spend less time on things like doing interviews with the press, public speaking, and going to boring board meetings."

Shelby Davis is a long-term investor, doesn't believe in market timing, and calls the compounding of money the eighth wonder of the world. "We are not traders," he emphasizes. "We are old-fashioned investors doing research, taking three-year time horizons and trying to know management. We want to pick a collection of business partners that we can own for extended periods of time."

He further attempts to minimize risk by looking for low multiple, moderate-growth companies, rather than the sexy stories or fads of the day. Right now, the financial sector is his favorite area of the market, and he has close to half of the assets in his funds invested there. "We think this is the decade of financial assets and that inflation and interest rates will stay in a trading range with a gentle trend upward," he explains. "The demographics clearly favor accumulation of financial assets. The defined contribution plans and the consumer taking control of their financial futures with packaged financial products makes sense."

Beyond that, Davis looks for business that he can understand with solid balance sheets, a strong market share, and multinational reach. "We want management to be able to answer these questions: Where are you going in the next three to five years? What are your hopes, dreams, and goals? And how are you going to get there?" Most importantly, he demands that companies allocate capital well and recognize that it has a cost. "We also try to develop themes," he says. "For instance, in addition to financial stocks, we also like the energy area and think technology will continue to capture a bigger share of the gross national product."

Davis divides his time between homes in Florida, Wyoming, Maine, and New York. In between keeping up with his six children, he enjoys hiking, sailing, and swimming. But he's never far from Wall Street, taking his Bloomberg terminal with him wherever he goes. One thing's for sure: He currently has no plans to retire and is not interested in selling his firm. "What's great about this business is you're not tied to one company," Davis surmises. "You can look at the whole world and figure out which industries and companies you like."

Occupation: CEO and Chief Investment Officer, Davis Selected Advisers, LP
Santa Fe, New Mexico

Birth Date: March 20, 1937

Education: BA, Princeton University, 1958

Biggest Mistake Investors Make: "Being too short-term oriented and not thinking of companies as a partnership instead of a number on a page."

Best Investment: Fannie Mae (First bought this stock ten years ago, and has multiplied his money at least 75 times.)

Worst Investment: Memorex (Purchased for $50 in 1960. It went up to $160 and then down to $1. He got out around $30.)

Advice: "Find an area that interests you and let it become your circle of competence. Then, look for investments within your circle of competence. Search for good managers with integrity and become partners with them."

Market Outlook: Bullish. "I expect to see Dow 10,000 in the next few years, assuming we don't have a major recession."

MICHAEL DiCARLO

DFS Advisors

Mike DiCarlo has always had a knack for making money. Even as a teen, he had his own business managing a number of local bands. It was a profitable venture, and DiCarlo found himself with an abundance of cash. He reasoned that the best thing to do was put it to work in the stock market. "Having run my own company, I was familiar with the kinds of things companies faced every day and that helped me to make investment decisions," he says.

His initial interest in equities was purely for pleasure and to build his personal wealth. In college, he prepared for a career in politics. But as graduation day drew closer, he had a change of heart. "The more I saw my politician friends having to go through lots of scrutiny, the more I said that's not for me," he recalls. So he took a job as a bill processor with John Hancock. He worked his way up over the years, eventually taking over management of the top-ranked small-cap Special Equities Fund in 1988 and later becoming the company's chief equity officer. Because he's always been an entrepreneur at heart, it came as no surprise when he left John Hancock in July 1996 to form his own investment firm with two other partners. "It was something I always wanted to do and the timing just felt right," he says. "I had been at John Hancock for 18 years and was looking for a new challenge."

DiCarlo still manages Special Equities, thanks to a special arrangement with his former employer, but he also runs a $60 million hedge fund. Both invest exclusively in small-cap stocks, but the hedge fund can take more risk by shorting stocks and buying exotic securities.

"I think small-cap companies are interesting because they attack a niche in the market, which is easily definable," he shares. "It's clearly one of the riskiest areas, but if you have a disciplined approach to doing things, you can take out and mitigate some of the risk."

He uses four yardsticks to measure his stocks, all of which can be applied consistently in any kind of market or economic environment. "First, we try to find companies that are growing by 25 percent or better before the momentum investors get a hold of them," he says. "Next, I look for companies that are self-financing and in a leadership position in their particular market. Finally, and most importantly, I look for a management that's focused on generating shareholder gains. You've got to sit down with the managers and grill them about their business, what their margins and new products look like, how their competition is doing, and what their exit strategy is. Then you go talk to vendors, distributors, customers, competitors, anyone you can to make sure what you're being told by the top of the house is actually being executed throughout the entire company. You also want to see management have a lot of their net worth tied up in the company."

Most of DiCarlo's companies have market capitalizations between $100 and $750 million when he makes his initial purchase, although he'll hold his winners even if they grow beyond that range. "If a company continues to give me the kind of growth I bought it for in the first place, I'll stay with it even if it exceeds those parameters," he adds.

His sell discipline is also clearly defined. "I'll get rid of a stock when it goes down 12 percent from what I paid for it," he reveals. "Also, because I'm always fully invested, if I find a new candidate for purchase, I'll sell one holding to buy another."

When DiCarlo and I talked recently, he was having a tough time. His mutual fund was down almost 20 percent and small stocks in general were getting creamed. "It's painful and tough to see this, but I believe if you take a long-term perspective, everything will be all right," he concedes. "The kinds of stocks I invest in are clearly high-quality, emerging growth companies, but they also happen to be more volatile than any index you could create. When the market turns around, I outperform to the upside in a big way and make people forget all about the downside. Small stocks are so inexpensive right now, I think we're leading up to another time like 1991–1993 where stocks can double, triple, and quadruple from where they're at today."

DiCarlo maintains there are four things you need to be successful in the investment business, and an MBA isn't one of them. "It takes hard work, skill, luck and, most importantly, common sense," he says. "We all try to make this job, for whatever reason, sound more complicated than it really is."

Occupation: Founding Partner, DFS Advisors
Boston, Massachusetts

Birth Date: March 6, 1952

Education: BA, University of Massachusetts at Boston, 1980

Biggest Mistake Investors Make: "Sticking with their losers too long."

Best Investment: Infinity Broadcasting (Started buying as an IPO, and it was eventually taken over by Westinghouse.)

Worst Investment: Hunter Environmental (Paid up to $5 a share for the stock several years ago, and it dropped down to $1 in one day.)

Advice: "Use your common sense. Like my father said, 'if it sounds too good to be true, it's probably not real.'"

Market Outlook: Bullish, especially on small-cap stocks.

DAVID DREMAN

Dreman Value Advisors

If investment genius is truly in the genes, David Dreman owes a lot to his 87-year-old father. "He was always sort of a natural contrarian, so the instincts came very naturally," he says. "Bull and bear markets have always been second nature to me." Dreman's dad runs a small investment and commodities firm in Winnipeg, Manitoba, and Dreman grew up watching him work. In fact, there was never any question in his mind that he'd spend his professional career picking stocks. After graduating with a business degree from college, he worked for his father several years trading stocks on the Toronto exchange before venturing to the United States in search of more excitement.

"The American markets seemed to be much broader and volatile, which created more opportunity," he remembers. "I thought that was more interesting, because the Canadian market was primarily composed of industrial and mining stocks. I came here for what I thought would be a one-year look at the U.S. markets and I've been here ever since."

Dreman started out as a research analyst and later senior editor with Value Line, before becoming an investment officer with the brokerage firm J&W Seligman. He finally went out on his own in 1976 and has been practicing his low PE, contrarian strategies ever since. "I define a contrarian as someone who buys out of favor stocks that are cheap relative to the market," he explains. "Major opportunities almost always come at times when markets are panicky. That's when major monies can be made. We seem to have one crisis or another every two or three years." Dreman attempts to profit from the doom-and-gloom predictions that he figures are a bunch of nonsense. For example, he made a lot of money in 1990 when analysts began bad-mouthing the banks. Then, when the threat of health care reform emerged and the White House began trashing the pharmaceutical companies in 1993, Dreman scooped up drug shares at around eight times earnings.

Dreman's father always told him the consensus of the experts is usually wrong. That's why he believes his contrarian strategy works so well. "One of the most important things to money managers is finely tuned earnings estimates," he observes. "What I've found in my research is that the chances of an analyst in 20 quarters being within a plus or minus 5 percent range of his or her estimate are one in 100 billion. It shows you how this is a loser's game." Contrarians, on the other hand, don't try to forecast the future precisely. If anything, they take advantage of the fact that earnings surprises create temporary havoc with good stocks.

A low price-earnings ratio is important to Dreman, because studies show inexpensive stocks perform best over time. That's why he begins his search for companies by running a computer screen that brings to his attention names selling at PE multiples below that of the overall market. "I also want an above average dividend yield and good fundamentals," he adds. "I'm trying to buy companies that are likely to increase earnings at an above average rate relative to the S&P 500 for the foreseeable future."

It's no surprise that Dreman often finds his best ideas after reading about some impending disaster. "I like bad news from a good stock that isn't permanent," he reveals. "I like to exploit the market's overreaction. But I won't touch a company that has real serious problems. I'm looking for a crisis that I believe the Street and analysts have overreacted to and is not as serious as it looks at first glance." Once he buys a stock, Dreman sets a moving target based on valuation. "I'll sell a stock when it reaches a market multiple," he says. "I'll also get rid of it if the economic conditions change and I see bad times ahead or am wrong in my fundamental analysis. Finally, if a stock doesn't work out over a three- to four-year period, I'll sell."

In addition to managing the Kemper Dreman High Return Fund, Dreman oversees some $2.5 billion in private and institutional money. He has written several books on investing and is a columnist for *Forbes*. Today, he spends much of the year working out of his home in Aspen, Colorado, although he's starting to get somewhat sick of the snow. Nevertheless, he claims his passion for investing is stronger than ever. "The markets are like a 19th century battlefield," he says. "There's smoke and you're masked in an enormous amount of contradictory information. It requires good decision making, and there's an enormous amount of tension. Most people seem to buckle in. I love it."

Occupation: Founder and Chairman, Dreman Value Advisors, Inc.
Red Bank, New Jersey

Birth Date: May 6, 1936

Education: Bachelor of Commerce, University of Manitoba, 1957

Biggest Mistake Investors Make: "Not looking at the long-term records of stocks and the probability that certain situations will work out and others will fail."

Best Investment: Old Republic International (Bought for $8.20 years ago, and it has increased more than 50-fold since.)

Worst Investment: King's Department Store (The stock went from $12 to $1 about 15 years ago.)

Advice: "You don't have to take big risks to make money. Risk costs you money. You're better off buying a good diversified portfolio of safe, blue chip stocks, rather than trying to hit the ball out of the park."

Market Outlook: Cautious. (Expecting a correction or flat returns.)

JEAN-MARIE EVEILLARD

SoGen Funds

When it comes to investing, Jean-Marie Eveillard has a simple philosophy: "It's a big world out there beyond the borders of the United States, and there are bound to be opportunities in the developed and developing worlds, so don't close yourself off to them." In other words, Americans shouldn't just invest in companies here at home. "Many investors aren't very sensitive to that notion after a period where the U.S. market has done better than practically any other market in the world over the past three years," he admits. "But that's not always the case."

Eveillard practices what he preaches. As manager of the SoGen International Fund, he searches the globe for attractively priced stocks and bonds, although his single-largest exposure right now is to the United States.

This consummate cautious investor is worried that too many folks are throwing money into the market expecting it to go nowhere but up. Yet he still doesn't see anything even resembling a mania. "The excesses in the American market are nowhere as bad as what I saw in Tokyo in the late 1980s," he shares. "But it bothers me that so much money has marched into mutual funds, especially because a lot of it has come from safe bank accounts."

Eveillard was born and raised in France and still speaks with a beautiful French accent. He was forced to work as a trainee during his last year of college, where he studied business, and was offered a job writing for the investment section of a weekly financial magazine. That's where he first developed an interest in the equity markets. He then took a job with the French bank Sociètè Gènèrale after earning his degree.

Before long, he was managing money. The bank sent Eveillard to New York in 1968 to help serve as an analyst for the SoGen International Fund. At the time, it was only open to French citizens and invested exclusively in American companies. Six years later, he returned to France and was promoted to managing a global fund of his own. However, he had to answer to an investment committee and yearned for more freedom. His big break came in 1978, when the French manager of SoGen International wanted to return to Paris. Eveillard came back to New York and was named chief portfolio manager of the fund. He immediately changed its focus, making it truly an international offering. "I decided to run the fund as if it were my own money, which it was to a modest extent, because much of my personal money was invested in it," he recalls.

The investment process for Eveillard and his five analysts begins by looking for individual companies, not countries, to invest in. He reviews dozens of research reports sent in from around the globe each day in search of stocks that look like great buys. "We try to get fair businesses at a good price, but we occasionally buy good business at a fair price," he explains. "The easy part is determining whether a stock is reasonable. It's much harder to make a medium- to long-term assessment about the company's prospects."

He does a lot of fundamental research, looking at PE and price-to-cash flow ratios, along with differences in accounting methods and relative valuations among the various countries. "We are more inclined to investigate opportunities in countries where we think the overall market may be unduly depressed," he says, noting that he's having a hard time finding any market that fits that criterion right now. "I must admit I am starting to get my feet wet in Japan again, and Europe appears to be much cheaper to me than the United States."

Although he likes to hold his stocks for several years, he'll sell a holding for one of two main reasons. "Either after a year or two we have to acknowledge we made a mistake in our original assessment of the company, or as the price of a stock goes up, we ask ourselves whether the company is better than we thought it was," he says. "If not, and the price has moved up, we'll start selling it."

Although he is married to an American and has lived in this country for more than two decades, Eveillard remains a French citizen. He now manages more money than he ever dreamed of, \$5 billion, and his funds have some 100,000 shareholders. He admits to being under a tremendous amount of pressure and tells me there's a good chance he may retire within the next five years. But don't expect him to just sit at home doing nothing. "My grandfather worked for the French railroads," he shares. "The day he retired, he was completely bored because he had no outside interests. In my line of work, I can continue to run my own money in a leisurely manner."

Occupation: President/Manager, SoGen Funds
New York, New York

Birth Date: January 23, 1940

Education: Graduate of Écoles des Hautes Commerciales, 1962

Biggest Mistake Investors Make: "Having a lack of patience."

Best Investment: SAP (a German technology company). The stock has risen more than tenfold since he bought it in 1992.

Worst Investment: Buying several media stocks in the United Kingdom during the 1980s, right before the government began charging hefty TV license renewal fees. The stocks fell by more than 50 percent in a matter of weeks.

Advice: "Have patience."

Market Outlook: Cautious. "It will be a hard year to make money around the world."

HAROLD EVENSKY

Evensky, Brown & Katz

Harold Evensky has a message for America's mutual fund companies: You charge too much and are about to be held accountable for it. "For me, the easy standard is what would a fund manager charge to manage institutional money," Evensky says. "It seems to me the expense ratio should be in that range (which is generally 1 percent or less). That's why I have trouble understanding why management fees for retail funds are significantly higher than that." The average stock fund's expense ratio is a shade above 1 percent, but some go as high as 3 percent or more.

Evensky realizes he alone can't do much to reverse this trend, but he's a member of an influential organization that believes it can. It's called the Alpha Group, and it's comprised of 13 financial planners from eight investment firms across the country. Together, Alpha controls some $2 billion in client assets, most of which is in no-load funds. The group hopes to use its muscle and proxy voting power to pressure fund companies to cut costs. "We'll reject managers solely on the basis of high fees," Evensky boasts. "The reason it hasn't been more of an issue until now is because returns have been so high, no one has noticed how much they were paying."

Nevertheless, Evensky invests most of his clients' money through funds. He uses both index and managed funds, because the indexes often beat the professionals. "We use active managers in areas where we believe there's a possibility they'll outperform net of costs and fees," he says. "We also use managers who, even if they don't beat the index, are likely to provide downside protection. I'm also convinced that investors are more comfortable knowing that someone is at least trying to protect them on the downside, even if it's not true."

Evensky is a true pioneer in the field of financial planning. He became a stockbroker 19 years ago after a short stint running his own construction company. Unfortunately, he wasn't very good at cold calling for clients. "I read about financial planning, which was something brand new back then," he recalls. "I enrolled in a program to learn about it and started giving seminars on financial planning to develop my business." He soon began targeting more sophisticated and wealthy clients and rejoined his old business partner from the construction business to start his own investment firm in 1985.

"We opened as a financial planning practice," Evensky shares. "We did big, multihundred-page comprehensive plans for a very substantial fee, and then implemented them on a commission basis." When discount broker Charles Schwab introduced a program allowing independent planners to trade no-load funds with minimal transaction costs, he switched over and became a totally fee-based adviser, charging his clients a percentage of the assets under management, instead of a load or commission. "We are not money managers," he emphasizes. "We hire money managers (usually through funds). Our focus is on the asset allocation, not the selection process."

Evensky chooses his funds using a clearly defined top-down approach. "First, we don't use sector funds or those that use aggressive strategies, like short selling," he explains. "That eliminates a lot off the top. Then we decide where in the economy we want to be, such as emerging markets, large-cap value or whatever. Next, we screen for what we consider to be fatal flaws, like high expenses. We then check turnover and things like that. The final screen is to really look closely at the fund."

This usually means interviewing the manager, often in a conference call with other Alpha Group members, in search of three important characteristics: philosophy, process, and people. "We want to know why the manager thinks we should give him some of our clients' money," Evensky says. "It's the answer to that question that's most important to us. We want to know their vision. If that sounds good, then we'll want to know things like what are your trading costs? How do you make buy and sell decisions? How do you reward people who work with you? If that sounds good, we want to know more about the people there. By the time we've gone through all that, we usually have a pretty good feel for whether or not the fund is for us." He steadfastly avoids what he calls "the *Money* magazine hot fund of the month," because he contends what's on top this month is likely to be at the bottom next month.

Occupation: Partner, Evensky, Brown & Katz
Coral Gables, Florida

Birth Date: September 9, 1942

Education: BA, Cornell University, 1965
MA, Cornell University, 1967

Biggest Mistake Investors Make: "Not knowing what they want to accomplish and not having an investment plan."

Best Investment: Marrying his partner, Deena Katz. (She was brought into his firm as a partner seven years ago, and they were married a year later.)

Worst Investment: Managers Intermediate Mortgage Fund. (Bought it four years ago, and when interest rates spiked up, he lost 15 percent of his investment.)

Advice: "Make a plan before you invest."

Market Outlook: Cautious. "I'm hoping for 9 to 12 percent returns in 1998, but deep down I'm scared it could be an awful year."

AL FRANK

The Prudent Speculator

Al Frank makes no bones about why he likes value stocks so much. "I'm a cheap guy," he says. "I'll still go to a discount gas station a mile away to save three or four cents a gallon, even though I hardly need to these days." He traces this respect for cash back to his childhood. Both of his parents were uneducated tailors who never made a lot of money. Frank hated school himself and wanted to do nothing more with his life than work at a print shop. "I had no intention of going to college," he admits. "I was a very mediocre student. I graduated in the lowest quartile of my class."

Because all of his high school buddies enrolled at Los Angeles City College, Frank decided to join them. "It was the best educational institution I ever attended," he contends. "I was still planning to be a printer and thought I'd take a business major for two years to learn how to run my print shop. But when I got there, I decided I didn't want to be a business major after all." So he transferred to UCLA with the dream of becoming a cinematographer. He practically flunked out and enlisted in the Army instead. After hitchhiking to New York, working briefly for the *New York Times* and marrying his first wife, he came back to California and earned a bachelor's degree at UC Berkeley. Next, he moved to Las Vegas, back to New York, then to Europe, before returning back to California to get his master's degree, before ultimately returning to UCLA to work toward a PhD.

Frank is unquestionably a man who loves adventure. But his search for what to do with his life ended one day after his mentor at UCLA introduced him to the stock market. He quickly developed a passion for it. "I was studying the stock market, while working as an assistant professor," he recalls. "In 1977, one of my friends suggested that I write a newsletter, and another wanted me to manage money. I decided to register with the SEC and started *The Pinchpenny Speculator,* which is the original name of *The Prudent Speculator.*" It was just a hobby at first. He mailed out around 100 letters and managed some $65,000. That all changed in 1983, when *The Hulbert Financial Digest* started to follow his publication and ranked it the number one performer for the year. "All of a sudden I had 1,000 subscribers and then 6,000," he exclaims. "Before long, I was making $2 million a year." Everything was going great until the crash of 1987 came along. Frank was fully margined, and his model portfolio lost more than 55 percent of its value in one day alone. "I personally had a $2 million portfolio," he dreadfully recalls. "After the crash, it was worth $400,000. I made the money back in two years, but the subscribers I lost never returned."

The performance of Frank's newsletter is back on top and so is he. He now works out of his home in Santa Fe, New Mexico and maintains an office in Laguna Beach, California, where his assistant John Buckingham does most of the actual stock research these days. Frank follows about 700 companies at any given time and pays close attention to such fundamental factors as price-to-book value, price-to-cash flow, price-to-sales and PE ratios, along with debt and return on equity. "In the beginning, when I was doing this myself, I bought Barron's. Twenty years ago you could find stocks selling for six times earnings, 60 percent of book value, and yielding 6 percent," he remembers. "They were called 'The Triple Sixes.' I also wrote some very simple spreadsheet programs early on."

His computerized database is much more sophisticated now, but stocks that cheap are hard to find in today's market. Nevertheless, Frank's overriding goal remains the same: to find stocks that he expects to double within three to five years. "Once I spot a company that looks promising, I send for 10-Ks and 10-Qs," he adds. "I then estimate a value for each stock, and if the current selling price is below 50 percent of my target, it's a buy." Frank rarely visits the company or talks with management. "I've never found a chief executive who didn't see the problems at his corporation as anything but opportunity," he notes. Frank is a big believer in diversification and has learned a lot from studying the work of his mentor, Benjamin Graham. "His was one of the first books I ever read," Frank reveals. "His idea that you should buy undervalued stocks because they provide a cushion of safety is very impressive to me." Frank readily admits that about 25 percent of the stocks he recommends are never profitable. "But the other 75 percent range from barely profitable to exceptionally profitable," he claims.

Occupation: Publisher, *The Prudent Speculator*
Laguna Beach, California

Birth Date: April 19, 1930

Education: BA, UC Berkeley, 1956
MA, California State University Los Angeles, 1962/1965

Biggest Mistake Investors Make: "Being impatient and panicking out before the market realizes the value of a corporation."

Best Investment: Western Pacific Industries. (Bought for $12 in the late 1970s and sold out for $163 in less than seven years.)

Worst Investment: A couple of savings and loans that were forced out of business and went down to zero in the 1980s.

Advice: "Be patient, diversified, and selective. Stock selection is easy. Patience is difficult."

Market Outlook: Bullish.

WALTER FRANK

Moneyletter

Economics has been a lifelong passion for Walter Frank. After serving in the Armored Division for three years during World War II, Frank earned an undergraduate degree in history and literature at Harvard University. Then, after spending a year in Paris working for Radio Free Europe, he returned to study economics.

"Economics was incredibly important when I was growing up during the 1930s," he says. "I further realized while working as a correspondent for Radio Free Europe that economics was at the basis of everything, and I wanted to know more about it."

Frank also had a strong interest in stocks. "As soon as I got back to Harvard, some friends of mine inherited a fair amount of money and wanted to know if I would be interested in managing their portfolio," he recalls. "I said yes."

That sparked a career that has lasted more than 45 years. Frank's first job after college was writing a monthly newsletter for a New England bank. "After a while, the bank asked me to consult on the general economic outlook for their trust department," he says. "Meanwhile, I picked up a couple of more portfolios on my own and started to build up a reasonably sized advisory business."

In the mid-1960s, he and a partner on Wall Street formed a hedge fund, which they ran through the beginning of the bear market in 1973. "We went long stocks, like the aggressive growth funds of today, and that was a good period for it," he recalls. "We bought IPOs and played all of the games, but we didn't short stocks."

In a bull market, that's wonderful. But when the great bear emerged, it was a disaster. "The hedge fund didn't survive," he laments. "I wandered in the wilderness for awhile. I continued to consult, write the newsletter and do articles for *The Economist*. I even consulted for Congress at one point."

He ultimately left the stock market altogether and began playing around in real estate when it was hot during the early 1980s. "Then, in 1985, an opportunity came for me to work on *Moneyletter,* and at the time I needed to accept the offer," he says. The newsletter was published by William Donoghue back then, but has gone through several owners since, most recently being bought out by Agora Financial Publishing.

Frank not only writes *Moneyletter* out of his hometown of Ashland, Massachusetts, but also does market forecasting and selects the recommended funds. He considers overall asset allocation the most important part of his job. "The first thing I do is look at the economic outlook, mainly in terms of my view on interest rates, because this determines the justifiable price-earnings ratio for stocks," he explains. "Then I examine the various asset classes, both in the United States and overseas."

Next, he decides whether it makes more sense to be in equities, bonds, or cash, and to what degree. "I spend no time on whether I want aggressive growth, value, or high and low beta," Frank admits. "That's because I developed a computerized fund selection system to go along with the asset allocation strategy that chooses the funds automatically for me."

You might think of it as a momentum strategy, because it only takes into account performance over periods of not more than one year, without regard for who is actually managing the fund. "One of the things you'll find if you use a momentum strategy like this is there is the danger of having five funds in your portfolio that all turn out to be, for all intents and purposes, exactly the same," Frank warns. "So I do some fundamental work to make sure this doesn't happen."

Frank is convinced funds are the best way for most people to invest. "Despite what Peter Lynch says, I don't think individuals should be investing in individual securities, unless they make it a full-time job," he argues. "The ordinary Joe is in no position to compete with the institutional world in terms of knowledge, and knowledge is what makes this whole thing go."

While Frank has watched the mutual fund industry grow exponentially over the past few decades, he thinks it has much more steam left. "If we have some bad markets, some funds aren't going to make a lot of sense and you'll see them disappear and be bought out," he predicts. "However, I don't see that the fund industry has anywhere to go but up. The assets may go down in bad years, but they'll be back."

Occupation: Editor and Chief Investment Officer, *Moneyletter*
Baltimore, Maryland

Birth Date: March 31, 1924

Education: BA, Harvard University, 1949
MA, Oxford College, 1952

Biggest Mistake Investors Make: "Having a lack of patience, plus the inability to hold on and look ahead."

Best Investment: Loew's (Bought in the late 1960s, and the stock multiplied several times.)

Worst Investment: Several high-tech IPO's he purchased in the early 1970s, one of which went completely broke.

Advice: "Know your limitations, and don't be too greedy."

Market Outlook: Cautious. "I'm more interested in international markets. I don't see anything to suggest a bear market, but can't see how U.S. stocks can go much higher."

ELAINE GARZARELLI

Garzarelli Investment Management

There's no question Elaine Garzarelli is one of the most powerful and influential women on Wall Street. But the past year or so has been pretty tough. After calling the 1987 stock market crash and earning a loyal following, Garzarelli stumbled in July of 1996 by issuing a "sell" signal on the market when the Dow Jones Industrial Average was at 5390. As testament to her influence, the market promptly fell 44 points once word of her pronouncement hit the press. But the Dow continued its upward rise the very next day, going on to jump through the 6000 mark. Garzarelli finally reversed herself six months later by sending out a "buy" signal, although those who followed her previous advice had missed out on a gain of more than 20 percent.

Garzarelli's past forecasts have been eerily accurate. So what went wrong? "I have a set of indicators that I look at, including cash flow and earnings," she explains. "In the past, they both moved together. This time, they didn't. The cash flow indicator had the highest weighting in my timing model and when it became unfavorable, it prompted the model to flash a sell signal." But she noticed earnings were still strong. And after doing additional digging to see what the problem was, she found out cash flow wasn't being reported the same way it used to be. "Companies were no longer providing numbers before tax depreciation in a timely and accurate manner," she says. "Therefore, I tossed out the cash flow indicator and replaced it with earnings in my model. When I did that, the market was a buy."

Garzarelli took a lot of heat in the press for her less-than-accurate call, but claims her institutional clients took it all in stride. She also reportedly lost few subscribers to her popular *Garzarelli Forecast* newsletter, which boasts a circulation of more than 70,000. Besides, Garzarelli's no stranger to controversy or pressure. She became a senior vice president at Drexel Harriman Ripley at the age of 23 at a time when women were moved up the ranks rather quickly. "The company made me head of a whole team of rocket scientists," she recalls. "Our job was to build econometric models and determine what made the stock market go up and down." But none of her older male subordinates would take orders. So she called her dad for help. "I asked him what to do," she recounts. "He told me to do what everyone does when they get promoted: Fire one of them. After I did that, there was no problem. They did everything I wanted them to."

Garzarelli remained in relative oblivion for some 11 years, perfecting her model to predict market moves and earnings estimates for 90 different industries. "I had been very useful to the firm internally, but the sales force started to notice me in 1992, when I called the bull market," she says. "The new director of research said my work was the best-kept secret on Wall Street. He told me to be on the *Institutional Investor* All-America team and go on *Wall $treet Week*, and that my bonus would be dependent on it." In essence, the firm wanted to make her a star to bring in business.

But her initial foray into the spotlight was rather disappointing. "My first *Wall $treet Week* appearance was so bad, my mother actually ended up with a nervous condition and was in the hospital trying to recuperate," she admits. Her new employer, Lehman Brothers, asked her to start managing a mutual fund in 1986. Because she was expecting the crash, her fund went up 5 percent in October of 1987, while the market dropped 35 percent. "*The Wall Street Journal* wrote that I predicted the crash, and by then the news media was all over the place," she remembers.

Garzarelli follows 85 different econometric models and talks with leading economists in various industries to determine which sectors of the market are undervalued and likely to outperform in the months to come. To be attractive, a sector must have an expected earnings growth better than the S&P 500 and a PE ratio that's below its historical range.

Despite her latest faux pas, this sector analyst has an excellent long-term record. The fact that she is so precise may be one reason she lost her $2 million job at Lehman Brothers in 1994. The firm's top brass thought she was wrong to be bullish and got rid of her. She turned out to be right. Now she runs three investment companies of her own. Garzarelli spends two weeks out of each month working on her research report from her home in Florida. The rest of the time she's usually out traveling the country or visiting with clients.

Occupation: Chairman, Garzarelli Investment Management
Chicago, Illinois

Birth Date: October 13, 1951

Education: BA, Drexel University, 1971
MBA, Drexel University, 1977
Doctorate, Drexel University, 1992

Biggest Mistake Investors Make: "Panicking. It causes them to sell at the bottom and buy at the top."

Best Investment: Buying General Motors in 1974. (The shares jumped 150 percent in just a few months.)

Worst Investment: Purchasing steel stocks in early 1977. (They went down 20 percent shortly thereafter.)

Advice: "Unless you're a really good market timer, stay invested."

Market Outlook: Bullish.

SETH GLICKENHAUS

Glickenhaus & Co.

When Seth Glickenhaus graduated from Harvard some 63 years ago he had two choices: He could go to work on Wall Street or enroll at the Columbia Law School. He chose law school, but Herbert Salomon of Salomon Brothers wouldn't take no for an answer. "I agreed to take a job with him for three months under the condition that if it didn't work out, I'd go back to school," Glickenhaus recalls. "It worked out, but I left in 1938 because I was generating about $25,000 a week in profits for the firm, but they were paying me just $48."

Though he still earned his law degree by going to school at night, he started working for a little municipal brokerage shop that went out of business a few months later because, as Glickenhaus puts it, "The owner was a dipsomaniac." His initial reaction was that it served him right for leaving such a cushy future at Salomon. But Glickenhaus and a colleague managed to convince the firm's principals that if they were allowed to take over, they could generate enough business to return the $25,000 they had invested in the company. "They agreed and in a few months we had paid them back and turned it into our own brokerage shop," he recalls. "We ran it through 1946, although I went off to war and my partner took over until I came back." That was when he started what was in effect the first hedge fund. "We set up a deal with our accountant to work for $15,000 a year and to give each limited partner 6 percent up front and 50 percent of all the profits," he says. "If someone had invested $10,000 with us, by the time we wound the fund up 13 years later, they would have walked away with something on the order of $300,000."

By that time, Glickenhaus himself was a multimillionaire and realized his performance to this point would be a tough act to follow. So he decided to get out of Wall Street to become a medical doctor at the age of 46. "I did my premed work at Columbia and was admitted to the Einstein Medical School," he says. "Then the lure of Wall Street got to me. I started my own firm, Glickenhaus & Co. All I did at first was trade for my own account. It was lovely. I had no responsibilities, customers, or limited partners. If I made money, I kept it. I made a lot of money and quit work every day at 3:00 PM. I'd then have the rest of the day to go play squash or visit art galleries. This went on for about ten years."

Then some rich friends asked him to manage their retirement accounts and he agreed. Since that time in 1972, his firm has grown to overseeing $4.7 billion of other people's money. Clearly, Glickenhaus hasn't lost his touch in all of these years. His firm is ranked by Thomson Investment Software as the number one investment management company in the nation over the past ten years, with a cumulative total return of 523 percent, compared to 312 percent for the S&P 500.

Glickenhaus calls himself a cautious investor who is more concerned about downside risk than the quality of earnings. "When I look for a stock, I want to find outstanding management," he reveals. "I'm also very price conscious. I love companies that have come down in value for one reason or another that I feel is invalid. I also like companies with a lot of cash flow that will be used to buy back the stock." Furthermore, he seeks out names that are either industry leaders or low-cost producers, and he wants to buy them for less than intrinsic value, or what a reasonable person would pay if it were broken up and sold. "I also look for stocks selling for very low price-earnings multiples," he adds.

Glickenhaus deals almost exclusively with large-cap stocks, because of the huge amount of money he manages. He has several strict sales disciplines. "Let's assume we buy a stock and we think it's going to go up 60 percent in two years," he explains. "If it does that, and it's not a bargain any more, we'll sell it. Another reason is if a stock goes up too much too fast, we'll get rid of it to avoid losing our gain."

Even though he's about to turn 84, Glickenhaus believes every investor should keep most, if not all, of their money in stocks, not bonds. "Bonds are a very reckless investment," he contends. "But the place to be is not in equities, but in well-chosen equities. There is no such thing as a stock market. There is, however, a market of stocks with the characteristics I've outlined that has enormous potential. The rest, I call them the Rembrandt/Picassos, are overpriced and not worth owning."

Occupation: Senior Partner, Glickenhaus & Co.
New York, New York

Birth Date: March 12, 1914

Education: BA, Harvard College, 1934
LLB, New York University Law School, 1938

Biggest Mistake Investors Make: "Unwittingly putting their money in mutual funds without realizing they have gotten so large in many cases that they have lost their flexibility and are very vulnerable."

Best Investment: Global Marine (Bought for around $2 five years ago, and it's now worth more than $20.)

Worst Investment: An entertainment company (he forgets the name) that went from $23 to zero in 1994.

Advice: "Hunt out good discretionary investment managers, and invest your money in equities."

Market Outlook: Bullish, although he's expecting a pretty flat year.

MICHAEL HIRSCH

Freedom Capital Management

Michael Hirsch was investing in mutual funds long before they were cool. "I started managing money using funds in 1975 and remember I got a 45-minute interview with the assistant pension officer at Chrysler back then trying to get them to give me some of their money to manage," he says. "I spent the first 30 minutes of that time explaining to him what a mutual fund was. He had no idea."

Hirsch is often credited with pioneering the concept of using funds to build an entire investment portfolio. "I saw what was happening with the market even in the 1970s, in terms of volatility and what not, and realized funds were an efficient way to diversify," he recalls. His underlying thesis was that, because institutional investors constantly change their preferences for sectors and styles, you must be ready to shift around at any time, and funds offer the most flexibility. Back when he started out, there were just 125 funds. Today there are more than 8,000 in the United States alone. "There are too many in my opinion," he contends. "Funds are becoming like commodities and that confuses the hell out of the public."

Nevertheless, Hirsch continues to be a big advocate of the fund industry and manages the FundManager family of mutual funds, which invests exclusively in other funds. "Funds are the way to go because the markets are moving more rapidly and the individual has no way to effectively compete with the institutions by going directly into stocks," he argues. "What bothers me is the naivete that's out there. The problem is most people, are new to funds and expect the market to keep going up. They have unrealistic expectations and will bail out at the first sign of trouble." So far, that hasn't happened. But Hirsch isn't the only investment adviser sounding such an alarm of caution.

When choosing funds, Hirsch always prefers the tortoise over the hare. "Slow but steady wins the race," he maintains. "I get nervous when one of my funds winds up in the top 10 percent." He looks at what he calls his "three Ps" when evaluating individual funds: performance, people, and the process. "I want consistent performance over the long term, not spectacular performance over the near term," he explains. "If you look at funds that have stayed in the top half of their peer group for the last three years, that will knock out 90 percent of all candidates."

Next comes people. "I like funds run by individuals, not committees," he says. "I believe investing is an art, not a science. You can't paint the Mona Lisa by committee. I want strong-willed individuals with demonstrated investment management talents who are putting their reputations on the line each day." Hirsch points out that the major difference between managers who oversee private money and those with funds is that a fund manager's record is on public display each day, while private managers are only accountable to their clients, and even then it's not always clear-cut how well they're doing. Additionally, he wants fund managers who can describe their investment style and discipline in 25 words or less, and he demands that they do their own research, instead of turning to analysts from other brokerage firms. "People who rely primarily on third-party research are doomed to mediocrity," Hirsch insists.

The final "P" is the process. "I have to satisfy myself that each manager is bringing a different area of expertise to the totality of our clients' portfolios," he says. "I don't look at labels. I look at the investment approach. That's how you build in the downside protection, because any particular investment will fail at some point."

Hirsch recommends that investors keep at least 10 percent of their portfolio in bonds at all times. Believe it or not, he insists a portfolio can easily have 30 to 40 different stock funds and five to ten bond funds without being overdiversified. "That's because I'm trying to create safe, steady returns," he notes. "I do believe that more is better." He concedes that such an approach prevents him from ever being at the top, in terms of performance, but insists he'll look like a genius during the next bear market. "I do make sure each fund owns different stocks, and I stay in regular contact with all of my managers," he adds. "I'll sell a fund when assets get too big and the manager can't deal with it anymore."

These days, Hirsch works out of both New York and Israel. Although he has three older kids from a previous marriage, he and his wife adopted two young boys and decided to raise them in Israel. The children, ages 9 and 11, live in Tel Aviv year around with their mother. Hirsch flies back and forth from New York every other week. "We felt Israel was a better environment for our family," he shares. "It's a society that really revolves around the children. It's wide open and nourishing for kids. People who have visited Israel tell me it's what small town America was 30 years ago."

Occupation: Portfolio Manager, Freedom Capital Management
New York, New York

Birth Date: February 7, 1945

Education: BA, Brooklyn College, 1966

Biggest Mistake Investors Make: "Buying at the top and selling at the bottom."

Best Investment: Won't say, to avoid offending any of his managers.

Worst Investment: Won't reveal this one either for the same reason.

Advice: "Have a long-term perspective, buy a good basket of funds, and stick with them."

Market Outlook: Cautious.

KEVIN LANDIS

Technology Value Fund

It sounds somewhat ironic to hear Kevin Landis talk about how Warren Buffett and Peter Lynch are his biggest heroes. After all, Landis runs a technology fund, and both Buffett and Lynch generally avoid investing in such companies. Unlike Landis, these two luminaries admit they don't understand what many high-tech firms do. But Landis maintains the investment principles they espouse work like a charm. "I believe in having my cake and eating it, too," Landis says. "I like companies with substantial growth prospects, but want to avoid paying high multiples for them."

Landis is a relative newcomer to the field of investing, yet his Technology Value Fund has produced chart-topping returns, turning in gains in excess of 60 percent in both 1995 and 1996. Landis was born and raised in California's Silicon Valley, home to many of the world's leading technology companies. He studied electrical engineering and computer science in college, before getting his MBA and landing a job as a semiconductor analyst for a high-tech market research firm. "I learned how to rigorously analyze fast-changing markets," he says. "But I got itchy to dive back into technology, so I went to work for a chip company called S-MOS as their new products marketing manager."

While at S-MOS, he began dabbling in stocks on the side and realized he was making more money from trading than he found in his weekly paycheck. "I determined my true calling was to be investing in technology," he claims. "So I left S-MOS in the summer of 1993, and my partner and I started this new company."

His partner, Ken Kam, who owned a medical-device company, is also somewhat of a virgin to the stock business. The two have been friends for years, since forming an investment club in 1987. "Stock picking had been a passion of ours for many years," Landis says. "We sat down over Christmas at the end of 1992 and decided to start an investment firm. It took awhile for us to get up and running since neither of us had any direct experience in the industry."

Because the two wanted to make their investment services available to a large number of professionals in the technology field, they decided to start a mutual fund. The fund invests in two primary sectors: electronics and medical technology. Landis manages the electronic side, while Kam is in charge of picking the medical stocks. "When we finally got our SEC clearance (in May 1994), the money that came in was strictly from people who knew us and had confidence in us," Landis says. "Now, it's coming in as a result of our strong performance and style."

Unlike most technology funds, which are willing to pay dizzying multiples for fast-growing companies, Kam and Landis want to buy their stocks on the cheap. "We look for securities that are mispriced," he explains. "We pay attention to all of the normal value statistics, like price-to-earnings, price-to-sales, and the total market capitalizations for companies that aren't making any money."

Management is also important, although Landis contends that when it comes right down to it, customers don't buy managers or PEs—they buy products. "Companies that demonstrate they can come up with the right products at the right price points at the right time are the real winners," he maintains. "So we find our favorite companies and then have a patient eye for value, meaning we will only buy when we can get a stock at the right price." He is also patient with his investments and is willing to give companies time to make their products successful.

"There are two good reasons to sell a stock," he offers. "One is simple outrageous appreciation, to where you can't make a case for buying or even holding it anymore. Another is when you are incorrect in your initial analysis and realize a stock is not worth owning in the first place."

Landis maintains that two of the primary advantages he has over his competitors are his strategic location and industry contacts. "There aren't any other mutual funds headquartered in the Silicon Valley," he points out. "We are also set up in such a way that our investors can continually educate us and bring new ideas to our attention, which they do. Superior information is the most important edge you can have."

Occupation: Portfolio Manager, Technology Value Fund
San Jose, California

Birth Date: April 28, 1961

Education: BS, University of California at Berkeley, 1983
MBA, Santa Clara University, 1988

Biggest Mistake Investors Make: "Trying to time the market."

Best Investment: Iomega (Bought in late 1994 for a split-adjusted $4 a share, and sold out from $35 to $48 within six months.)

Worst Investment: Silicon Valley Research (Purchased in 1996 for $4 to $5, and it dropped down to $1 within a few months.)

Advice: "Don't let market volatility discourage you from investing in the technology sector."

Market Outlook: Bullish. "My prediction is the world will have a greater need for the products technology companies produce by the end of 1998 than at the beginning, but I could have said this about any of the past 20 years and felt pretty comfortable I'd be right."

VIVIAN LEWIS

Global Investing

Vivian Lewis once lived a life most journalists only dream about. She was a foreign correspondent who covered stories throughout Western Europe during the 1960s and 1970s, living in London, Brussels, and France. Like most who wind up with glamorous jobs, she got into the business by accident. After graduating with a history degree from Radcliffe in 1962 at the age of 20, she planned on a career in academia. "I got married to a foreign correspondent while I was working on my PhD thesis, and we ran out of money," she explains. "I didn't think a married woman should ask for tuition assistance from her dad, so I took a job with *Business Week* as an office assistant. A year and a half later, I was bureau chief in Brussels."

But when Lewis got pregnant with her first child, she was immediately fired. "When I say this today, people ask why I didn't sue them," she notes. "They told me if I sued them I would never get another job in journalism, and I believed them. I was scared to make waves about being treated badly." Fortunately, she managed to land back on her feet, and went on to work for such publications as *The Economist* and *Institutional Investor*, writing about foreign companies and the financial markets. The magazines were thrilled to have her on retainer because she was stationed overseas, which saved them on travel costs.

"When my husband was posted back in the United States by his employer *The New York Times* nine years ago, I went sashaying in to the *Institutional Investor* offices and said, 'Hi, I'm here.' Their faces dropped. I told them this was their opportunity to make use of my brilliant European connections in the United States. They replied, 'We're not going to send you to Europe and let you run up expense accounts. It was great having you write for us while you were over there and we could get you cheap, but now it's a different story.'" Lewis looked in the mirror and realized she was in her 40s and not immediately employable. "The reason I started *Global Investing* is because I decided there was a niche in the market and I needed a job," she admits. "I was covering this stuff for the institutional market, but wanted to cover it for U.S. retail investors who were not and still are not being given any information about internationalizing their portfolios."

Global Investing is a monthly newsletter that highlights select foreign stocks that trade as ADRs in the United States. "ADR stands for American Depositary Receipt," Lewis points out. "These were invented in the period right after the first World War for a specific purpose—for foreign-based companies to raise money on the U.S. capital markets. Shares of securities from these overseas companies are deposited in a foreign bank, and a U.S. bank creates a certificate to prove they are there. You then trade the receipts, which settle in the United States under the same system as U.S. stocks." Lewis still does a fair amount of traveling to uncover new ideas, but she also has a team of freelance reporters from around the world who contribute stories and ideas to her publication.

While Lewis is a big advocate of foreign investing, she cautions against buying shares directly through overseas markets, as opposed to using ADRs. "Most people do not have custodial accounts on foreign exchanges," she reasons. "If you want to buy foreign stocks over ADRs, there are all kinds of obstacles for retail investors. The minimum trades are much higher in foreign markets, and they don't like limit orders. Plus, you don't get 1099s nor the same kind of information regarding quarterly and annual results as you do with the ADRs. You're also not treated as well when it comes to rights offerings and stock splits."

Admittedly, it's not easy getting good information about a company in another country when you live thousands of miles away. That's why Lewis, who speaks several foreign languages, calls evaluating ADRs more of an art than a science. "For one thing, you should know more about the country and other stocks in the industry when considering a foreign stock," she advises. But why take such risk? Isn't it a hassle to research and find foreign companies? Wouldn't it be better to just keep your portfolio invested solely in U.S. stocks that you could keep a close eye on? "No," Lewis says. "You shouldn't put all of your eggs in one basket," she points out. "Two-thirds of the stocks in the world are outside the United States. It's idiotic to ignore them. I think people should have one-quarter to one-third of their portfolio invested overseas."

Occupation: Publisher, *Global Investing*
New York, New York

Birth Date: June 19, 1951

Education: BA, Radcliffe College, 1962
MA, University of California at Berkeley, 1963

Biggest Mistake Investors Make: "Not taking profits."

Best Investment: The Japan Fund (Bought it while living in Europe throughout the 1980s. Her earliest investments had returns of some 5,000 percent.)

Worst Investment: Corimon (a paint company from Venezuela). She paid $5.35 on average per share at the end of 1995 and has been unable to sell it because trading was suspended.

Advice: "Don't let taxes determine your investment strategy. Pay the taxes and take the profits."

Market Outlook: Bearish on the United States, but more optimistic about Europe and Japan.

BOB MARKMAN

Markman Capital Management

Bob Markman is hoping to cash in on the seemingly endless stream of new mutual funds popping up these days. While funds used to be a simple alternative to investing in individual stocks and bonds, today there are more than 8,000 to choose from. That means finding good funds has become more complicated and difficult than ever, and with new offerings being introduced each day, it's only going to get tougher. Markman is convinced this will lead to a proliferation of what are known as "fund of funds"—mutual funds that invest in other funds. Instead of choosing ten different stock funds on your own, you can simply put your money into an aggressive growth fund of funds, for example, and let the manager research and select the underlying funds for you. Markman runs three such fund of funds for conservative, moderate, and aggressive investors.

"The fund of funds concept is starting to catch on, but it's taking a while for both the public and media to figure out what this stuff is," he says. "People don't know whether it's just another fund for their portfolio or a substitute for professional management." Markman views it as a little of both. "It's for the do-it-yourself investor who wants some help," he says. "It lets them buy professional management without entering into a marriage contract." Markman also notes that to hire him directly, it takes at least $500,000. But you can get into one of his funds for much less.

If things had been different, Markman might be managing the futures of some big Hollywood stars instead of mutual fund portfolios. After graduating from Northwestern University, he worked at the William Morris Agency before leaving to pursue a career in advertising. In 1980, he became fascinated with the financial planning field, which at that point was still in its infancy. So he took a job selling load funds with Private Ledger. The idea of charging his customers a commission each time they purchased a fund never made sense to him, especially after the crash of 1987. "It occurred to me that, even if someone had shown me *The Wall Street Journal* two weeks in advance, and I could've known there was a crash coming, I couldn't have done anything about it," he reflects. "I had all my clients' money in load funds and didn't have the discretion." That prompted him to go out on his own, managing money through no-load funds on a fee-only basis. Today he oversees some $400 million, half of which is invested in his fund of funds.

Portfolio building for Markman revolves around what he calls the "daisy" concept. In the center of the daisy, which accounts for roughly 60 percent of the overall total, he selects a few long-term, reliable performers with good managers. The remaining petals consist of more speculative funds that may be traded with greater frequency. The whole process begins by uncovering the best places to be invested. "We look at our fund portfolio as a team of players with different roles," he explains. Once he's determined which roles he needs to fill, he searches for the best players. This usually calls for finding funds with strong current relative strength compared to their peers. He then digs a little deeper to see if that performance can be sustained.

Unlike some of his colleagues, Markman spends little time interviewing individual fund managers, although he concedes the person pulling the trigger is important. "The dirty secret of this business is that it's rare to find a manager who is a real jerk," he reveals. "They are all very sharp guys. The benefits of interviewing managers might be outweighed by the risk of falling for a relationship with them."

Markman's funds and private accounts used to experience a high degree of turnover from week to week. But not anymore. He claims to have reduced the number of trades he makes each year by 50 to 80 percent. "We did a study and found we would have been better off buying funds on New Year's Eve and holding them for an entire year, instead of constantly switching around," he shares. "Sometimes we know too much for our own good in the short term. I won't buy a fund unless I think I can own it for at least a year, although that doesn't mean I will." Because he has become less heavy-handed, Markman insists his returns have dramatically improved.

Markman invests all of his own personal money in funds, noting that the last stock he bought ten years ago went bankrupt. He also says the best thing investors can do is look for long-term consistent returns, instead of constantly trying to find the hot fund of the moment. "If people invest on a regular basis and make 10 to 15 percent a year, they'll have more money than they'll know what to do with," he adds.

Occupation: President, Markman Capital Management
Edina, Minnesota

Birth Date: August 20, 1951

Education: BA, Northwestern University, 1973

Biggest Mistake Investors Make: "Taking too much risk and not diversifying enough."

Best Investment: SoGen International Fund (He still owns it.)

Worst Investment: Benham European Government Bond Fund (He bought it in September 1992, 48 hours before the European exchange rate mechanism fell apart. The investment lost about 9 percent of its value in three weeks.)

Advice: "Diversify, cancel your *Wall Street Journal* subscription, and spend more time with your kids."

Market Outlook: Bullish.

CAPPY McGARR

McGarr Capital Management

Who says a small-town boy from Texas can't make big money in the stock market? Certainly not Cappy McGarr's well-heeled clients. The Dallas hedge fund manager has generated annualized returns of almost 27 percent over the past ten years. He's also ranked the number one U.S. growth and value equity manager in the nation by *Nelson's Directory of Investment Managers.* Not bad considering that McGarr had no career goals growing up, let alone a desire to invest. "In San Angelo, Texas, where I was raised, I don't think we'd ever heard of stocks," he quips.

McGarr wound up on Wall Street almost by accident. He majored in both journalism and government in college, but found the jobs he was qualified for didn't pay much. So he decided to go back to school for an MBA and landed a job with Goldman Sachs after graduation. After spending about 12 months in New York, the firm sent him back to Dallas. Four years later, he decided to go into business for himself. Today, it takes at least $5 million to get into his hedge fund. He presently has some $160 million under management.

Originally, McGarr raised money for various private deals. He started the hedge fund in 1984. It's clearly not as exotic as some. He doesn't get involved with currencies, commodities, futures, or derivatives. Instead, he invests primarily in large-cap, household names, with an average market capitalization of $11 billion, because of the liquidity they offer. The most adventurous thing he does is short anywhere from 5 to 40 percent of the portfolio, although he maintains it makes sense to always have a bias toward the long side.

"Over time, managements get up every day to make shareholders money," he reasons. "They may execute a wrong strategy, be in a bad business or be unintelligent. But if they have integrity and are trying to do what's right, the only goal management should have is to increase shareholder value."

McGarr believes earnings are what ultimately drive the price of a stock. But the people in charge are also important, and he checks to make sure their interests are aligned with his. "We spend a lot of time looking at management and what they own of their own company," he says. "We want to see what stock options they have and how much stock they are mandated to own. That's very important because obviously if management owns stock, they're going to have the same interests as the shareholders because they are shareholders."

In addition, a strong financial standing and reasonable share price is essential. "A solid cash flow and earnings growth rate is very important to us," McGarr maintains. "If you can find companies that are selling below their growth rate, by definition you're going to be buying a stock that's cheap. We try to purchase stocks that are selling below their growth rate. In other words, their PE sells at a discount to their growth rate."

A final requirement for every stock McGarr owns is it must be a proven leader. "We like companies that have a dominant market share and are number one or two in the areas they deal in," he says. "We find all of this out by constantly poring over research, reading periodicals, and running computer screens."

These elements are so essential because McGarr runs a highly concentrated portfolio of just 10 to 15 names on both the long and short side. "Over time, this has helped us to substantially outperform the S&P," he points out. "We try to earn a 20 percent net return for our investors each year. In order to achieve that goal, we attempt to make sure each stock in the portfolio can go up at least 25 percent in a year." Although he hasn't always achieved that goal, McGarr has never had a down year.

His latest project is starting a new small-cap hedge fund. "A lot of times, we'll find stocks that are very compelling either on the long or short side, but they don't have the liquidity we need," he explains. "So we're going to close the new fund at $100 million and will be investing in companies with market capitalizations of less than $750 million."

McGarr says his other full-time job is taking care of his wife and two young daughters. "One of my girls likes sports, and the other will either be president or a stand-up comic," he quips. She may have inherited that talent from her dad, because in college McGarr used to do some 35 different voices for a radio show. Today, he claims, the only voice he uses on a regular basis is his own.

Occupation: President, McGarr Capital Management
Dallas, Texas

Birth Date: August 1, 1951

Education: BA, University of Texas at Austin, 1973/1975
MBA, University of Texas at Austin, 1977

Biggest Mistake Investors Make: "Having a lack of patience."

Best Investment: Dell Computer (one of *Wall Street's Picks for 1998*).

Worst Investment: PageNet (Bought in 1996 for $19 and finally sold out several months later for just $10.)

Advice: "Do your homework and have a list of criteria that you think are important to determine value."

Market Outlook: Bullish, assuming earnings remain strong and inflation is kept in check.

MICHAEL MURPHY

California Technology Stock Letter

Could it be that Michael Murphy is about to leave Wall Street for Hollywood? The *California Technology Stock Letter* editor and mutual fund manager's second passion in life is producing feature films. His first flick, titled "Llamathon," is in the can and looking for a distributor. Murphy produced the film with his partner, in both business and life, Lissa Morgenthaler. It deals with, what else, but a technological breakthrough. "It's about a guy who has cancer, and his sister gets him into a biotechnology clinical trial to try and cure it," he says. "The guy raises llamas, and at the end of the film, he's able to run in a race called a Llamathon, which is a real event on the California coast."

Of course, Murphy's not about to quit his day job just yet. He started investing in technology stocks as a computer programmer with American Express in 1968. He was asked to analyze the company's investment operations and spent 18 months researching the stock market to better understand his assignment. A short time later, he was tapped to become a computer analyst, and ultimately wound up on the investment committee managing money.

He launched the newsletter in 1981 after spotting an unfulfilled need in the area of technology stock research. "There was really nothing for individuals that provided fundamental analysis of these companies," he recalls. Murphy now covers both computer-electronics and what he calls "medtech-biotech" companies, noting that there's a big difference between the two. "On the medtech-biotech side, you are dealing with development-stage firms," he explains. "In the electronics and computer area, you don't mess around with development-stage companies."

That's because there's a real model and path set up for getting legitimate electronics companies funded and profitable before they go public, most commonly with the help of venture capitalists. But such support isn't normally available to biotechnology companies, and they often have no choice but to offer stock. "It costs so much money to develop a drug and there is no way for venture capitalists to keep these things private through to profitability," Murphy contends. "They take them public early, but keep a close eye on them to make sure they stay on track."

On the computer-electronics side, Murphy wants to buy companies that show at least 15 percent annual growth in both profitability and return on equity. However, he's somewhat of a bargain hunter and only willing to pay a fair price. To determine what that is, he begins by calculating a potential candidate's "growth flow" rate, which represents earnings plus research and development per share. He then calculates the share price-to-growth flow rate, and if the result is ten or less, the stock is usually a buy. Ironically, the more a company spends on R&D, the less Wall Street usually likes it because it depresses current earnings. Murphy has a different opinion. "R&D is where new products come from," he insists. "New products are what create all this sales growth, regardless of what the economy's doing, and usually new products carry higher profit margins."

Murphy has another approach for evaluating medtech-biotech companies, which he points out carry more risk. "The capital markets pay people to assume risk, and these are clearly risky development-stage companies," he says. "But when they ultimately succeed, you can make 30 to 40 percent per year compound rates of return." Unfortunately, you can't use the growth-flow exercise to evaluate attractiveness, because most of these companies don't have any earnings. "So we have a measure that we call the 'M-score,'" he offers. "We look at how much money they've spent on research and development in the last five years and add that up." He then examines the stock's total market capitalization. The ratio between the market capitalization to R&D gives him the stock's M-score. "In normal times, this ratio will be eight to ten, which is fair," he says. "On the other hand, in tough times, it will fall to three or five. The lower the M-score, the better."

Other things to look for when evaluating technology companies, according to Murphy, are the quality of each company's scientific advisory board (it should be composed of prominent, well-published names) and whether they have any blue chip marketing partners. But the bottom line, as is often the case when it comes to investing, is to use common sense. "If a company makes something that you think is goofy, whatever it is, don't mess with it," Murphy cautions.

Occupation: Editor, *California Technology Stock Letter*
Half Moon Bay, California

Birth Date: December 29, 1941

Education: BA, Harvard College, 1963

Biggest Mistake Investors Make: "Acting without information. Buying on tips and not even getting an annual report."

Best Investment: Chiron (Bought it at $1 seven years ago and now it's around $20.)

Worst Investment: Telios Pharmaceuticals (Purchased for $8 and it ultimately went bankrupt.)

Advice: "Buy stocks in a growth universe but use value criteria. Don't try to make money in things that aren't growing, but don't get sucked into the momentum investment theory."

Market Outlook: Bullish, especially on technology stocks.

WILLIAM NASGOVITZ

Heartland Advisors

There's no question that in strong bull markets, like the one we've been in for the past several years, growth investing is a lot of fun. But over time, Bill Nasgovitz is convinced that value techniques will produce greater profits. "Value investing has stood the test of time," he says. "It's what one of my colleagues calls the 'sleep well' investment philosophy. This means the growth guys will probably beat you in up markets, but you'll sleep well in down markets knowing you'll eventually make money because there's substance behind your stocks."

Nasgovitz began investing as a teenager, using paper route money to buy shares in companies based in his hometown of Milwaukee. He's always been a fan of undiscovered opportunities, which is what originally led him to mine for stocks in waters few others dare to wade. As manager of the Heartland Value Fund, he's an expert at investing in micro-caps, which he defines as equities having market capitalizations of less than $100 million. While it may seem there aren't a lot of choices in this area, the opposite is true. Nasgovitz notes that of the 14,000 or so publicly traded companies out there, around 90 percent meet his criterion in terms of market value.

After spending time after college as a broker at Dean Witter, he started his own investment firm in 1982. His company suffered greatly during the crash of 1987. However, he quickly recovered, founding Heartland Advisors in 1988. The firm now manages more than $2 billion in both private accounts and several mutual funds. Although Nasgovitz continues to focus on micro-caps, he has expanded his firm's list of offerings to include large- and mid-cap stocks as well. "I like micro-caps because they represent the fastest growing part of the U.S. economy," he says. "These stocks perform best over the long term, and it's a joy finding something that nobody else knows about." Indeed, although Wall Street is starting to give these tiny gems more attention, they remain in relative oblivion compared to their larger brethren.

Nasgovitz traces his entrenched value investment philosophy back to the bear market of 1973–1974, when the Dow crumbled and the average stock plummeted by 70 percent. He reread Benjamin Graham's work and vowed to only buy stocks based on a list of specific value parameters. "Low PE, low price-to-cash flow, low price-to-book value, financial soundness, things like that," he explains. "What we're trying to do is capitalize on the upside potential of small stocks, but limit the downside risk."

He locates candidates through all sorts of channels. He and his analysts look for such characteristics as financial soundness, positive earnings dynamics, high insider ownership, capable management, hidden analysts, and some kind of catalyst in each company they consider. They have built up a library of micro-cap ideas over the years and revisit it from time to time to see if their value parameters have been met. They also get hundreds of external research reports each year.

"We're looking for companies that not only have a value safety net, but also have upside potential," Nasgovitz says. He notes that stocks in this area generally have a small number of outstanding shares, so prices can gyrate tremendously from day-to-day, making them much more volatile than larger companies. That's why he admits individual investors need to own at least two dozen different micro-cap stocks to have a properly diversified portfolio. His value fund has 260 names.

"This is a very inefficient market and prices rarely equate the true worth of a company," he adds. "We like to discover companies selling for a ridiculous price." Although he's a fundamental analyst, Nasgovitz always views stock charts to see where a company has been, and therefore, its potential once the price recovers. He likes to buy at bases and sell into uptrends. Nasgovitz rarely touches initial public offerings, although he files them away for consideration down the line after the excitement has subsided.

Nasgovitz admits his discipline requires patience, because the market often takes time to recognize value. But he's willing to wait up to two years to see a story unfold as expected. If nothing happens by then, chances are he'll take his money off the table and move on. He'll also sell once a stock's value is realized and it moves from being undervalued to overpriced. To thaw out from the cold Milwaukee winters, Nasgovitz recently bought a home in Santa Barbara, California, where he has set up a new office. "I love the weather, and you can actually grow a garden there," he exclaims.

Occupation: President and Chairman, Heartland Advisors
Milwaukee, Wisconsin

Birth Date: October 8, 1944

Education: BA, University of Wisconsin—Madison, 1966

Biggest Mistake Investors Make: "Not paying attention to what's going on in the bond market."

Best Investment: Payco (First bought the stock for $4 in 1980, and those shares eventually went up to $40 within three years.)

Worst Investment: Mid-America Waste (Bought for $4 a share in the late 1980s and eventually sold out a couple of years later for $1 before it went bankrupt.)

Advice: "Pay attention to competitive returns in the bond market, and equate those returns to earnings yields from stocks."

Market Outlook: Cautious, and hoping for a correction.

LOUIS NAVELLIER

Navellier & Associates

Why do professional managers have such a hard time keeping up with the S&P 500 index? Louis Navellier has one explanation. The ace stock picker, newsletter editor, and mutual fund manager says all but 22 stocks in the S&P are efficiently priced, which makes it tough for any one person to gain a competitive edge. That's why he's devoted his life to finding those names at the opposite end of the spectrum. "Stocks usually get inefficiently priced because of the flow of funds," he says. "Any time a stock's being discovered or institutionalized for the first time, or when Wall Street hasn't properly discounted the fundamentals, it is inefficiently priced."

That's why Navellier has always focused primarily on small-caps, which are often neglected by the major institutions. He determines whether a stock is inefficiently priced or not by looking at its so-called alpha factor. "A stock's return correlated to the market from week to week over the past year is the beta, and the return uncorrelated to the market is this mysterious alpha factor," he explains. "There are a lot of stocks out there that are totally correlated to the market, and 85 percent of big-cap stocks have alphas at or near zero."

Navellier first began honing his investment skills as a finance student in the late 1970s. He didn't buy the conventional wisdom that the stock market was always efficient. "I knew back then there were money managers beating the market," he recalls. So, with the help of two professors, he developed several computer models to prove he was right. It's a system he has refined over the years and still uses today. "We're continuously testing and monitoring what works on Wall Street and rebuilding our models," he says. "I'm really more of a modeler than anything else."

In other words, Navellier uses his computer to find out which stocks the majority of investors are in love with at the present time. His theory is that if you want to beat the market, you must buy stocks that aren't simply moving in tandem with it. He puts his database of 7,000 stocks through several bottom-up screens each week. Predictably, he starts off by calculating each company's alpha factor. "We then take the alpha, divide it by a stock's volatility and get a reward/risk ratio," he says. "The quantitative screens are designed to stack the odds in our favor and that's what we try to do. The whole process is automated. There's no subjective judgment to it at all."

The computer puts his entire list of stocks through 23 back-testing models, which check various ratios such as price-to-book, dividend discount, cash flow, and PE, along with earnings momentum. "We're trying to find what Wall Street likes fundamentally (at any given point in time) because what it likes does change," Navellier reasons. "We're overlaying fundamental anomalies on my high alpha stocks to tilt the odds in my favor." Based on the results of this and the risk/reward ratio calculation, the computer sorts each stock in terms of relative attractiveness and the top 10 percent form Navellier's buy list.

As a final step, he uses an optimization model to determine how to mix and match the final list of stocks to get the highest returns with the least amount of risk. "The model will often say put 5 percent in this stock, 2 percent in this stock, 3 percent in this stock, and so forth," Navellier reveals. "What it's trying to do is find stocks that complement each other and represent different industry groups, while attempting to lower the overall volatility."

Navellier is always highly diversified and has a strong discipline, keeping his average holding a mere six to eight months. "Typically, when I buy a stock, I'll watch it move up in price," he says. "As it moves up, it tends to become risky. My allocation model will tell me to cut back on it, not because it's a bad stock, but because it's getting increasingly risky and less predictable."

Admittedly, Navellier's strategy is hard for individual investors to follow, because it's based on a proprietary computer model. That's why he publishes his research in his monthly *MPT Review*, which is ranked as the top-performing newsletter by *The Hulbert Financial Digest* over the past ten years. Navellier also manages a series of mutual funds that follow his quantitative strategy. So what does Wall Street like right now? "Earnings surprises," Navellier shares. "Earnings momentum is also coming back into vogue as liquidity improves."

Occupation: President and CEO, Navellier & Associates
Reno, Nevada

Birth Date: November 22, 1957

Education: BA, California State University, Hayward, 1978
MBA, California State University, Hayward, 1979

Biggest Mistake Investors Make: "Getting emotional and holding on for too long. You should sell good stocks to buy better stocks."

Best Investment: Ascend Communications (He first bought the stock in mid-1995, and it jumped more than 530 percent in ten months.)

Worst Investment: Digitran Systems (It suspended trading and ultimately went down to zero.)

Advice: "Be very diversified and balanced. As stocks increase in risk, you should cut back on them."

Market Outlook: Bullish.

JAMES O'SHAUGHNESSY

O'Shaughnessy Capital Management

The only way to be consistently successful in the stock market is by tirelessly following a proven investment strategy no matter what. That's the conclusion of Jim O'Shaugnessy, who back-tested various strategies over a 40-year period to see which techniques came out on top. "There is underlying empirical evidence that shows there are certain ways that work very well, and others that perform very poorly," he says. "For example, every strategy that bought high-priced stocks, in terms of what you had to pay for sales and earnings, underperformed during the period I examined."

Why is it so important to stick with a strategy? For the same reason doctors tell their patients not to smoke, O'Shaughnessy explains. "They know there is underlying empirical evidence that proves smoking is bad for your health. The same is true for investing. If you don't stick with a strategy, and just go with the hunch of the moment, you're going to be an accidental investor thinking with your heart rather than your head."

O'Shaughnessy should know. He first learned the perils of investing by using his heart after graduating from college. He had some money in the bank and decided to make a living by trading options, which was a disaster. "I realized how difficult it was to trade well over long periods of time," he shares. "I started doing some research and it indicated that the people who made piles of money were investors, not traders. After coming out whole, I changed my focus and became an investor."

He started his own money management firm in 1988 and recently launched a series of mutual funds that follow the various strategies he has found work well over time. One follows a version of the popular "Dogs of the Dow" technique, which calls for buying the ten highest yielding stocks in the Dow Jones Industrial Average and holding them for exactly one year. Then you go through the process all over again and replace any names that no longer make the grade. "How often does Dogs of the Dow beat the S&P 500?" O'Shaughnessy asks. "Almost 97 percent of the time over rolling ten-year periods." This technique has gained widespread publicity in recent years and is no longer the secret it once was. But O'Shaughnessy insists this strategy is still extremely valid. "The fact that billions of dollars are going into these stocks alone can probably make up for that fact that the Dogs are yielding less than they used to," he surmises. "You also have to remember that people may claim they're using the strategy, but many don't stick to it religiously like they're supposed to."

If you have access to a computer, and are looking for a more sophisticated technique that works well over time, you should consider what he calls his "price momentum strategy." "Stick with low price-to-sales ratios and high relative strength," he advises. "In other words, buy cheap stocks that have done well on a price appreciation basis. You limit yourself to the stocks in your database with a price-to-sales ratio below 1, PE under 20, or price-to-book ratio below 1, which are all indications a stock is cheap. You then marry that to strong price performance over the previous year. What you're doing is buying a stock the market may have hated, but is starting to change its mind about." This strategy turned a $10,000 investment in 1951 into $14 million by the end of 1994. During that same period, a similar investment in the S&P 500 only grew to $1 million. O'Shaughnessy also emphasizes the importance of diversification. For him, this means owning at least 50 different stocks, although he says individuals with smaller portfolios can do well with around 25 different names.

As for company fundamentals, he looks at management, new products, or other factors that could foretell its future prospects, O'Shaughnessy claims that's all worthless information for investors. "Study after study proves that when you put too much emphasis on that stuff, you end up doing worse in the end," he insists. "There are two ways to invest: the proud way and the humble way. The proud way is how most of us invest. We think we're smarter and better than everyone else and can make selections on a stock-by-stock basis. That doesn't work, and 80 percent of all managers can't even beat the S&P 500. The humble way recognizes that no one of us is as smart as all of us. So it searches for empirical evidence and sticks with what works. The human forecaster always loses, but models never vary."

Occupation: President, O'Shaughnessy Capital Management
Greenwich, Connecticut

Birth Date: March 24, 1960

Education: BA, University of Minnesota, 1985

Biggest Mistake Investors Make: "Letting their emotions make decisions for them, and thinking with their hearts, rather than their heads."

Best Investment: The time he spent writing and researching his best-selling book *What Works on Wall Street.* (It brought him more than $100 million in new business from readers who were impressed with his work.)

Worst Investment: Buying an insurance company stock at age 22 because of a takeover rumor. (He lost more than 30 percent of his money in a short period of time).

Advice: "Stick with a superior strategy that has been proven over long periods of time."

Market Outlook: Bullish on the prospects of the stock market consistently providing returns of around 10 percent a year.

JOHN ROGERS

Ariel Capital Management

As a kid growing up in Chicago's Hyde Park area, John Rogers always looked forward to Christmas and his birthday. That's because starting at the age of 12, he knew he would get stock in a blue chip company as a gift from his dad. "As the years went by, I started to get more and more interested in reading annual reports and the stock market letters that my father subscribed to," he recalls. "It was fun."

Rogers's dad was a lawyer by profession. He's a judge in the juvenile court system today. But he had an important reason for giving his son stock certificates instead of toys. "Dad felt that his peers in the African-American community didn't know about the stock market," Rogers explains. "It was important to him that his son didn't grow up with that hole in his learning." Rogers clearly learned his lesson well. At the age of 18, his dad gave him total control over the portfolio, which is when he began to think about investing as a possible career. He majored in economics at Princeton and started off in the business as a stockbroker with William Blair & Company. But he never liked that job very much. "I was already developing my own investment strategy that was based on long-term patient value-oriented investing," he says. "Being in the brokerage industry didn't really make sense. You had to make transactions happen in order to get paid, which forced you to only think about the short term."

Two years later, he and a friend decided to join forces and start their own investment management firm. "We opened an office on Michigan Avenue in Chicago with the dream of starting a money management and mutual fund company," he remembers. "The thing we had going for us is we were both lifelong Chicagoans, so we knew a lot of people and could get in some doors." The two went to parents, family, friends, and their brokerage clients to raise seed capital before launching the Ariel Fund, which at the time was legally run as a partnership. "It was a way of building a track record," he concedes. "Starting in the summer of 1983, I had about $500,000 under management. Every quarter after that I would go to prospective clients and say, 'I'm 24 years old, but here's how I've done, and this is what you will get if you hire me.'" Today he oversees more than $1.5 billion in private accounts and mutual funds.

"We call ourselves value investors," he says. "There are three things we focus on. First, we want stocks that are cheap and out of favor. We look at the PE and price-to-cash ratios first. Then we try to figure out what a reasonable person would pay for the business if it were to be sold." Interestingly enough, Rogers claims to find most of his investment ideas through reading. "I read all of the business publications that are out there, as well as mutual fund newsletters and books," he reveals. "I am constantly searching for companies and industries that are doing well." However, some of his best buys come from reading stories about companies that are having trouble. If an article is negative on a stock, Rogers will often get an itch to check it out further

"We spend a lot of time trying to truly understand the management team of every company we consider," he says. "We want to know all we can about their background, where they were educated, where they worked before, what roots they have in their community and what they've accomplished. My experience has been that when you encounter any type of disaster down the line, it's usually because of a problem with management."

In addition, Rogers puts each company through a series of social screens. "They revolve around the fact that we stay away from industries we do not think are right for us long term," he reasons. "We stay away from tobacco stocks and those that aren't environmentally friendly. We don't think tobacco is a growing industry and are convinced companies that aren't concerned about the environment will have a hard time being successful. We also try to be sure that there's a culture in the companies we invest in that appreciates diversity. But the bottom line is that we believe these social screens will lead us to making better investment decisions."

Ariel's motto is "slow and steady wins the race," which alludes to Rogers's aversion to pulling the trigger. "The major reason we'll sell a stock is when we lose confidence in the quality of the product being produced or management's ability to grow the business at above average rates over the next three to five years," he adds. "We strongly believe that patience is what wins in our business. You find a good company and hold it forever. The message is 'think long term.'"

Occupation: President, Ariel Capital Management
Chicago, Illinois

Birth Date: March 31, 1958

Education: BA, Princeton University, 1980

Biggest Mistake Investors Make: "Always looking backwards and picking stocks and funds that did well yesterday, thinking they'll do well in the future."

Best Investment: T. Rowe Price (Started buying after the crash of 1987 at $5 per share. It's been as high as $54 since then, and he still owns it.)

Worst Investment: Payless Cashways (Began purchasing in the spring of 1993 at $13. Sold it for $2 in 1996.)

Advice: "Look forward. Find fund managers that have done well in many markets over the long term, and stick with them."

Market Outlook: Bearish.

ERIC ROSEMAN

Global Mutual Fund Investor

If you think it's bad that there are some 8,000 mutual funds here in the United States, consider that there are about 42,000 of them around the world. "Without question, we have far too many funds right now," contends Eric Roseman, editor of the *Global Mutual Fund Investor* newsletter. "The fact is, more money has flowed into mutual funds since 1991 than in all of the years since 1966 combined. The key to finding good funds is focusing on the world's best management companies and weeding out the rest." In addition to writing his monthly publication, Roseman manages money for offshore corporations and entities using a combination of hedge funds and mutual funds from his office in Canada.

Roseman has been bearish on U.S. stocks for a long time. He's convinced his pessimism will turn into reality once the Federal Reserve begins to aggressively raise interest rates. "It's happening already," he insists. "This is going to do damage to all dollar-denominated markets. It's a normal process called a correction. You've got an overvaluation problem that you have to deal with."

He's also convinced investors are too euphoric and complacent about their equity investments. "I'm seeing a lot of elderly people who are 80 percent in stocks," he says. "They're way overweighted. You have to be a sophisticated investor today. When you look around and see how well you've done over the past seven years, you must realize it's time to be careful."

You could certainly argue that Roseman is too young to be so cynical. At 31, he's the youngest member of this year's panel. Surprisingly, though, he's as concerned about the plethora of inexperienced managers in charge of funds today as many of the old-timers who have been on Wall Street for decades. "It's extremely important that you stick with proven people who have been around the block and experienced up and down markets," he advises. "There are far too many young guys managing all of this money."

Roseman is a graduate of McGill University in Montreal. He began his career doing global research for a private Canadian investment holding company. Since then, he's developed his own strategy that combines undervalued world markets with what he deems to be top-performing mutual funds, using the time-tested teachings of mentors like Sir John Templeton and Benjamin Graham. His research concentrates on the long-term, macroeconomic prospects of both developing and mature economies, as well as the underlying fundamentals of different asset classes, like equities, bonds, currencies, commodities, and precious metals.

Roseman believes that American investors should have at least two-thirds of their stock portfolios invested overseas, although he's pretty down on virtually all equity markets right now. "The U.S. market is only about a third of the total picture, and opportunities abroad are definitely increasing as a percentage of stock markets around the world," he points out. "Another reason to be abroad is that the U.S. market has already boomed. You don't want to come in and buy after it's had a big move. If you're a global investor today, you should also be hedged to protect yourself against a potential downturn."

Roseman is convinced that investors will do best using foreign mutual funds, instead of American Depository Receipts (ADRs), which he thinks are a ripoff. "ADRs have high fees," he explains. "There are fees for the brokers who trade them. There are commissions to trade them. If you want to play foreign markets, buy a fund with a good manager." While he occasionally recommends single-country closed-end funds, Roseman generally touts diversified open-ended funds with holdings in many different countries. What's more, he won't touch a closed-end fund under any circumstance unless it's selling at a discount.

Roseman considers himself to be a contrarian value investor who likes to find managers who buy securities below their intrinsic worth. To make his recommended list, a fund must outperform its benchmark index for at least five years, follow an investment discipline similar to his own and stay away from using derivatives or leverage. Of all the places to invest in 1998, Roseman has one clear favorite. "You should definitely overweight in the emerging markets of the world," he insists. "That's where the growth is going to be going forward, especially in China."

Occupation: Editor, *Global Mutual Fund Investor*
Montreal, Quebec, Canada

Birth Date: October 18, 1966

Education: BA, McGill University of Montreal, 1989

Biggest Mistake Investors Make: "Being too impatient. The bull market has damaged investor expectations."

Best Investment: Telebras (Scooped up shares of this Brazilian telephone company in March 1995 at $33 and sold it for $130 in 1997.)

Worst Investment: Buying several U.S. restaurant stocks in 1997, including Lone Star and Outback Steakhouse. (They all dropped 25 percent in a matter of weeks.)

Advice: "Pick your investments carefully, and don't rush into anything. Also, if you don't understand something, don't invest in it."

Market Outlook: Bearish.

ROBERT SANBORN

The Oakmark Fund

While low PEs, reasonable price-to-book value ratios, and high dividend yields are the gauges most value investors use to define "value," Robert Sanborn follows a different track. "All of these things are meaningless to me, even though I think of myself as a core value investor," he says. "I look at what a business is worth to an owner who owns the whole thing."

It comes as no surprise that Sanborn would have a bias toward finding companies on the cheap. The Boston native grew up in a middle-class family and quickly learned the importance of making every dollar count. "I have a younger brother and sister, and my parents never had a lot of money," he reflects. "We did all of our shopping at discount stores like Filene's Basement. We were always looking for a bargain."

While studying at Dartmouth College, he grew interested in economics and contemplated becoming a professor. But shortly after starting graduate school at the University of Chicago, he decided the lifestyle of an academic wasn't for him. "I found I really enjoyed investing and decided to get an MBA instead of a PhD," he says.

Sanborn became a securities analyst for the Ohio State Teachers Retirement System pension fund after graduation. A few years later, he left to become a portfolio manager at Harris Associates, the respected Chicago value investment firm. At the time, Harris only managed private accounts. But, in 1991, Sanborn convinced company brass to let him launch The Oakmark Fund. Talk about a grand entrance: In its rookie year, Oakmark was up 48 percent, compared to a gain of 9 percent for the Standard & Poor's 500. Oakmark quickly became the number one fund in the nation, turning Sanborn into a star in the world of personal finance.

Sanborn admittedly attributes part of his great start to a combination of good luck and great timing. But his savvy stock-picking skills deserve much of the credit as well. "My view is very eclectic," he says. "I can look at a very high-growth company, and if it trades below its value to an owner who is going to own it for its duration, I'm interested. I buy great companies, but everything depends on value." He also wants to make sure any stock he considers is backed by a strong business. "The longer I'm in this field, the more skeptical I am of buying lousy businesses at any price," he reasons. "I'm very comfortable with our investment style. I can't see approaching the investment process any differently."

To determine how much a company is worth, he examines a multitude of different factors. "We look at transactions in the marketplace and try to make sense of them and whether they are reasonable," he explains. "We then try to apply those valuations to comparable companies." He also pays much more attention to cash flow than PE ratios. "The 'E' is accounting earnings, which we find is often not reflective of a company's true financial situation," he says. "That's why we like to look at cash flow more closely than reported earnings."

Sanborn follows five guidelines in his investment discipline. First, of course, he pays attention to value. Next, he wants to invest in a company with owner-oriented management. "I will not invest with a lousy management team hoping either someone will take them out or that things will somehow get better," he says. "We always assume the current management team is the one we will be dealing with. If we can't find owner-oriented management, we won't buy the stock."

In addition, even though he manages a $4.4 billion portfolio, Sanborn prefers to concentrate his holdings. "I like to have 65 percent of my portfolio in the top 20 names," he says. Finally, Sanborn thinks independently. "I don't even know the name of my salesmen from the major brokerage firms," he insists. "We do all of our own research here and rely on our own people."

Sanborn hates to sell a stock, and will only pull the trigger if he has misjudged the management team or if the stock approaches 90 percent of his estimated value. Turnover in his fund averages a meager 20 percent a year.

When he's away from the office, Sanborn loves to read about economic history and politics and is very involved with the Libertarian political party in Illinois, although he has no plans to launch a campaign of his own anytime soon. "To me, the Libertarian philosophy is right on the money," he insists. "But I have too many skeletons in the closet to run for office myself."

Occupation: Portfolio Manager, The Oakmark Fund
Chicago, Illinois

Birth Date: March 8, 1958

Education: BA, Dartmouth College, 1980
MBA, University of Chicago, 1983

Biggest Mistake Investors Make: "Letting their emotions rule their heads."

Best Investment: Liberty Media (He owned the stock from 1991 to 1994 and saw his money multiply more than ten times.)

Worst Investment: Nike (The stock was a mediocre performer when he owned it. He eventually lost his patience and sold out, right before the stock doubled.)

Advice: "Know yourself, and invest for the long term."

Market Outlook: Bullish.

STEPHEN SAVAGE

Value Line Mutual Fund Survey

Steve Savage is by no means a computer nerd, but he's built his career compiling electronic databases for mutual funds. He got into investing through journalism. In college, he was hired by a Canadian newsletter publisher to write for one of its New York-based investment publications. "I got a chance to interview some pretty well-known fund managers," he says. "I learned a lot fast because I was immersed into the financial culture quickly." He joined the publisher full time after graduation and convinced his bosses to let him start a mutual fund research publication, called the *Blue Book of Mutual Fund Reports*. It featured single-page research reports on each fund, similar to what the *Value Line Investment Survey* did with stocks. "I went out and bought a computer and learned how to set up my own database and generate my own full-page reports," he says. "I put the whole thing together myself."

The service was marginally successful, but the publisher was facing hard times because of a postal strike in Canada and decided to shut the publication down after a year. That was in 1986, right about the time when a then unknown firm called Morningstar launched its first fund research publication. Savage left the company to start his own fund newsletter, but had a hard time building his subscription base and decided to sell out after just seven months to go work as an editor with Wiesenberger, a company known for its meticulous fund research and performance tracking service. "That job schooled me in the real fine points of mutual fund data and statistics," Savage says. "It gave me an opportunity to learn the production and data collection aspects of the business, as well as editing and product management."

After being named director of his division, Savage was charged with modernizing and computerizing Wiesenberger's massive database. "We still had stuff that was being tracked on index cards and hand calculators," he notes. "I brought in the resources to build a computerized database and put up a PC network. What used to take 20 hours to calculate now could be done in 30 minutes."

In the winter of 1993, Savage learned that the CEO of Value Line wanted to talk with him about a job. "I called to politely turn her down, and we wound up talking for six hours," he remembers. "What they wanted me to do was very exciting. They wanted to build a mutual fund information division from the ground up, applying the Value Line formula to mutual funds, and competing head-on with Morningstar." Savage was intrigued by the challenge and accepted the offer.

"The day I started, there was nothing more than a drawing on a page of what they wanted to do," he says. "There were no computers or research analysts and

I was supposed to get the product together in six months." By working late nights and weekends, Savage's team almost met the deadline, and the *Value Line Mutual Fund Survey* was born in 1993. The company offers both print and online versions of the product. Savage claims there's a clear philosophical difference between his products and those put out by archrival Morningstar. "I would characterize Morningstar as supporting fundamental research on funds, where the effort is put on finding good funds on an individual basis," he explains. "We are much more supportive of the asset allocation approach, where determining an appropriate asset allocation plan is equally as important as the individual funds."

Unlike Morningstar, Value Line also provides subscribers with model portfolios and specific recommendations. In addition, instead of a star rating, it ranks each fund with a number from one through five, with one being best. But Savage cautions against giving too much weight to this or any other ranking system, because it is based solely on past performance, which can be misleading. "When you look at the posted track records of mutual funds in this country, and compare them to the actual results received by investors, you'll find they are very different," he maintains. "Investors are getting much lower results because the money flows in after a good portion of the record has been racked up and then flows out over the weak periods."

Savage and his staff like to interview portfolio managers, which they believe are the key to a fund's success. That's why he doesn't like indexing very much. "My philosophy is to come up with a sensible asset mix and find funds that are good representatives of those asset classes without doing indexing," he adds. "Instead, buy funds where the manager is hopefully going to add value over time."

Occupation: Executive Director, *Value Line Mutual Fund Survey*
New York, New York

Birth Date: June 23, 1961

Education: BA, Hunter College

Biggest Mistake Investors Make: "Chasing performance."

Best Investment: Buying the Benham Target Maturities 2020 portfolio in December of 1994. (It went up 61 percent the following year.)

Worst Investment: Citel (He purchased the stock in 1985, and the company went out of business.)

Advice: "When you're most excited about an idea, stop and let some time pass and see if you're still excited about it then."

Market Outlook: Bullish, but expects annualized returns from equities to be in the 8 to 10 percent range from now on.

THURMAN SMITH

Equity Fund Research

To Thurman Smith, picking good mutual funds is a bilateral process. "It requires using both sides of the brain," he surmises. "You begin by screening them using the performance numbers, then you look at the fundamentals." Smith examines these statistics, using various computer programs that he has developed over the years. That's actually how he got started in the business. He was a computer applications programmer for several different investment companies, including State Street Bank, Loomis Sayles, and Fidelity Investments. After doing this for awhile, he decided he would rather invest the money instead of creating programs that allowed other people to do it. Besides, he was qualified for the task because he had an MBA in finance and investing from Babson College. So, in 1983, he took the plunge and started his own firm, putting money to work for clients through no-load mutual funds.

"I like funds because your universe is under control and you solve the problem of diversification for clients who don't have large accounts," he explains. "An account under $1 million would probably be better off in funds, rather than individually managed stocks, in terms of efficiency, reward-risk, diversification, and expenses."

While he enjoys his current job more than his previous ones, he still spends most of the day in front of a computer screen, trying to uncover tomorrow's top performers. "I realized it was possible to evaluate managers using some computer tools to generate reward-risk ratios for individual funds. This type of analysis is more useful for evaluating funds and predicting their performance than simply using calendar year figures," he reasons. "I had developed enough software and data to generate a newsletter prototype, and launched *Equity Fund Outlook* (a monthly publication) in 1988, figuring if I had all this information, I might as well get something out of it and some national exposure as well."

Smith's custom-built program may sound complicated, but the rationale behind it isn't. "I compare up and down market performance over the past three years," he explains. "During that time, we've had 12 up periods and six down ones. That's more useful than looking at beta or standard deviation or anything else I can find. I examine the actual behavior of the funds relative to the Wilshire 5000 index in those up and down periods, which have nothing to do with calendar periods." Smith's database contains 300 funds, which he selects using other computerized products, including Morningstar, and by reading various financial publications.

Once he's run his screens, he gives each fund a grade, which determines whether it winds up on his buy or sell list. To get an "A," a fund must do well in good markets and not fall as much as its peers in bad ones. "Given the same risk level, it would have to have the highest growth potential or reward factors, as measured by its upmarket performance," he points out. However, even if a fund is explosive during bull markets, it if goes into a free fall when the market turns south, he won't even consider it.

Once Smith finds a fund with good numbers, he moves on to evaluate it more closely, including an analysis of the person running the show. "The data are just the initial ABC screening," he admits. "I want to know who's behind the wheel." He also likes new funds managed by proven talent. "Everything else being equal, a new fund can be much better than an old one, mainly because of the smaller asset base," he adds. Smith will sell and replace a fund once its growth and risk numbers start to deteriorate. He's certainly not afraid to pull the trigger. Turnover in his momentum-based tax-deferred portfolios can be as high as 100 percent a year.

One thing Smith has noticed over the years is that one style consistently seems to land on top. "Growth at a reasonable price is a discipline that tends to consistently do the best," he reveals. "This technique is a mixture that captures both the growth potential of a stock while paying attention to the price you pay for it."

As the name of his firm suggests, Smith only follows equity funds. He contends that even the most conservative investor should stay away from bonds. "Bonds just don't return enough, and they don't necessarily offset movements in stocks," he maintains. "They're not really an opportunity for risk control. You can be conservative with equity funds. If you're nervous, you could use an equity-income or value fund instead of bonds." For clients who need a monthly income check, he simply puts them in stock funds that offer a systematic withdrawal program. Smith believes the average investor should own eight funds in different asset classes for proper diversification.

Occupation: President, Equity Fund Research
Boston, Massachusetts

Birth Date: May 9, 1942

Education: BA, University of North Carolina, 1965
MBA, Babson College, 1976

Biggest Mistake Investors Make: "Not having a properly diversified portfolio."

Best Investment: Oakmark Fund (Purchased it in 1991.)

Worst Investment: IAI Capital Appreciation (The stock went straight down as soon as he bought it in early 1997.)

Advice: "Make sure your funds are well-managed, and do your research."

Market Outlook: Cautious.

LOUIS STANASOLOVICH

Legend Financial Advisors

The first rule of mutual fund investing, according to Louis Stanasolovich, is you should never simply buy a fund, but rather a manager. "I won't invest in a fund without getting to know the person who is running it," he says. "I also ask for biographies of all the key analysts and traders, because if you have a lot of turnover among your underlying staff, that will create chaos in the organization."

Stanasolovich has an accounting background and started out as a cost analyst for U.S. Steel Corporation out of college. "I was trying to find somewhere to put the extra money I was making, and all I knew about were credit unions, savings bonds, and things like that," he reflects. "A buddy of mine was taking an investment course, and I joined him." Soon after completing the class, he read about the International Association for Financial Planning (IAFP), an industry trade association, and decided he wanted to get into the business. He joined a financial planning and asset management firm after receiving his securities license, and started his own company, Legend Financial Advisors, four years ago.

"Most of my clients come in with money they've either invested on their own or through a broker who was selling a product," Stanasolovich says. "It's hard to tell whether someone earning a commission is working in your best interest. I would say 97 times out of 100 they aren't. I work strictly on a fee-only basis and believe that's the future of the brokerage industry. It's what the investing public wants. It used to be half of my clients would start off by asking how I'm compensated. Now I'd say that number is closer to 95 percent."

Stanasolovich builds each portfolio by first figuring out which investment styles and markets he wants to target. Then he puts money to work through buying funds that represent each of those areas. "We do it all on a valuation basis," he says. "Right now, we think U.S. large-caps are extremely expensive. We're not out of that area completely, but we've cut back on our allocation. We also have between 13 and 18 percent of our clients' money in real estate funds." He prefers funds over individual money managers because they give him more options and have documented performance records. "You can get a huge amount of diversification by using several funds, rather than just placing your money with one manager," he maintains. "I believe when you buy a private manager, you're buying sex appeal. On a $500,000 portfolio, I might use 15 to 25 mutual funds, depending on the circumstances. I could never get that kind of diversification with a private manager. I believe you need to have all of the major styles covered."

The typical account under Stanasolovich's control contains components of large-cap growth, large-cap value, small-cap growth, small-cap value, two different real estate funds, a contrarian fund, a small-cap international fund, and a couple of developing markets funds. He tries to choose one manager for each targeted style and prides himself on doing thorough individual fund analysis. "Generally, the funds I pick are run by owner-managers," he explains. "This means they're an owner or shareholder of the fund company. I also want to make sure they have a contract with provisions to keep them there for awhile."

In addition, Stanasolovich favors funds which reward managers for good performance and tends to avoid fund families like Fidelity and Putnam, which are known for having high turnover. He avoids index funds altogether, claiming most of his managers can outperform the averages, and emphasizes names with low expense ratios. "I watch all of my funds very closely to make sure they're keeping up with the indexes for their investment style," he says. "I don't have a lot of turnover, maybe two or three funds a year. I find it strange in our industry that fund managers are expected to go out and visit companies, yet advisers don't go and research the managers they are recommending."

While Stanasolovich likes to personally get to know each fund manager, that's not easy for the average investor to do. Therefore, he recommends reading various financial publications and using quantitative statistics, like past performance over several years, as a start. "You only want to look at those with good performance," he advises. "Next, check the assets, and if they have grown substantially in a small stock fund, chances are it will not perform as well as it used to."

Occupation: Founder and President, Legend Financial Advisors, Inc.
Pittsburgh, Pennsylvania

Birth Date: February 5, 1957

Education: BS, Pennsylvania State University, 1979

Biggest Mistake Investors Make: "Reading popular magazines and therefore buying yesterday's news."

Best Investment: Templeton Developing Markets Fund (Bought at the end of 1992 and has doubled his money so far.)

Worst Investment: An oil and gas penny stock he purchased in the 1980s that went belly-up.

Advice: "Hire a good adviser and/or seek out good sources of information."

Market Outlook: Bullish, although he doesn't expect great things for the U.S. stock market. "I think it will be a better year for bonds than stocks, and am more attracted to foreign markets than the United States."

MICHAEL STOLPER

Stolper & Company

Michael Stolper is a little embarrassed. His new twin-turbo Porsche is the fastest car being raced on the San Diego auto cross. Unfortunately, he doesn't have the fastest time. "For someone who's not particularly well-coordinated and doesn't see well, it's all you can do to shift gears when flying around a course at 90 miles an hour," he says. "You're basically running against the clock." Racing is something he's enjoyed since he was a teenager. But away from the track, he also looks for winners destined to finish the race first, only in this case we're talking about mutual funds.

Stolper has his feet on both sides of the mutual fund fence. As an investment adviser and president of a firm that matches wealthy individuals with money mangers, he often recommends funds to his clients. But as a director and shareholder of three fund companies, he empathizes with the business concerns they face, including the need to pay for an enormous amount of overhead. That's why a fund's total expense ratio is of little concern to him. "My attitude on fees is that if you don't like it, don't buy it," Stolper says. "If you think you're buying a Camry and it's priced like a Lexus, go down the street. There are 6,000 products to choose from. You're buying intellectual skills. I want the best skill I can get, and I'm perfectly willing to pay up for it."

This Oklahoma native has had a lifelong interest in the stock market, though he's not exactly sure why. "I just sort of got the bug," he says. "I thought it was a fascinating business. It looked like easy money without a lot of work. That's probably what appealed to me." After earning a master's degree in finance, Stolper originally planned to get into investment banking, which he viewed as the most glamorous job on Wall Street. Unfortunately, the big firms weren't impressed by his degree from the University of Oklahoma. "I ended up in the retail brokerage business," he shares. "I was 22 and not well-credentialed, so that was the only avenue available to me." He took a job with Bateman, Eichler in 1968 and began using investment advisers to manage money for his clients in the early 1970s. "It became clear to me that it was easier to make judgments about people managing money than about individual securities," he maintains. "I was choosing stocks on my own and also had some clients who were being advised. The advisers were doing better than I. So I had to reluctantly acknowledge that these people were more clever and capable of investing the money." A short time later, Stolper founded a firm specializing in matching the rich with the right people to oversee their portfolios.

While Stolper uses both funds and individual managers, he insists that when clients leave the decision up to him, funds are always his preference. "The main advantage to funds is simplification," he insists. "The main disadvantage is their tendency to overdiversify." When it comes to choosing funds, however, the manager in charge remains his most important consideration. "That's the only thing that matters," he contends. "If you don't believe that, you should just find an index and put your money there."

Judging managers isn't easy though. "What you're looking for is a pattern of success," Stolper explains. "I not only want statistical data, but also to talk with these folks. I want to believe there's something intellectually compelling about them. Typically, my worst mistake has been hiring bright guys who weren't moneymakers. Some people will dazzle you with their intellect, but they can't put the numbers up."

Stolper reveals that the best managers he's come across tend to be socially underdeveloped. "We interview about 150 to 200 firms a year in their offices," he says. "One thing you'll always find in great managers is that all they can talk about is stocks. There's a clear change in the conversational pattern and body language when that subject comes up."

A more difficult consideration is deciding whether to sell a fund. "The reality is you sell when you run out of patience," he admits. "We're real slow to add names. If you run a screen, you'll find 88 percent of underperformance is style driven. The market doesn't like what the manager is buying, yet they own the same stocks that attracted you to the fund in the first place. If I can't find anything else wrong, I'll stick with the manager and go back to sleep."

Occupation: President, Stolper & Company, Inc.
San Diego, California

Birth Date: August 15, 1945

Education: BA, University of Oklahoma, 1967
MBA, University of Oklahoma, 1968

Biggest Mistake Investors Make: "Thinking and overmanaging their investments."

Best Investment: Investing in three privately held mutual fund companies (Janus, Meridian, and the Pasadena Group).

Worst Investment: An oil limited partnership he bought in the 1980s that became worthless.

Advice: "Never forget that in this business you make most of your money by just showing up. The influence of participation and compound interest is substantially greater than cleverness or asset allocation."

Market Outlook: Cautiously Bullish. "I'm looking for a basically flat market, because I think it's time for a rest."

GARRETT VAN WAGONER

Van Wagoner Capital Management

Garrett Van Wagoner knows just how fleeting fame can be. In 1996, he was the fund manager that could do no wrong. His face graced the pages of almost every major personal finance magazine, and he was often touted as the heir apparent to former Fidelity Magellan manager Peter Lynch. It's no wonder why. After posting chart-topping returns as skipper of the Govett Smaller Companies Fund, Van Wagoner started his own firm, and his three upstart funds posted returns from between 30 and 60 percent during the first half of the year. This attention and performance helped to attract more than $1.2 billion in six short months, making Van Wagoner Funds the fastest growing new fund family in history.

But a funny thing happened on the way to superstardom. The share prices of Van Wagoner's funds began to drift in the opposite direction and never looked back, just as a huge flood of cash came flowing in. During the first five months of 1997, this downdraft continued. His Emerging Growth offering alone fell by as much as 37 percent, before staging an impressive comeback. Almost overnight, Van Wagoner's phone stopped ringing, and the press didn't even want to talk to him. The tone of the letters he received from shareholders also changed. "Before, I was getting nothing but glowing comments about how wonderful I was and how their son wanted an interview and their daughter wanted to marry me," he candidly admits. "Now I get my share of people asking what's wrong and telling me how disappointed they are."

But this kind of roller coaster ride is nothing new for Van Wagoner. It's simply part of his style of investing. As he's shown in the past, you have to put up with a considerable amount of downside volatility if you expect to achieve the kinds of eye-popping returns Van Wagoner has posted during his short yet highly successful career. And, as Van Wagoner puts it, those who are willing to stick with him through the occasional bumps in the road will likely be very pleased at the end of their journey.

Van Wagoner was introduced to the stock market as a third grader in New Jersey. He was forced to write a column for his school newspaper and wanted to cover sports. Unfortunately, that job was already taken, and investing was about the only beat left. Van Wagoner was attracted to the whole concept of stock market investing right from the start. "The idea of making money without working was intriguing in that you could buy something and sell it and get more money for it without shoveling snow or mowing a lawn," he says. "I really didn't understand back then that stocks could also go down."

This money manager in the making bought his first stock at age 14, purchasing ten shares of his favorite department store. He became even more interested in business and finance as a student at Bucknell University and landed a job at a Washington, D.C. bank after graduation. "I was hired to be the entire equity research department," he recalls. "Management wanted somebody to come in and look for stock ideas." He then took a job with another regional bank in Miami and got a 50 percent pay raise, from $14,000 to $21,000 a year. One week before the bull market began in August 1992, Van Wagoner was hired by Bessemer Trust as a large-cap equity manager. The firm transferred him to New York and put him in charge of small company stocks. Back then, the division had a mere $1 million in assets. "It was an area nobody else wanted to cover," he confesses. "We eventually developed what we called an emerging growth fund." Van Wagoner managed the investment pool for eight years, before being hired to take charge of the Govett Smaller Companies Fund. Although he originally operated his current firm as a one-man-band operation, today he has a staff of five, including three analysts, a trader, and marketing director.

When searching for investment ideas, the first thing Van Wagoner looks for is companies offering a leading product or service in their industry. "On top of that, I want to make sure the management team has both the qualifications and ability to execute the business plan necessary to grow the company," he explains. Additionally, he demands that company executives have a vast majority of their own net worth tied up in stock or options. "I want their longer-term business interests to be aligned with mine," he reasons. He further looks for companies growing by a minimum of 20 percent a year and admits that the toughest part of his job is figuring out what price to pay for a stock. "I do have one rule that I don't violate very often, and that is I won't pay more than one times the growth rate," he shares.

Once he makes a purchase, the newly married Van Wagoner stays in frequent contact with company management and will hold on as long as he's confident those in charge are continuing to execute their stated business plan.

Occupation: President, Van Wagoner Capital Management
San Francisco, California

Birth Date: September 27, 1955

Education: BSBA, Bucknell University, 1977

Biggest Mistake Investors Make: "Chasing trends."

Best Investment: Ascend Communications (It jumped 800 percent in 1994.)

Worst Investment: Quarterdeck Office Systems (Bought the stock for $24 at the end of June 1992, and it fell to $6 by the middle of August.)

Advice: "Be patient and only invest as much as you can afford to lose."

Market Outlook: Bullish.

CATHERINE VOSS SANDERS

Morningstar Investor

The most coveted prize a mutual fund manager can receive is not a big bonus or even getting on the cover of *Money* magazine. Rather it's a five-star rating from Morningstar, the influential mutual fund tracking service that was born in a Chicago apartment back 1984. Among those involved in awarding the stars is Catherine Voss Sanders. She is publisher of the company's monthly publication *Morningstar Investor*, which contains a handpicked list of the 500 funds deemed most worthy of attention.

Voss Sanders admits both investors and the fund companies alike put too much emphasis on those familiar stars. "The star rating is a good introduction to a fund, but not a good conclusion," she admits. "It's a great place to start. It gives you a good idea of where a fund sits in the spectrum of all other funds. But if you stop there, you're probably not going to get where you're trying to go." A fund can't wine and dine its way to five stars. It's all based on a quantitative screening, which calculates how a fund measures up in terms of risk and downside volatility. "There are a lot of risk measures that look at both upside and downside volatility, like beta and standard deviation," Voss Sanders reveals. "We designed this risk measure to just look at the downside volatility, thinking that what people are really concerned about is not making more than they expected, but the chance of losing money. So we look at how often and by how much a fund underperforms a risk-free asset on a monthly basis, specifically a three-month T-bill, and come up with a score for that."

As a result, a fund with three stars could have a better performance record than a five-star fund, if it took significantly more risk to achieve it. That's why Voss Sanders warns against building a portfolio of nothing but five-star funds without doing further analysis. "You can put together a really lousy portfolio by just stopping at looking for five-star funds," she says. "We're always the first to say if you see a five-star fund, it's likely there's something good going on. But you have to ask if the past is likely to continue and if the people who built that record are still there."

Voss Sanders started out, not in finance, but as a writer for an investor relations agency. Before long, she tired of having to articulate the spin of corporate bigwigs and, on a whim, sent a resume to Morningstar in 1991. To her surprise, they called and offered her a job as an analyst. She used to edit the company's biweekly newsletter *Morningstar Mutual Funds*, before having her second son two years ago. Now she works part-time on the monthly publication and oversees the entire operation.

Without question, she's got her hands full, both at work and at home, where she's mother to two children under four. That's why she and her copywriter husband hired their own live-in aupair. "We have this woman from Austria who's here staying with us for a year," she explains. "It's part of a government-sponsored program. You pay them a small stipend and give them room and board and they are supposed to help watch your kids for 45 hours a week. It's sort of like a half babysitting, half foreign exchange student kind of thing. It's working out real well."

Morningstar was the brainchild of Joe Mansueto, a former investment analyst who noticed that the fund industry was starting to explode in the early 1980s. He decided to bring professional analysis to funds, similar to what already existed for stocks. He began by compiling fund performance data in an annual directory, and his business grew right along with the fund industry. "We've grown from a company of about 40 employees when I started in early 1991 to more than 350 today," Voss Sanders shares. Morningstar's product line has also expanded significantly, even in the past few years. In addition to the print publications Voss Sanders works on, the company has introduced several computerized and Internet-based programs, and has products that analyze individual stocks as well.

When it comes to the fund industry, Voss Sanders' major beef is that most companies charge too much for managing money. "The reason they do is because they can get away with it," she says. "There's no real pressure on funds to keep those costs down. The fund companies have a great thing going. They can charge their expenses in basis points, without you ever having to send them a check. You don't notice what you're paying, and it doesn't seem like a big deal."

Occupation: Publisher, *Morningstar Investor*
Chicago, Illinois

Birth Date: July 31, 1966

Education: AB, Duke University, 1988
MSJ, Northwestern University, 1989

Biggest Mistake Investors Make: "Failing to properly diversify and not knowing how funds interact with each other."

Best Investment: Buying zero coupon bonds in 1991, without even knowing what they were. (They went up 17 percent in the months before she realized she made a mistake and decided to get out.)

Worst Investment: Berger 100

Advice: "Pay attention to a fund's holdings when diversifying your portfolio. Also, keep an eye on costs."

Market Outlook: Bullish, but expecting returns to be a more normal 8 to 9 percent.

JOHN WALLACE

Robertson Stephens Investment Management

When a friend of John Wallace's first suggested that he get into the securities business, Wallace figured it must have something to do with locks. Why should he think otherwise? After all, he had been living as far away from Wall Street as you can imagine: Ecuador. Wallace fell in love with the South American country after spending a year there in college studying Spanish. "I liked it so much I went back in 1979 and started an import/export clothing manufacturing business with a partner from Denmark," he says. "We were selling hand-knit sweaters, hats, and some cotton skirts and tops."

While the company was successful, Wallace quickly grew tired of it and ultimately turned the reins over to his girlfriend before the two returned to her hometown of New York. "We got married, and she said somebody's got to work for a living," he recalls. "So I went back to get my MBA at night. At the same time, I had a friend in the money management business, and he set up some interviews for me."

As it turned out, Wallace was in the right place at the right time. About three months after having lunch with Diane Jarmusz, a portfolio manager at Oppenheimer & Co., he was offered a job as her assistant. "That was in 1986, which means I started in this business when I was 32," he says. "This is really a second career for me." Jarmusz ran the Oppenheimer Equity Income and Total Return Funds, and Wallace helped her out. But, a short time later, the firm launched what it called the Main Street Fund and told Wallace it was his baby. "Oppenheimer was very entrepreneurial back then," he says. "It was known as a shop that would give its people a chance to run money sooner than later compared to other fund companies."

His big break came in 1990, when Jarmusz decided to do something else and gave Wallace control of the Total Return Fund. His performance was so good, both Main Street and Total Return quickly ballooned in size. "When I left, the Total Return Fund had about $1.8 billion and the Main Street Fund had around $2.5 billion," he says. At one point, Main Street was the number one fund in the country over a five-year period under Wallace's leadership. This strong performance captured the attention of San Francisco-based Robertson Stephens Investment Management, which offered Wallace a chance to run its new Growth and Income Fund in 1995. (If you read the 1997 edition of *Wall Street's Picks*, you know that Bob Markman selected Robertson Stephens Growth and Income as his top fund selection for the year.)

Wallace defines investment management as an art, not a science, and he continues to refine his stock-picking skills as the years go by. "I come to work every day literally trying to find stocks that I think have the potential to double within two to three years," he shares. "If I'm able to do that, I'm compounding money for shareholders at 25 to 30 percent annually."

Of course, that's easier said than done. So how does he find such stocks? He begins by looking for a catalyst that can drive earnings and therefore the stock price higher. "It could be a new management team, a new product launch, new markets they are expanding into, a restructuring or a realization of an undervalued asset," he explains. "Finding this catalyst is all based on information flow. I'm in constant communication with the sell-side research firms, meeting with managements and suppliers and talking with other traders and brokers." Although Wallace has a growth bias, and tends to concentrate on small- and mid-cap issues, valuations do matter. "I like stocks trading at two-thirds to 80 percent of their growth rates," he maintains. "I do occasionally invest in IPOs and some of the faster-growing high PE names."

Wallace sets a price target for each holding in the portfolio using a simple formula of A x B x C. " 'A' is the forward earnings estimates of the company," he explains. " 'B' is the market multiple of the S&P 500. 'C' is whether or not the company deserves a premium or discount to that multiple." As a stock approaches 90 percent of that target, and assuming there's been no fundamental change, he'll get rid of it. He also sells part of his position in any stock that goes down 15 percent or more from his entry point or if he finds a better place to put the money.

Occupation: Portfolio Manager, Robertson Stephens Investment Mgt.
San Francisco, California

Birth Date: April 8, 1954

Education: BA, University of Idaho, 1978
MBA, Pace University, 1987

Biggest Mistake Investors Make: "Not understanding how their money is being managed. A lot of mutual fund shareholders are betting on five-year track records where the guy who produced this performance isn't even there anymore."

Best Investment: Millicom International Cellular (Started buying in 1991 for $3. Sold it in the mid-$20s. Now it trades above $40.)

Worst Investment: Iwerks (Bought as an IPO for $18 in 1993. It immediately doubled before crashing down to $3 in about one year. Wallace got out around $6.)

Advice: "Do your homework. Understand your money manager's process. Look at the stocks in your portfolio and see if they are the types of names you can sleep with at night."

Market Outlook: Cautious. (Thinks we'll have a trading market in 1998, where traders will have no sympathy for mistakes.)

MARTIN WHITMAN

Third Avenue Funds

Although some might take offense at constantly being referred to as a "vulture." Martin Whitman considers it to be a compliment. "It sure beats being called an asset allocator or academic," he says. "Those folks don't know what they're talking about. To be a vulture investor means you know what you're doing and can read a document."

Whitman earned his vulture reputation by building a career out of investing in distressed companies, those that Wall Street often expects to go out of business. "There's almost nothing we go into where the near-term outlook isn't terrible," he points out. It's a field of expertise that he got into almost by accident. "After serving in the Navy, I originally planned to teach economics," he remembers. "But after finishing graduate school, I saw there wasn't much of a future for me as an academic, so I went to work on Wall Street."

He started out in research, before moving into investment banking, managing private money and doing control investing. Whitman first began specializing in distressed companies in the early 1970s, when he decided to start his own firm. "I wanted to do corporate finance, but I didn't have a lot of money," he says. "There were two fields that were wide open, where I didn't have to compete with the big firms like Morgan Stanley and Goldman Sachs. They were bankruptcy and shareholder litigation. I built quite a reputation in both areas." Originally Whitman just gave advice to these troubled companies. But he soon figured out he could make more money by investing in them as a portfolio manager. Today, in addition to managing both private accounts and two mutual funds, including his original Third Avenue Value, he teaches control investing at Yale.

Whitman invests in the stocks and bonds of distressed companies, depending on where he finds the most opportunity. And while many view this as an area of great risk, he disagrees. In fact, safety is his top concern. "You can't use the word risk without putting an adjective in front of it," Whitman argues. "There's no such thing as general risk. If you know what you're doing, you can guard against investment risk, but you can never guard against market risk."

To protect himself from investment risk, Whitman never buys the common stock of a distressed company. Instead, he sticks with secured debt, because he wants the most senior issue available that will participate in any potential reorganization. When he does buy stock, it's usually from companies with large market capitalizations. "For credit securities, I always assume there will be a credit default," he says. "Then I figure out how I would come out in the event that this happens."

For equities, he demands that potential investments be backed up by strong cash positions. "I want to be the most senior person to participate in the reorganization," he reasons. "If you get a well-financed company, obviously the most senior is the common stock. I also look at pricing compared to what I think the businesses are worth as private entities or takeover candidates. For high-tech small-caps, I want to see an exceptionally strong financial position and try not to pay a premium of more than 60 percent over book value. The theory is that it roughly simulates the price a first-stage venture capitalist would pay."

Whitman is clearly a value investor, but he pays little attention to traditional indicators of value, like dividend yields and PE ratios. "Graham and Dodd (the two noted authorities on value investing) are all screwed up," he maintains. "I analyze companies just like Warren Buffett. I analyze the values in the business and stop. The basic analysis of all the amateurs, including Graham and Dodd, is to try and determine at which price a stock will sell. You carry an awful lot of excess baggage with that kind of methodology."

Whitman's portfolio turnover averages less than 15 percent a year. "Most of my companies get taken out through mergers and acquisitions," he says. "If I'm doing it right, in any six-month or one-year period, there ought to be a lot of takeovers. I will sell on my own if I conclude I've made a mistake, like when management burns cash and has bad operating results, or I find out the guy in charge is a crook." Whitman admits some 20 to 30 percent of his stocks turn out to be clinkers. But the gains from his winners more than make up the difference in terms of performance.

Occupation: CEO and Chief Investment Officer, Third Avenue Funds
New York, New York

Birth Date: September 30, 1924

Education: BS, Syracuse University, 1949
MA, New School of Social Research, 1956

Biggest Mistake Investors Make: "Paying attention to the market."

Best Investment: Nabors Industries (Paid 40 cents a share for the stock in 1987, and it's now worth more than $20. He's also a director of the company.)

Worst Investment: Union Federal (Bought for $2 a share in 1993, and it ultimately went to zero.)

Advice: "If you pay attention to bottom-up fundamentals, you can do reasonably well on a fundamental basis, provided you invest in an economy where there's political stability and an absence of violence in the streets. In other words, don't pay attention to all that nonsense about interest rates and Dow Jones."

Market Outlook: "I don't have a clue," he admits.

DONALD YACKTMAN

Yacktman Asset Management

Don't tell anyone, but Don Yacktman sometimes gets scolded by his colleagues for dozing off during the day. That shows how little attention he pays to the minute-by-minute fluctuations of the market, even though he manages $1.4 billion in both personal accounts and two mutual funds. It's also a good indication of how comfortable he is with the companies he owns.

It stands to reason that Yacktman wasn't very happy working for his previous employers. He started out in the business as a portfolio manager at Stein Roe, but his more research-driven fundamental investment process kept clashing with the one they espoused. "They were momentum investors, constantly buying high and selling low, and I don't operate that way," he says. "It was a continuous source of frustration." He then went on to manage the Selected American Fund (which is now run by fellow *Wall Street's Picks for 1998* panelist Shelby Davis). Yacktman's performance was excellent. He managed to steer the fund to an annualized return of 18.2 percent over an eight-year period. The fund was ultimately taken over by Kemper Financial. But when fund operations were transferred from one subsidiary of Kemper to another, he knew he had to get out. "The culture was suddenly very different," he reveals. "We had a very entrepreneurial culture before, and it became very bureaucratic."

That forced him to go out on his own in 1992, when he launched the Yacktman Fund (which was selected as one of *Wall Street's Picks for 1997*). Yacktman and his team follow a strict discipline that he developed over a decade of working in the investment field. "What we're ultimately looking for are businesses that are growing rapidly, faster than the S&P 500, but how we're different from most growth managers is that we buy at a big discount to their fair market value," he explains. "We're disciplined in our buying process. We use value techniques, in effect, to buy growth businesses. We buy on weakness not strength. The derivatives are you end up with a portfolio that's growing faster than the S&P, but selling for less."

Yacktman's corporate logo is a triangle, symbolic of the three characteristics he demands of each company he owns. First, he wants a good business. "We look for high returns on tangible assets," he says. "We calculate this by examining the amount of cash a company generates after paying for capital expenditures." Next, he seeks a shareholder-oriented management team that will spend that cash wisely. "Managers can do five things with their excess money," he notes. "Funnel it back into the business, acquire a competitor, repurchase shares, pay off debt, or make a dividend distribution. I would rank their importance to us in that order." Finally, the stock must sell for a low purchase price. "We capitalize the cash flows that are generated after capital expenditures and subtract the debt, which gives us a valuation for the business," he says. "We then wait patiently for a big gap to occur between the public and private market value of the stock." If he had to sum up his investment philosophy in a mission statement, Yacktman says it would be to earn the highest returns consistent with minimal risk. "I will sell a stock when it gets very close to its private market value or swap it for something else," he adds. "In other words, when a better business comes along selling at the same price, or I find one of comparable quality selling at a lower price, I'll trade one for the other."

Because of his strict value criteria, Yacktman is often at odds with momentum players, like those he used to work for. "The problem is if you focus just on earnings and price momentum, you're likely to buy stocks too close to their private market value and expose yourself to great vulnerability on the downside in the event of a disappointment," he reasons. "There is great liquidity on the upside, but not on the downside. That's when those people get nailed."

Yacktman has such faith in the companies he ultimately decides to buy that he's not afraid to take highly concentrated positions. In fact, his new fund, Yacktman Focused (one of *Wall Street's Picks for 1998*) will only own around 15 stocks at a time and his original Yacktman Fund has almost 70 percent of its total assets in the top 12 holdings. "I think Mae West said it best: Too much of a good thing is wonderful," he maintains. "In my mind, there's no substitute for knowledge. If one has researched correctly and can determine the private market value of a company with a high degree of confidence, those stocks selling at the deepest discounts to their private market value with give you the highest returns over time."

Occupation: President, Yacktman Asset Management
Chicago, Illinois

Birth Date: September 12, 1941

Education: BS, University of Utah, 1965
MBA, Harvard College, 1967

Biggest Mistake Investors Make: "Doing superficial research. They get a call from a broker and buy without even knowing what they own."

Best Investment: Berkshire Hathaway (Paid $400 a share in late 1982. At last check, it was trading at $44,600)

Worst Investment: First Executive Life (Bought the stock for $10 in 1989 and lost most of his money.)

Advice: "There is no substitute for knowledge. You need to know what to buy and how much to pay for it. If you don't know how to do that, hire a professional manager."

Market Outlook: Cautiously bullish.

UPDATE

on Wall Street's Picks for 1997

Those of you who read *Wall Street's Picks for 1997* might be wondering, "What should I do with those stocks and mutual funds now?" Well, wonder no more because the answer to that pressing question can be found on the following pages. I went back to each of last year's panelists and asked, "How do you feel about your pick from last year going into 1998? Do you now consider it to be a buy, sell, or hold?" You'll find their responses on the following pages.

Just so we're clear on definitions, *buy* means that they still recommend their pick for purchase at current price levels; *hold* indicates they suggest holding on, if you already own the investment, and *sell* is a sign to take your profits (or losses) and move on.

Some of the stock-picking experts were sort of on the border, advising a *buy/hold* or *hold/sell* strategy. Buy/hold is a signal they're lukewarm on the pick and aren't strongly advising any new purchases, while hold/sell suggests they consider the stock to be a weak hold and are on the verge of getting rid of it.

THE TOP STOCKS FOR 1997—UPDATE

STOCK	PANELIST	CURRENT ADVICE
Alcoa	Michael Metz	BUY
Angeion	Garrett Van Wagoner	BUY
Ascend Communications	James Collins	HOLD/SELL
Canadian Pacific	Jean-Marie Eveillard	HOLD
C.P. Pokphand	John Dessauer	HOLD
Crop Growers	Larry Jeddeloh	1
First Data	Alan Bond	BUY
First USA	Robert Sanborn	2
General Electric	Vita Nelson	HOLD
General Motors	James O'Shaughnessy	SELL
General Re	Shelby Davis	BUY
Greif Brothers	Philip Carret	BUY
Huffy	George Putnam	BUY
Hyperion Software	Margarita Perez	BUY
Intel	Al Frank	HOLD
Louisiana Pacific	Richard Huson	HOLD
Mattson Technology	Michael Murphy	BUY
McDonald's	Elaine Garzarelli	BUY
Moog	Mario Gabelli	HOLD/SELL
Phoenix Technologies	Sally Anderson	BUY
Photocomm	R. Max Bowser	BUY
Reuters Holdings	Robert Stovall	BUY
Seattle Filmworks	Art Bonnel	BUY
Stillwater Mining	James Dines	HOLD
Transocean Offshore Drilling	Louis Navellier	SELL

1–Company acquired by Fireman's Fund.
2–Company acquired by BancOne.

THE TOP FUNDS FOR 1997—UPDATE

FUND	PANELIST	CURRENT ADVICE
ASM Fund	Burton Berry	HOLD
Brandywine Fund	Craig Litman	BUY
Cohen & Steers Realty Shares	Sheldon Jacobs	HOLD
Dreyfus New Leaders	Paul Merriman	SELL
Robertson Stephens Gro & Inc.	Bob Markman	BUY/HOLD
Turner Small Cap	Thurman Smith	HOLD
U.S. Global Leaders Growth	Michael Stolper	BUY
Vanguard International Growth	Earl Osborn	BUY
Vanguard Specialized Energy	Don Phillips	BUY
Warburg Pincus Intl. Equity	Jay Schabacker	BUY
Yacktman Fund	Harold Evensky	BUY

GLOSSARY
of Investment Terms

American Depositary Receipt (ADR)—Receipt for the shares of a foreign-based stock that are held by a U.S. bank and entitle shareholders to all dividends and capital gains. It's a way for Americans to buy shares in foreign-based companies on a U.S. stock exchange.

annual report—Yearly statement of a corporation's financial condition. It must be distributed to all shareholders of record.

ask or offer price—The lowest amount a seller is willing to take for shares of a stock.

asset allocation—Act of spreading investment funds across various categories of assets, such as stocks, bonds, and cash.

beta—A coefficient measure of a stock's relative volatility in relation to the Standard & Poor's 500 index, which has a beta of 1.

bid price—The highest amount a buyer is willing to pay for shares of a stock.

blue chip—Common stock of a nationally known company with a long record of profit growth, dividend payments, and a reputation for quality products and services.

bond—Any interest-bearing or discounted government or corporate obligation to pay a specified sum of money, usually at regular intervals.

book value—What a company would be worth if all assets were sold (assets minus liabilities). Also, the price at which an asset is carried on a balance sheet.

bottom-up investing—The search for outstanding individual stocks with little regard for overall economic trends.

broker—Person who acts as an intermediary between a buyer and a seller.

buy and hold strategy—Technique that calls for accumulating and keeping shares in a company over many years, regardless of price swings.

cash ratio—Ratio of cash and marketable securities to current liabilities. Tells the extent to which liabilities could be immediately liquidated.

chief executive officer (CEO)—Individual responsible for the overall operations of a corporation.

contrarian—Investor who does the opposite of the majority at any particular time.

convertible bond—Security that can be exchanged for other securities of the issuer (under certain conditions), usually from preferred stock or bonds into common stock.

current ratio—Current assets divided by current liabilities. Shows a company's ability to pay current debts from current assets.

debt-to-equity ratio—Long-term debt divided by shareholder's equity. Indicates how highly leveraged a company is. (A figure greater than 1.5 should raise a red flag.)

diversification—Spreading risk by putting assets into several different investment categories, like stocks, bonds, and cash.

dividend—Distribution of earnings to shareholders.

dividend yield—The cash dividend paid per share each year divided by the current share price.

dollar cost averaging—The process of accumulating positions in stocks and mutual funds by investing a set amount of money each month, thus buying more shares when prices are down, less when they are up.

Dow Jones Industrial Average—The oldest and most widely quoted stock market indicator. Represents the price direction of 30 blue chip stocks on the New York Stock Exchange. (Doesn't always give an accurate view of what's happening with the market as a whole.)

fair market value—Price at which an asset or service is or can be passed on from a willing buyer to a willing seller.

Form 10-K—Annual report filed with the Securities and Exchange Commission showing a company's total sales, revenues, and pretax operating income, along with sales figures for each of the firm's different lines or businesses over the past five years.

good-till-canceled order (GTC)—A brokerage order to buy or sell shares of a security at a given price that remains in effect until executed or canceled.

growth stock—Stock of a corporation that shows greater-than-average gains in earnings.

institutional investor—Organization that trades a large volume of securities, like a mutual fund, bank, or insurance company.

intrinsic value—Worth of a company; comparable to the prevailing market price.

limit order—Order to buy or sell a security at a specific price.

market capitalization or market value—Calculated by multiplying the number of shares outstanding by the per share price of a stock. One can also categorize equities into several different classes, including micro-cap, small-cap, mid-cap, and large-cap. The general guidelines for these classifications are as follows:

- micro-cap—Market capitalizations of $0 to $100 million.
- small-cap—Market capitalizations of $100 to $750 million.
- mid-cap—Market capitalizations of $750 million to $2 billion.
- large-cap—Market capitalizations of $2 billion or more.

market order—Order to buy or sell a security at the best available price.

mutual fund—An investment company that raises money from shareholders and puts it to work in stocks, options, bonds, or money market securities. Offers investors diversification and professional management.

Nasdaq Composite—An index (formerly the National Association of Securities Dealers Automated Quotation System) weighted by market value and representing domestic companies that are sold over the counter.

net current assets—Calculated by taking current assets minus current liabilities. Also referred to as working capital.

price-earnings ratio (PE)—Price of a stock divided by its earnings per share.

price-to-book value ratio (P/BV)—Calculated by dividing shareholder's equity by the number of outstanding shares. If under 1, it means a stock is selling for less than what the company paid for its assets, though this is not necessarily indicative of a good value.

Standard & Poor's Composite Index of 500 Stocks (S&P 500)—Tracks the performance of 500 stocks, mostly blue chip names, and represents almost two-thirds of the U.S. stock market's total value. It is weighted by market value. (As an equity investor, your goal should be to beat the return of the S&P 500. This is not an easy task, and roughly 75 percent of all mutual fund managers fail to do so.)

stock—Represents ownership in a corporation. Usually listed in terms of shares.